A Living Testimony and Autobiography of Alter Pain

The
He♥rtest Story
Finally Told

Jesus's Glory Divinely Bold

Alter Pain

WESTBOW
PRESS®
A DIVISION OF THOMAS NELSON
& ZONDERVAN

WestBow Press books may be ordered through booksellers or by contacting:

WestBow Press
A Division of Thomas Nelson & Zondervan
1663 Liberty Drive
Bloomington, IN 47403
www.westbowpress.com
1 (866) 928-1240

ISBN: 978-1-5127-6518-2 (sc)
ISBN: 978-1-5127-6519-9 (hc)
ISBN: 978-1-5127-6517-5 (e)

Library of Congress Control Number: 2016919430

Print information available on the last page.

WestBow Press rev. date: 12/19/2016

This is a true story, but because of its nature, I used a pen name and altered other names, including those of companies, institutions, and so on, for privacy concerns. I have generalized geography, events, and dates, but they're accurate enough for my purposes—to offer a true-life testimony.

I did not want to expose anyone; rather, I wanted to expose the power of God and how He can change anyone's life. I have been challenged to open pasts doors.

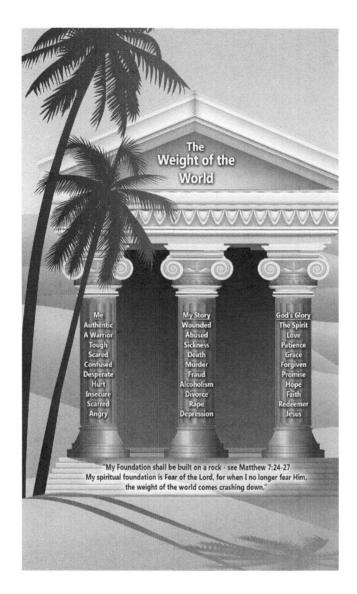

The pillars on my foundation

A good foundation can support these three pillars, which make up life. All three pillars need to be present for life to exist. Without me, you, or our stories, there wouldn't be any need for God's glory. Without God, nothing is possible—no earth, stars, moon, sun, or life.

With a good foundation and this trifecta of pillars, we can support the weight of the world.

Contents

Foreword

2 Corinthians 12:9 NLT Each time he said, "My grace is all you need. My power works best in weakness." So now I am glad to expose my weakness, insecurity, fear and doubt, so that the power of Christ can work through me for His divine purpose.

I wrote this book due to the courage of my conviction that was driven by a power within that came from God and His Living Word, the Bible. This is my true autobiography. I have struggled as I listened to God lead me and orchestrate His purpose in my life.

For quite some time, He has been asking me to share my story with the world. For years, I avoided His commands. I was fearful. I hid from the fact God wanted to transform me into a warrior so I would glorify His mighty power and love. I felt exposed and vulnerable as I wrote this book. I was spiritually naked from word one, and I was in the same state when I finished writing. I was born in uncharted waters and am still in those waters. I have never found dry land.

My calling to ministry began in 2000. Today, after sixteen years of my hiding from it, God called me to put my servant's hand to paper, extend my heart to yours, and share my story to encourage you. It's an honor and privilege that He gave me this opportunity to share with you this messy, personal testimony of my life. So bust out the popcorn, get cozy, then buckle up; we're taking a journey together.

Acts 20:24 NLT "But my life is worth nothing to me unless I use it for finishing the work assigned me by the Lord Jesus—the work of telling others the Good News about the wonderful grace of God.

I am who I am because of everything I have done and said and everything that has happened to me and has been said to me. I am the sum of every experience I have had, including my upbringing.

We all have a paradigm, a story to tell. We are the sums of our stories. I plan to sacrifice my paradigm, to give up my life for something much greater than me. God can do so much more with my story than I could ever dream of doing on my own. He doesn't want me to hang onto my past, but He wants me to share it with the multitudes. How can I do that without having to live in the past? God is a surgeon. Watch Him work with detail and precision on my life.

God told Noah that there would be a great flood and that he had to build an ark. Though he faced a formidable task, Noah obeyed God and ultimately saved himself, his family, and the animals. Here again is an example of three pillars: first, Noah existed, second, he had a story, and third, God was the power behind Noah's passion to do as he was told. Noah kept his eyes pinned on God, who was in front of Him lighting his path.

In Exodus, Moses was given the power to part the waters and do magic through God's powers. God turned his staff into a snake and back to a staff in front of the Egyptians. Even with all the bells and whistles and powers from God, Pharaoh's heart was hardened and he wouldn't let the slaves go. Nonetheless, Moses believed the Israelites would be saved from the Egyptians because God said so. The Lord stayed ahead of Moses and the frightened Israelites and commanded them to not look back; their salvation was in front of them, not behind them. Had they not listened, they would have been wiped out by the Egyptians. Instead, none of the Egyptians survived the pursuit; they drowned when the waters God had parted came back together. Never look back unless God tells you to; always look forward to Jesus's outstretched hand and the path He has lit for you.

In my fifty years of preparation to be a godly warrior, I chose to look back many times and lost sight of God, who was in front of me. On this new journey God is orchestrating for me, He has made clear that I'm ready to look back again, but this time, He is holding my hand and I have chosen to let Him take me back in time so He can make me a testimony of His power, authority, and love. The journey was frightfully dark, scary, and nerve shattering. I wouldn't have come back in very good shape without Jesus's help; I came back a warrior armed with the power to live wholly thanks to God's grace.

God, you are my rock, my salvation, and my only Father. You have rescued me from some very bad circumstances. As I start my ministry at age fifty, let it be yours, amen.

Note: All biblical verses are from the YouVersion Bible app NLT.

Dedication

I dedicate this book to a wonderful and godly woman who found Jesus Christ as her Lord and Savior and transformed her life. The challenges she has overcome have been an example for me and have profoundly affected the way I fight for life, love, and God.

Mother, I love and respect your warrior heart. Our lives are exposed in the greater good of Jesus and all He can accomplish for others through us.

You are my teammate in life, my friend, my mother. I am so proud of you and love you with all my heart.

A Special Thank You

I give thanks first to God and then my wife, for being such a strength and rock while believing in me during this time of my being so exposed and vulnerable. You have witnessed many raw emotions that resurfaced as I went back in time. You carried me as you always have. You are simply the best.

Thank you, Mr. and Mrs. Bill and Barry Lyons, my dear, special friends, for being great listeners, great advisors, and great supporters on this mission. I love you.

Mr. and Mrs. (Pastor) Tim and Beverly LaHaye, thank you for your time, wisdom, and mentoring as I embarked into uncharted territory. And you cook a great steak. Actually, Black Angus does, but thanks for paying for it. I hope I earned it by being good company. Love you guys!

Pastor Tim McKenzie, your service to the body of Christ is an example of accountability for me and helped me write this. I love you, pal, and thank you.

Friends and family, thanks for the hours of listening and for the grace and hospitality you showed me during our visits, phone calls, meetings, and more. If I sell one book, it will be because God had that one person in mind who will be inspired and do many good things all for His glory. Love you guys.

Chapter 1

❧ ⚘ ☙

A Revelation

In the dark of night, I am driving recklessly with my wife and three kids to an unknown destination. The fog is thick, but it appears only below the windshield as though I were erratically driving on top of the clouds. It's as though I wasn't supposed to see what lay beneath the grayness. It's a cold, snowy, wintery night. The heat is turned up as high as it will go inside our Ford Expedition, but we're still chilled to the bone. The cold in the air isn't natural, and the heat isn't helping.

There is intermittent chaos around me as I drive. I'm navigating around police cars and passing other cars effortlessly as if I were racing in the Indianapolis 500. Full-sized SUVs should not be able to maneuver like mine is. It's as though if I took my hand off the wheel, the vehicle would drive itself. I ask myself, *Am I really this good, or is the traffic making way for me?*

Our SUV rules the road. Even the fog and snow are parting for me. I feel I'm in another great exodus. I'm strangely enjoying the excitement even though I'm also petrified. *What's going on? Why is this happening?* Nothing feels natural; I feel like I'm in a movie or rehearsing for something much bigger. Am I running from something? What could I be running from? Maybe we're running toward something!

I sense that a pathway is being made in front of me, but I don't know who or what is doing that. I think I'm losing my mind. *Come on, Alter boy, keep your eyes on the road.* I can't wrap my mind around any of this. The chaos seems to be orchestrated as if I were playing a video game or were a character being manipulated in one. Some kind of weird ... or

1

is God preparing a path for me and my family? He'd promised to light my path if I would follow Him. I know He does what He says.

My stepkids—Kevin, Kara, and Steven—are in the backseat crying and afraid. Kara is screaming hysterically. She is an emotional, melodramatic young lady and sounds as if she needs this excitement to aid in her already very colorful array of emotions.

My wife is repeatedly asking me, "What are we doing, Alter?" She bursts into tears. "Where are we going?" I have a death grip on the steering wheel. After several well-executed maneuvers around traffic and accidents, I say, "Honey, I don't know!"

Every time we pass an accident, I see amoeba-like dark clouds swooshing around aimlessly over the road. I pass them off as exhaust from engines even though they seem more animated than that. Oddly, I don't feel threatened by them; they're keeping their distance from us.

Cars around us are skidding and crashing into each other. As I follow one of the dark clouds up, I notice several helicopters flying erratically. They begin flying so low that the windows and the dash of our SUV start vibrating. They are Hueys based on the *clop clop clop* noise coming from the blades breaking the sound barrier. We naturally duck when they fly by us so low. I'm calm and relatively confident; I'm not my usual self when under tremendous stress. His Word tells me not to worry; in fact, it's a command. As a middle-aged, trained warrior, I'm amazed at how in control I am. At least for the moment. I'm even feeling a bit cocky.

The ambulances, fire trucks, paramedics, and police are out rescuing vehicles that have slid off the road. People are dying in crashes everywhere. I want to stop and help, but I can't. Something has a grip on me. I feel I'm a puppet. I start thinking I could even take my hands off the wheel. Okay, I'm almost positive I'm not really driving this SUV. *God, who is driving this vehicle?* I cautiously let my hands off the wheel and wait for the next turn. If I'm wrong, we'll end up in the trees ahead hurt or dead. If I'm right, our vehicle will turn by itself.

I take my foot off the gas, but we're still going a steady fifty mph. We're headed for a cluster of trees. Jan screams. Our car turns right and follows the road. "Jan! This vehicle is driving itself! Honey, we're on cruise control, destination unknown! Ha! Wooo! God is real! Give me some skin, honey!"

Jan lets out a scream that could curl hair and some words that don't sound like compliments on my driving. Whap! My right arm takes her blow. "Sheesh, honey, it's a good thing I didn't have my hand on the wheel."

My humor is not welcomed. I have to find my serious side again fast. My wife had always said that I was the only one who laughed at my jokes. I reckon she's right. I was only trying to give my psychologically distressed and nearly emotionally paralyzed family a reason to laugh.

I focus on the clouds more. Their number and intensity have increased exponentially. Just as I start thinking they're harmless, cinematic special effects, one comes swooshing down straight into the windshield. Jan and the kids scream. So do I. This creature-like cloud seems alive and as if it's trying to say something. It doesn't stay with us long; it parts like the fog and snow. But another one comes. And another. One has eyes—deep, dark, lacking, and sad. It seems to demand that I notice it or rescue it from something. My wife screams again and grabs my right arm so tightly that she nearly dislocates my shoulder.

I try to figure out what these clouds are. One has a human form, and the next looks like an amoeba that can change its shape. We can hear their cries for help. The temperature suddenly starts dropping even lower; our breaths create fog in the car. I begin to feel sick for him, her—whatever it is.

"Alter!" Jan shouts. "They're spirits!" She points at a fresh wreck, and sure enough, I see black clouds ascending from the vehicle and then flailing around like a bunch of cats chasing mice through a maze at breakneck speed and with extreme accuracy. Dark spirits swirl around our SUV and nearly cover it. *Yes, they had to be spirits. Jan's right.*

Wherever there's another crash, there's at least one death. Each spirit represents a death. Another dark spirit ascends and flails around violently with no apparent direction and then another and another. Their shrieks deafen our ears; they're loud enough to shatter our already frozen bones.

The sounds are a combination of evil and good—a confused soul fading in and out of human form, the good, and the amoeba form, the

3

bad. My family and I decide that we, believers in Christ, are being safely escorted through this mayhem. "Are those spirits crossing over into death?" Jan asks.

"Yes," I reply. "The dark ones are the unbelievers."

We're in traffic in chaos; this or that car occasionally goes wildly astray as if spirits are infecting the drivers with something. "I'm not driving, Jan, so who is? Could it be God? I sure hope it is! Honey who else could it be?" I have so many other questions that I keep under my tongue; I don't want to scare the others. But I wonder why we don't become a traffic statistic like so many others we see. It's as though believers are surviving and don't even need to hold the wheel whereas nonbelievers are going out of control left and right. We see no dark spirits coming out of any of the vehicles that are driving in perfect harmony as if being orchestrated by a traffic conductor.

Jan and I decide now that we are breathing again to refocus on the kids. We began to prepare our kids for what we think is happening. "We no doubt have a destination," Jan says.

"We sure do, Jan. The vehicle is driving itself. I pray it's under God's command. I mean, He parted the water, turned a stick into a snake, made it rain for forty days and forty nights, and knocked the wheels off those Egyptian chariots. He can handle an SUV, right?" *God? Are we being introduced to something much bigger than us? Are we a choreographed convoy of vehicles driving effortlessly in the fog toward something good or an impending doom?* Though that's a valid concern, I feel oddly safe.

I start sweating and shaking. I go into a trance. "Jan, I'm … I'm …" I convulse and somehow hit the gas, but the car maintains its speed. My last thought as I'm passing out is that I'll end up one more dark spirit. Maybe my wife and kids too. After all, my life is not a rosy picture. *Am I in another dimension, or I am dreaming? My family! what about my family? No! No, God! No!* I slide into a dark hole at the speed of light. My ears begin to warm up. My stomach feels as though I'm on a roller-coaster ascending and descending but doing that backward. The streetlights are moving away from me as if they're streaking stars that went into a time warp in a *Star Trek* movie.

I remember so many space dreams I had when I was little. I go back in time. My head is spinning. I see my father, mom, sisters, disease, abuse, rape, violence, alcoholism, blood, death, murder, pain, and sorrow. How can this be? It's my life in less than a second. *Where am I going and why?* I had spent a lifetime trying to heal from my past only to be taken back through it all again in just a second.

Swoosh! I awake drenched in sweat. My hearing is back. My sight is back. I'm shaking and frightened. *Is this PTSD?* I'm crying. "What … what happened, Jan? Where am I?" I explain to her what just happened to me.

Her voice is quivering. "Alter, what's happening to you? You didn't even faint. You never even flinched. You've been here with us without skipping a beat."

Okay, again, lots of questions but no answers.

"Jan, did a dark spirit leave me?"

"No." She starts to cry and asks repeatedly if I'm okay. I'm so cold though the heat's on high. Kevin, my sixteen-year-old stepson, reaches over the seat and grabs my shoulder. I lock eyes with him through the rearview mirror; his eyes are sparkling with tears. "Alter, what's going on?" he asks. I feel I owe him an answer. I tell him what I've just been through. Steven, age nine, yells, "We're going to die!" Kara lets out with a mind-altering, shrill scream. "My friends!" she cries out. "Where are my friends? Will they be okay? Dolly, Romney, and Chisels! We have to go back and get them!"

Dolly is our black Lab. I have no problems leaving her behind because she's such a handful, but I don't say that because I don't want my stepkids to know my true feelings. But Romney and Chisels are our cats and almost worth turning back for. If I had more control of our destiny at that point, I might have turned around mainly for the sake of my precious Kara. Her sadness is a spear in my heart.

I realize we're not going home. I think we might be leaving our earthly home for good. I so hope this is the case and that we will end up with God. The book of Revelation tells us believers will not be left behind. "That has to be it, Jan! We're being rescued by God. We will be rescued from the tribulation. Jesus is here, right around the corner! I can feel it. Can't you, Jan?"

"I'm not having that same thought."

I had been through so much in my life that I often prayed the Lord would just take me, and I was thinking maybe, just maybe, the time is now. *But not Kara, Lord! She's so young, such an angel. No Lord, take me and not her.* Then I realize how foolish I'm being. *Yes God, take Kara too. Take Kevin, Steven, and my precious wife, Jan. God, take us all. Is this it? Could this really be it? The Rapture?* (Revelation 1:7) "Look! He comes with the clouds of heaven. And everyone will see him—even those who pierced him. And all the nations of the world will mourn for him. Yes! Amen!"

We all start yelling, crying, and freaking out again. I know I have to be the rock and demonstrate strength and unwavering faith for my family. I thought I did that already by letting go of the wheel just as we Christians are called to do, but I got whapped for it. It surely isn't helping for them to see me acting like a psychopath. I yell, "Quiet!" You could've heard a pin drop other than a couple of sniffles. "Listen to me! I can explain what's happening, but I need you to trust me and have faith in what I say, which is what God has taught us through His Word. Kevin, I have never let you down, and as crazy as this whole thing must seem to you right now, it'll all make sense to you soon. You'll be okay. Please trust me."

"I will, Alter," Kevin replies with only an ounce of self-assuredness.

"Kara, your friends will be okay as long as they've accepted Jesus into their hearts. Have they?"

"Yes," Kara whimpers. "I'm almost certain they all have."

I'm comforted by her reply. "Then you'll be seeing them soon." I realize she'd been hanging out with a pretty good crowd. "Will you trust me, sweetheart?"

"Okay," she murmurs.

"Stevie buddy, no one will die. In fact, it's the opposite. We're going to live forever."

Stevie smirks and asks, "Will Dolly, Romney, and Chisels be there too?" as if he's forming an alliance with his older sister on behalf of our pets. Stevie has always been the major animal lover in the family; animals have a natural affinity for him. I don't know if Dolly, Romney, and Chisels will be in heaven waiting for us. Based on his question, I wonder if Stevie recognizes where we're going. Praise God, I think he gets it.

I was about to explain to my kids and wife what I believed was happening—God was coming for us—when we saw a wondrous sight, a massive rock floating in the sky above with lights I had never seen in reality or even in movies. They're not manmade lights; they're natural lights coming from glorious clouds surrounding the rock. The lights aren't lightning, but they are electrifying. I can't stare at them too long not because of their brightness but because of their beauty and power. They're too glorious for the human eye. The helicopters are swarming around this massive boulder in the sky, an absolutely breathtaking sight.

"Jan, kids? You're about to meet Jesus. Are you prepared?"

"Awesome!" says Stevie. Then he thinks about it some more. "Wh … wh …what? You mean the real Jesus we learned about in Sunday school is coming?"

"Yeah, buddy, that Jesus. Are you ready to meet Him? I know our hearts are in love with Jesus because none of us ended up one of those dark spirits. They won't be seeing Jesus ever!" Stevie began to cry for them. *Nice job again, Alter.* I'd forgotten how huge Stevie's heart is. He's so sensitive; it's his greatest quality.

The SUV comes to a controlled stop. The locks on the doors pop up. We look at each other and ask, "Does this mean to get out?" I try to be calm. "I love each of you so much. If what I'm about to tell you wasn't true, I'd never say it. Have faith now and go see Jesus."

I encourage everyone to step out of the vehicle. We stand holding hands in a line in front of the SUV while staring at the beautiful rock. "I love you," I tell Jan. She finally looks calm. That indicates to me that she's ready for this. I can't help myself. "Oh … um … and I was right."

"About what?" she asks.

"About the steering wheel thing." I quickly cover my right arm.

We get lost in the beauty of the magnificent rock floating amid spectacular clouds. The light is bright, and the massive rock is slowly spinning. The hair on our arms and heads is standing straight up as though the air is charged with static electricity or maybe the polar magnetic fields are reversing. I cautiously blurt out as though I'd been given the words, "You will blink." I feel I'm dematerializing. It's a warm, vibrating sensation. I'm entering a new world, a new light, a new kind of something special. *Man, whatever this feeling is, I like it!*

"Hello? Hello?" I open my eyes and see nothing but whiteness all around. As my eyes begin to adjust, I see rock formations and lights. I can even see peace and joy, not just feel them. I see the silhouettes of people singing, kids playing and laughing … a celebration of celebrations … I am here, I am certain this is a vehicle to heaven. The only thing missing is Jesus.

My legs are weak. I can no longer support my weight. I sit on a rock bench shaped like a half moon. I study my surroundings and the holy place where I'm sitting. My family isn't with me. Oddly, I'm not worried about them. People are coming in as fast as we did.

I blink again and am standing weightless. I stare at the ground alone in a space that seems to have no walls but mysterious boundaries as though the mystical light were creating its own boundary. I know of no other way to explain it. It's a room filled with eternity. I feel a power I cannot describe. I feel safe, at peace, and in awe. I lift my eyes. I see Jesus. *Can this be true? Am I standing in front of the great I AM?*

I hear my name. My knees buckle. He holds me up without even touching me. I'm sobbing uncontrollably, but I eventually regain my composure. His robe is a bright white I've never seen before. I take in His long, flowing, dark hair, chiseled chin, and peaceful smile. My eyes meet His. I'm under His love spell. I realize He, my Father, the One who raised me, has spoken to me. I blurt out in a stutter, "You … y … really d … do …know me by name!"

He reaches out to me. We lock hands not as in a handshake but as in the way a loving Father embraces his son as if to say, *It's okay, I'm really here and won't leave nor forsake you.* He holds my hand in His with my palm facing up and visible. Someone asks, "Alter, how is your hand?" Jesus's lips aren't moving, but I assume He was the One who had asked that. I don't have an answer. Why can't I respond? We stand in silence.

I suddenly awake. *What? Seriously? That's it? "How is your hand?" That's all?* Man, I wanted more. So much more. *What does this dream all mean?* I lay in bed next to my wife. I'm soaked in sweat. I wake her. "Honey, I had a dream, and it seemed so perfect." It seemed and felt like flawlessly sequenced events that actually made sense. My dream was not a dream that one would have to study and decipher; it was clear, concise. Was this a dream? Was it a vision? Does God talk to us in dreams? Will I be alive on earth to experience the coming of Christ? I believe I will, but we are told in (1 Thessalonians 5:1-2) "Now concerning when all this will happen, dear brothers and sisters, we don't really need to write you. For you know quite well that the day of the Lord's return will come. Unexpectedly like a thief in the night."

Thirteen years ago, that dream changed how I look at my hand. I still needed an answer as to what Jesus might have meant if that had truly been He who had asked me the question about my hand. Bigger than that was the fact that I had stood with Jesus and had seen Him. This question might very well mean something significant to me. I will figure out what it means.

I've since read all about the significance of this "hand" in many theological sources. The hand can mean so many things biblically speaking, but I focus on its connection to helping, serving, assisting, and so on. *Well, how is my hand? Ouch. Have I kept my commitments with God? Am I a good servant? Am I following God's calling for me?* The sad answer was no. Even though I had that wonderful dream, vision, or whatever it was, I had resisted His calling for my life for over thirteen years. I feel heartbroken and clothed in fake garments. I want to be naked and afraid again. I want to have another chance to be clothed in His spiritually supplied garments.

One November day in 2015, I was upstairs above my garage working out on the elliptical machine while watching one of my favorite westerns. It was the night that would answer the question in my dream, "How is your hand?" I'm an owner-partner in a small business in the great Midwest that employs many. Where there are employees, there will be stress, and where there is stress, there must be exercise to clear the mind and body. It's the only way I can remain sane. Don't misunderstand me; I love our great people, but there's people drama in every gathering of two or more.

Our quaint, quiet town includes a beautiful, historic community whose people are wonderful. Our home is close to downtown, which looks almost as it did in the mid-1800s. Our place is pre–civil war. The garage in which I work out used to be a horse and carriage barn, but I've made it more comfortable than that.

As my workout and the western came to an end, I stepped off the elliptical machine and wiped sweat from my forehead. I was sure I was alone in the garage, and I knew the doors were locked. I heard footsteps coming up the creaky stairs. At first, I thought it was my wife, but whoever was making that noise was much heavier than she is. (Did you see how I just recovered from that? I'm sure Jan will be reading this.) I thought it could be a ghost.

Just as I started to feel weird about the footsteps, they faded, as if whoever it was had turned and was heading downstairs. I went down the stairs like the clumsy, fifty-year-old I am after a hard workout. "Anyone there?" I went through the entire garage and realized I was alone. I refused to believe I'd just been hearing things. I started sweating and going mentally black. *Oh no! It's happening again!* I'd had that feeling in my dream thirteen years earlier. How could I ever forget it? But that time, it was real. *I'm not dreaming. Am I having a heart attack?*

I began to shake and was feeling faint. I had a vision. I heard the same voice that had asked me about my hand all those years ago. It offered me an answer to that question. I was overwhelmed with awe and emotion. *My hand is my ministry. I am to put my hand on paper and share the story of my life.* I was taken back in time again during this mini blackout or actually more like a seizure, and I revisited my whole past in what seemed like hours. When I came to, I was still standing, so it must have been only for a second or two.

I became filled with the Holy Spirit and a passion to tell my story I cannot explain. My story had prepared me emotionally and without regret to be a warrior for this ministry. I was overcome by emotions but ran out of our garage, across the yard, into the house, and into my wife's arms. "Honey!" I said, "I have the answer to the dream I had about my hand. Remember that dream, Jan?" My heart was racing. I was pacing the floor. My ADD brain was in overdrive. I was bouncing around subjects of ghosts, dark clouds, footsteps on the stairs, my hand, writing a book, my calling, my ministry. "I have to write Jan. I have to reach out to the lost and hurting. God wants this."

I wondered why I had fainted as I had in my dream. I felt faint, but I hadn't passed out. I'd gone into a trance. It wasn't a dream, and I wasn't crazy. *Or am I? Was a power beyond my comprehension present when I faded out momentarily? Why the footsteps?* I was ready to explode with excitement. I suddenly started to chuckle. Though I knew little about the history of our house, I thought most likely someone had died in it. "Honey, maybe we have a ghost here." But I knew better. I felt God's presence.

So my journey officially began. My past had been revisited, my testimony was in place and ready, and I had been transformed into a warrior for God. After many years of running and hiding, doubting and procrastinating, preparing and growing in Him, I was ready to write my very personal story and share it. My ministry had begun.

This is not a story about me. This is another God story. It's real, raw, uncensored, and powerful. I pray that you will know me intimately after reading this story. I hope to one day know you the same way because there's a good chance you have a story too.

You're a child of God. You weren't made to be a clone of someone else but an authentic human being who stands out as an example of what a relationship with Christ looks like. Just because Christ was perfect doesn't mean your relationship with Him is. Exodus 19:5 tells us, "Now if you will obey me and keep my covenant, you will be my own special treasurer from among all the peoples on earth; for all the earth belongs to me."

Grab some popcorn, get cozy, have a box of tissue close by, and strap yourself in. We're going on a journey together. Ask God to be present with you on this journey for comfort, understanding, and clarity.

Chapter 2

❧ ❧

The Beginning:
Birth through Age Five

I was born on April 23, 1966 at ten minutes till one o clock PM, in New England a happy, healthy eight pounds four ounces. I joke about having slipped between the doctor's hands and landed on my head on the birthing table. I had wondered if this were true or just a joke told by mom to explain my goofy tendencies. This unfortunate accident could explain the many more unfortunate incidents to come. If I hadn't had bad luck, I wouldn't have had any luck at all. I never had a problem joking about myself and often joined in with others when they poked fun at me.

My mother, Barbe, was born in New England as well. She was an attractive, nineteen-year-old French woman, the daughter of Amelie. She was fresh out of a Catholic boarding school, and the world around her must have seemed large and new to her. Alphonse, Dad, was a handsome, twenty-two-year-old Frenchman who looked more Italian than French. He was also born in New England and was the son of my grandparents Chip and Lori.

Dad grew up in a wonderful family. He lived in a well-groomed, white-picket-fence neighborhood everyone dreams about living in. He was an officer for a well-known security company. He was five seven and weighed just 120, so I suppose his badge fed his ego. He had a million-dollar smile and the Hollywood looks of a bad-boy James Dean.

I was the second of three. Kristen was the firstborn; Pamela came after me. We are all about a year and a half apart. Kristen was a happy, cheerful baby born with a theatrical, dramatic flair. She was the type who could solve the world's problems if you gave her enough money and time. She had a servant's heart; she'd spend every last ounce of her love on anyone who needed it. Her baby face could melt anyone's heart. Pamela was born an instigator, but her cuteness kept her out of trouble. She could lure me into trouble in a New England second. I was stuck between a drama queen and an instigator; too much estrogen. But to know them is to love them.

I was a bit of a stunt baby and risk taker. I would jump up and down in my crib like a wild child. One day, I cleared the top rail and met the hard floor. I remember the jumping part but not the rest. My mother says I sustained a leg injury. This injury was a benchmark for my free-spirited, daredevilish ways that led to many other injuries later.

I was a quiet, polite, well-mannered baby in spite of my inner desire to reenact superhero stunts. I wasn't a big crier; I needed little to entertain me. I was very creative and had a wild imagination. I was always thinking outside the box. By age four, I was taking toys apart to figure out how they worked and putting them back together so I wouldn't get in trouble for that. I was an inquisitive little bugger who asked many questions. I have many memories of playing with my toys and my friends but very few memories of being held as a child or being read to. I don't remember playing games with my parents. I do remember a couple of times when I would sit up late and watch monster movies like *Godzilla* and *Tri-Clops* with mother. She would rub my head and tickle my arms. I remember that as if it were yesterday. I often yearned for the security I felt at those times; I was in love with Mom.

Most photos of me from my toddler to boyhood years have been lost or dispersed, some by me. I rarely had a smile on my face or was relaxed in the photos that remain. My pictures demonstrate some of my emotions, but I hid other emotions. I can look at a picture of me back then and tell you how I was feeling in it. A child lacking love, confidence, and security shows it. I tried to make up for that with an overabundance of false confidence. I remember feeling alone and being reclusive most of the time. Mother was often stressed; I sensed that even at a young age. Mother had been through a tremendous amount of stress in her early life.

Dad didn't affect me nervously quite as much as mother did, though he had his own demons. My insecurities were a problem for me in my teen years and are still a major component of my baggage today.

Chapter 3

❧

The Migration

Boxes were everywhere in our living room. I was confused and afraid. Mom kept telling me we were going away. Big people everywhere loading and unloading a big yellow and green truck and I couldn't figure out why.

Before long, we were on the road to the Southwest. Phillip, my older cousin who came along for the ride, made the road trip a fun time for us all. He was good with my sisters and me. It took forever to get to our new home. We stayed at a hotel one night. I did have my security buddy with me, though; there's nothing like waking up to your best friend licking your face. Loco, our dog, was trying to wake me as he always did. He and I were very close; we'd even been born the same year. My sisters, Loco, and I were cozy in the backseat of our sweet, deep-red GTO, the Red Baron. Naming our cars when we were young was fun.

Back to my best friend, Loco. He babysat me by lying on top of me. He believed he was protecting me. I was nearly suffocating, but I loved him so much I didn't have the heart to move him off me. He made me laugh and love life during difficult times. This brown-eyed mutt was my security blanket. He lived to be sixteen years old; my mom's boyfriend shot him. At least that's what I heard.

As a young boy, I would often pray but not know why or how to pray or what to pray for. I knew the name God, and that was the name I prayed to. I had many dreams alluding to a higher power that usually involved a godlike character. That should be enough proof that we're all wired by default to connect with God. I started praying at an early age. I'd do it privately. I was worried that it was weird to ask for things from something I couldn't touch or feel. I'd have dreams that God or something like Him would take me on journeys. I prayed a lot to this godlike entity that always felt so real. My dreams were always exciting, positive, and powerful. There was love all around me in my dreams and journeys. I attribute my becoming a prayer warrior to my dreaming.

I prayed often on our trip to the great Southwest to my imaginary but powerful friend who would protect me. I was confused and lost and didn't know what was going on. Mom and Phillip were in the front seat, and he helped us get safely to our destination. I don't remember where Dad was. The air was changing the longer we drove. It was hot and dry. I don't remember what time of year it was that we arrived in Arizona, but it was hotter than what we had been used to. Kristen, Pamela, and I were always thirsty; we couldn't get enough water. I could always tell when Loco had to go potty because he would walk in circles on my stomach as if he were about to use me as a patch of grass.

We were in the great Southwest. *Wow! Look at those big, giant, green things.* I was excited to see such a different world that included cacti. One was so huge that we got out of the car and posed for a picture by it. I knew then that I would like the desert.

Dad found a job as security officer for I think a grocery store and then later for some printing plants. Mom, a hair stylist, found work at a salon. My siblings and I attended a day care. I had a crush on a dark-haired woman who worked there. She would sneak me into the kitchen and feed me all kinds of goodies. She hugged me all the time. I called her Charlie Brown. I asked her, "Can I call you Mom?" She replied, "No. You have a mother already, silly." I was crushed. I sobbed. She held me close until I stopped crying, but she still refused to let me call her mom.

In my innocence, I told her some of my secrets because I felt safe and believed Charlie Brown would guard them. I trusted and loved her because she made me feel secure and happy. What kind of secrets could a four-year-old boy have? Probably not many, but they were my secrets.

Not long after we moved to the Southwest, Mom and Dad purchased our first home, a 1,100-square-foot, three-bedroom bungalow. I can still remember our address and phone number there. There was nothing but desert around us at the time. A carport was to the right of the olive-green house. The dead-center front door led into the living room. The dining room was toward the right, and the kitchen was toward the left and near Mom and Dad's room. My room was at the end of the hallway on the left. My closet became my hiding place. Kristen and Pamela shared the third bedroom.

I played outside a lot and made friends with kids close by, including Kenny, who lived four homes down on our side of the street. Mom and Dad eventually found us a babysitter who lived just around the block. Mrs. Eppleton had several older kids. Laurie was a blond girl about my age, Thelma was around twenty then, and Darlene was maybe fourteen. Mark was in high school. Later, Mrs. Eppleton brought her two nieces, Tana and Terri, from West Virginia and called them her daughters. The twins were a couple of years younger than me.

Not long after my parents purchased our home, Grandma Lori and Grandpa Chip, Dad's parents, came to visit. I always loved being around them. They made me feel the way a grandson should feel. Grandpa was a cool cat, and Grandma's little legs never stopped going. She was an energetic, four-foot-seven bundle of joy.

My other grandmother, Meme Amelie (Meme is French for grandma), was a very large and strict woman who believed kids should be seen and not heard. She must have had a hard life as she was not very nice to men or me for that matter. Meme was married to a very gentle and kind drunkard named Geralde. We called him Pepe, French for grandfather. Geralde had Meme on her last nerve; she divorced him and eventually remarried.

My new pepe, Jamie, seemed to me to be nothing more than Meme's puppet; she had complete control over Pepe Jamie. I felt sorry for him even when I was just four or five. Dad had a serious dislike for Meme, and the feelings were mutual; I could see that even at my young age. They had an ongoing feud years in the making and it wasn't pretty. We had moved across country to get away from her, but Dad's worst nightmare became true. Meme Amelie and Pepe Jamie moved to the southwest as well and ended up a stone's throw away from us. This and Dad's alcoholism would prove highly volatile in an already destructive and imploding marriage.

My spiritual dreams never stopped as a kid. I would often be in space and alone looking for something. Whatever I was searching for, I knew it was huge and powerful. I couldn't make heads or tails out of it then, but I needed a mental escape. I had a friend who was always present; I assumed this friend was God.

One night while I was sleeping in my closet as I did frequently, I had a dream about being in space and tumbling around. I woke up dizzy and weaved around my room. I realized I was in a dream within a dream because when I really awoke, I was back in my bed. In my dream, I saw stars floating around my walls as though I were in a planetarium but even more real. To this day, I'm not sure it wasn't real. Whenever I had a space dream, a godlike presence was there as my friend, protector, and guide who made me feel secure. I still equate space to heaven; I believe it's out there in another dimension.

Even as I grew, I would often hide from life. My closet was my refuge. I hid in it under my clothes when I couldn't sleep. One night while I was in bed, I had my first terrifying nightmare in our new home. My bed began shaking. I screamed for help. I jumped off and looked under my bed. Dad came running in, and the shaking stopped. Something or someone was trying to make a fool of me. Dad looked under my bed. Nothing. I called out, "God, come to me and be with me" as I had so many times before when He would come. Dad was perplexed. It was the first time he had heard about my space dreams with a God in them. He questioned me about it. I realized I had let my secret out of the bag. My only private comfort had become public information, but that never caused me to stop my relationship with what I thought at the time was God. I now know it was indeed God.

Dad asked me to tell him about my dreams. I did, and he never said another thing about it. I'm sure he figured that it was as good as anything else I could believe in and that if I needed a little make-believe friend, that would be a good one to have. I told him my God had come to me in my dreams.

Dad and I talked for a while until I calmed down. He kissed me goodnight as always and left my room. Alone in the dark, I began to pray to my God in space. I happened to glance up at the AC vent and was paralyzed with fear. Two beady, glowing, red, devilish eyes were staring at me from inside the vent. *Do I scream again? Is this real? It has to be! I can't just be imagining glowing, red eyes.* I let out a yell, and Dad ran back into my room. "Da ... Da ... Dad! It's in the vent! Red eyes staring at me! You have to turn the light off to see them." Dad turned off the light. The eyes were gone. He took me on a tour of my room. We turned over everything. We opened all my drawers, went through my closet, and looked under my bed again. He showed me the coast was clear. When he left, I ran to my closet and stuffed clothes under the door. I spent the night there.

I began wandering around our home when the others were asleep. I messed with the thermostat for the heat and AC. I turned the stove and oven on. I had no idea how to work the thermostat or the stove, but I had seen my parents do it enough times and thought I had the concept down pat. But I didn't know how to turn the controls off. I was always tempted to grab a drink of water, but I knew the noise I'd make jumping on the counter to reach a glass and turning on the faucet would wake my mother. So I would take a little walk to my neighbors' home in the wee hours and ring their doorbell. My neighbors would answer in their nightclothes and were always perplexed at my behavior. They were little Italians, and they loved Dad. They were kind to me and made me comfortable when I was around them. I'd ask them for a glass of water. I'd tell them I was afraid my mother would find out. I'd ask them to keep this a secret between us. They'd give me a glass of water, escort me to my house, and lock my front door. They eventually told my parents about this problem and admitted to having given me water each time until they learned why I wasn't allowed water before I went to bed—I wet my bed just about nightly.

I was reprimanded by Mom, who was sure I'd been sleepwalking. But I was fully aware of what I was doing and could remember why I did it—I was thirsty and scared. I couldn't sleep at night and couldn't wake up in the morning. This was a problem for a couple of years. I always woke up in my closet not knowing how I'd gotten from my bed to my closet, and then in the morning, I'd wake up in my bed not sure how I'd gotten from my closet to my bed. I would make sure I was in bed before mother came to get me ready for school. I'd fall into a deep sleep from having slept poorly all night in my closet and wandering around the house. Those deep sleeps caused me to wet my bed. That coupled with some psychological issues were the reasons for my bed-wetting. It wasn't a physical problem at all. I learned this as I matured.

As I grew older, my praying continued. Kristen often laughed at me because she would hear me praying in my room. She recalls how cute she thought it was. I kneeled by my bed and prayed. I didn't even know what caused me to pray in that posture to my friend and power. I couldn't see him but I could feel his presence. This started long before we started going to a Catholic church.

When I was six or so, all three of us kids were introduced to church. Mom had taken us to catechism classes and learned about God and the importance of communion. We were all dressed up for our first communion. I wore a blue-checkered suit, and Pamela and Kristen wore yellow spring dresses. They looked like angels.

Church scared me to my bones. It sounded like a bunch of people mumbling and moaning in unison. It felt impersonal. And the whole catechism thing was just too much for my confused, ADD mind. On my first day at catechism class, I hid under a decorative bridge in the front yard of the host family. I waited there scared out of my mind until mother showed up. When Mom went to the front door to get the girls, I jumped into the car as if nothing were wrong. I sat there waiting for Mom and my sisters. When Pamela and Kristen jumped in, Pamela asked, "Where were you, Alter?" "What do you mean, Pamela?" I asked with a don't-tell grin on my face she clearly didn't catch on to. Or did she want to get me in trouble? She was quite a little instigator.

I got in trouble; I got a good spanking when I got home. I was spanked a lot as a boy. Mom and Dad argued a lot; yelling and screaming matches were regular events at home. I was caught in the crossfire many times. Spankings would eventually turn to worse things; I feared the old wooden spoon my mother wielded. The abuse became mental as well as physical. For the most part, Pamela and Kristen escaped Mom's wrath. My closet became my refuge during the scary times in my life. My prayers went from being a temporary to a permanent way for me to stay sane. My space dreams were my escapes when sleeping. I continued to go into such deep sleeps, wet my bed, and not wake up in the morning. I tried not to wake up. I hoped I'd never wake up. Sleep was my only escape. I had told only my Italian neighbors and Charlie Brown of my fears.

I was afraid of Mom but was in love with her. If she had only told her story, distanced herself from Dad, and gotten help, she would have been freed much sooner in life. She's a special woman who has so much to offer, but she didn't know then how to handle the tremendous pressure she had to endure. She was as scared of Dad as I was of her. In some ways, I was her way out when her pressure pot blew and she could take no more. I reminded her of my dad—I was a shadow of him.

Knowing what I know today, I would do it over for her. I was a sacrifice for her. I love her so much and am so proud of her for who she has become that I would give my life for her. I ask you to not forget she too has a story as I move forward with mine. She was not evil but very confused at that time. She deserves the same Christian love from each of you that she and I share. We all have a story to tell. Mine gets uglier.

Chapter 4

❧ ❦

Child Abuse:
Age Six through Age Ten

In 1972, when I was six, I started school. I was petrified my first day; I didn't feel an ounce of excitement. I planned to run away the second I got to school so I wouldn't have to go home or to school ever again. This started a lifetime of hating school. And there was no security at home for me.

That day, I ran from the line of kids and hid behind an electrical box by the PE field. I planned on making my big break after the coast was clear. I stayed there several hours and watched the kids run out to the field for PE. A thin, dark, short-haired teacher with a stern look on her face came out of nowhere. "Young man, what are you doing crouched down behind this electric box?"

"I'm injured. The PE teacher told me to stay here."

"What's your PE teacher's name?"

"How'm I supposed to know? It's only my first day of school!" That lie was the first of many that I came to call survival lies.

The teacher started to walk away. I was relieved. I thought she had bought my story. She turned. "Oh, Alter?" I said, "Yes?" I realized I had given away my identity. I hadn't a clue I fit the identity of the missing boy she'd been frantically looking for.

I found out later she was my first-grade teacher. As if I weren't already afraid enough of my mother, I was petrified by my teacher too. She had it out for me from that moment on. She would ask me questions in front of my classmates. When I wouldn't answer because I was speechless and afraid, she'd pull me out of my chair by the earlobe and make me sit facing the corner with a dunce hat on. Was I the only one who was so afraid all the time? Why was I so different? What was I doing so wrong? I didn't know the answers to her questions at that age. I didn't know what normal was.

My first year was a disaster. I hated my teacher, and she clearly hated me too. I became a problem child. I eventually got to know every principal and dean of every school I attended. I was always on the dean's list, but it wasn't *that* dean's list. I was truly a gentle, kindhearted boy who would never have hurt anyone intentionally. God had given me a wonderful and tender heart, soul, and spirit. That was proof God was real in my life then. If I was kind with others, why were others so mean to me? I didn't know until later in life when I was given additional gifts of experience and wisdom.

I couldn't bear the stress of home life coupled with school life; that led to nightly bed-wetting and morning spankings. That abuse went on for years. Eventually, she had to pour a pot of cold water on me to wake me up. I was confused and dazed when I was finally awakened regardless of the method used. Mother raised her voice at me it seemed every morning because most mornings I was going to be late for school. She would drag me into the bathroom and brush my hair with those heavy, sixties- and seventies-style brushes. That was a typical morning for me. My sisters and I walked to school every day. I wondered if they knew I was wearing urine-soaked underwear in the 35- and 40-degree mornings. If I could smell them, I was sure others could as well.

My sisters didn't receive the treatment I did. I was a human sacrifice, a scapegoat for Mom's pain and anger toward Dad. I found it hard to muster up the guts to go to school, and when I'd come home, most days, Mother would be waiting with a wooden spoon in her hand. I started to cry long before I was even close to her, but I knew I had to keep going her way or my spanking would be worse. I tried to block the swings with my hands and arms. I don't know what hurt more—the licks on my rear end or those on my arms from having intercepted them.

I spent as many days as possible outside. It was a reprieve for me. I played with my friends and could breathe. We'd get into mud ball fights after hard rains at the construction sites nearby, which were prime playgrounds for us. We soiled our clothes beyond cleaning. After taking a bath one day after playing in the mud, I dried off, and mother came in and noticed my knees were still dirty. She went into one of her episodes, and I ended up with very sore and raw knees. When she finished scrubbing them, she made me scrub them too. She left the bathroom. I took the washrag and scrubbed my knees until she returned. I was too afraid to stop scrubbing for fear things would be worse when she returned. She came back to a crying little boy. I often blocked my face with my arms and hands out of impulse, but that time she felt bad. Her body language changed. She wrapped me in a towel and held me. She loved me. I know she struggled with the stress my father caused her.

Some nights when Dad got home, he'd sense I was being abused and would approach mother with anguish in his heart. That day, he noticed my knees had been scrubbed raw, and he questioned Mother about it. He said some mean things to her. Their arguments often led to violence that I thought was all my fault. Dad protected me, but I dreaded what he would do to Mother. I always thought of him as my savior. Though he would come home drunk most nights, I still couldn't wait for him to arrive. She never inflicted pain on me when he was around; he wouldn't let her. But he'd physically hurt her in ways that are hard to talk about or describe; use your imagination. Dad often came home late because he would spend a lot of time in bars. He loved his booze, and there were signs he liked other women. Regardless, he was the better option for me to hide behind.

Like most if not all kids, I'd pick my nose. Those nose nuggets as well as Crayola marks would end up on my bedroom walls. Mom came into my bedroom one morning, and I cowered in the corner knowing I had done wrong. It wasn't until later in life that I realized I desperately needed and wanted her attention. I was made to clean the walls in a very unconventional method until she returned. She must have forgotten about me; she was gone for what felt like an eternity. I could have quit licking the walls, but I was sure the consequences would have been worse if I had.

When she came in and found stains on the walls from my tongue, I thought she would faint out of guilt and remorse for what she had caused. She held me tightly and cried with me. I was secure in her arms. My suffering vanished. I didn't want her to ever let me go. I would have licked those walls forever if I could have experienced that feeling of being held by her as she had that day. "I love you, Mommy. Please don't cry."

Just as I started thinking I might actually like going to my school, I was moved to a new school due to overcrowding in the first. I don't remember my second- or third-grade teachers probably because they must have actually liked me. I ended up liking that school; most of my teachers through fifth grade were pretty neat.

Our family qualified for reduced meal stamps in school for most of my school life. Mom and Dad were embarrassed by that. One day while I was in the new library, I spied a pencil-dispensing machine. Pencils where a nickel each. We were required to bring a pencil to class each day. I didn't have a pencil or a nickel to buy one. I was worried I'd get detention if I didn't have a pencil. I tried to break into the pencil machine but couldn't. I served some time in detention that day. I swore I'd never be without a pencil or money again. That evening, I stole a nickel from Dad's change jar, and a new business was born. I hid the pencil machine between some shelves so no one could easily find it. I purchased a pencil and sold it for a quarter to a kid who didn't have a pencil. I capitalized off the fear of kids having to do detention. I changed my quarter for five nickels at a convenience store and started dealing in pencils. During every break and at recess, I sold them to kids in need for any coin other than a penny. Worst case, they'd have a nickel and I'd break even. Best case, they'd pay me the quarter they had to buy lunch. They'd rather go without lunch than spend time in detention.

Every day, I'd buy some candy and gum for myself but would also save some for pencils the next day. My average gross profit was about 60 percent as I look back. I'd hide my money, candy, and excess pencils in Fred, my stuffed animal whose mouth was more like a big pocket. Fred, a frog, was my savior. I also I hid my soiled underwear in Fred's mouth so Mom wouldn't find them and spank me.

That went on for months until the principal called me into his office. He was handsome, funny, and charismatic. He loved kids, but that didn't stop the chill that went down my spine when I walked into his office and saw my mother sitting with her legs crossed. I melted down. The principal had no idea why I was crying. He didn't know I was in for some rough times when I got home.

Dr. Gleeson kneeled in front of me so his eyes could meet mine. He laughed. "Mr. Pain, I'm very impressed with your entrepreneurial abilities, but what you're doing is wrong." I could tell he was holding back from laughing more. I was partly relieved that someone, particularly a principal, found humor in my business venture. "You cannot hide pencil machines and worse run a business with them. You're taking kids' lunch money, Alter, and they're going hungry. Moms are complaining, and you're compromising your integrity." He explained to me what integrity meant; I understood him. I remembered times I'd given pencils away to help a friend or two.

He and my mother were holding in their laughter. After my mother left, I contemplated asking my principal to tell Mom not to hurt me, but I couldn't muster up the courage. I was afraid it would be worse for me when I got home.

To my surprise, I didn't get in trouble. I actually slept well that night. But I had to give back what money and pencils I had to the school media center and apologize to each kid I'd profited off of. I think I had over $20 in cash and at least that much more in inventory (pencils and candy). And in '73 or '74, that was a lot of loot for a child. I did manage to hide most of my candy in my safe deposit box—the AC vent above my dresser, the same one in which I had seen those red, beady eyes. The screws that held it in place were easy to remove from the drywall they were barely stuck in. On my own accord, I gave most of my candy and the money I had made to my customers. Notice I said "most."

I was starting to like school; it was my hideaway from home. The kids liked me, and my fourth-grade teacher loved me. She was the most beautiful teacher in the world. She was blond, and she was very nice to me. I was her pet, and I'd find things to give her. I finally knew what it was like to be a teacher's pet. But one frightful day, she announced to the class she was getting married. I turned white as a ghost. I was in denial.

After she was married, she told me to start calling her by a different name. I couldn't do that for the whole year. I gave her a Valentine's Day card in which I had written, "You have hurt my heart." I thought she would cry when she saw the picture of a heart broken in two. She kept me after school one day to tell me I had to get over it. I didn't until sixth grade. She was my first crush.

After dinner one evening, everything was calm. Dad came home while I was doing my homework. The yelling started, but it was different from other arguments. Dad was going up and down the hallway violently thrashing about and damaging the walls and saying terrible things to Mother. He started coming home drunk night after night and becoming very abusive to Mother. Each week, the fights escalated. One night, Dad became out-of-control violent. Mother thought he was cheating on her, and he probably was. He thought she was cheating on him, but I don't think she ever did. Their arguments went from yelling and screaming at each other to Dad inflicting punishment on her.

I was in my bedroom burying my head in my favorite stuffed animal, Fred the frog, to muffle the sounds of the loud crashes and bangs, Dad's mean words, and Mom's screams. I ran out to see what was going on. Dad had Mom pinned against the wall and was inflicting violence and pain on her. I tried to muster up a few words to protect Mom, but all I could do was cry. Mom tried to talk some sense into Dad. "Alphonse, your son is watching this!"

Dad started to abuse me too, which was very rare. He was in a drunken rage. Even I, at age six, could tell he wasn't there mentally. He had blacked out. I felt I had to save Mom from death that night. Jesus had been abused, mocked, spat on, and cursed during His crucifixion. I felt Mom and I were being crucified. It was really bad.

Meme Amelie and Pepe Geralde, Mother's parents, were living in town then. Much to Dad's hatred, Meme loved to get involved in my parents' relationship. A woman who didn't like men had no business being married much less interjecting her wisdom into my parents' relationship. The fact that Meme was coming over so often wreaked havoc on Mom and Dad. It was a volatile situation that didn't take long to escalate out of control. I think in Meme's mind, she was protecting mother. In Dad's mind, she was Satan's wife.

The fights became more and more destructive to our family. On another occasion, Dad was so drunk he slurred his words so much I couldn't understand him. Pepe came over and got involved in another argument between Mom and Dad. Dad had once again started to abuse Mom, and I bravely tried to get between them. I didn't see the statue coming. It was about three feet tall and weighed maybe thirty pounds. Dad had tried to strike Pepe with it but broke it on my back. Fortunately, I wasn't hurt. God was there for me. Pepe and Dad were yelling at each other. Violence, yelling, and alcohol were the perfect ingredients for Dad's blackouts, scary events for a child to witness.

Dad followed Pepe out of the house with bad intentions. His temper caused a lot of destruction that evening. Neighbors were streaming out of their homes and were as scared as we were. Pepe ducked many of Dad's attempts to inflict pain and violence on him and somehow came out unharmed. We lived on a fairly quiet street; our house was the nucleus of dysfunctionality. The fights never ended, and I believed I was the cause of it all. I carried a big weight on my shoulders.

So now it's time to meet the neighborhood bully, Butch. Every neighborhood has one, right? His nickname matched his persona; he chased me around the neighborhood often. I was small for my age, but I could run fast. The last day Butch ever tried to hurt me, Dad was watering the yard. Butch chased me into the yard and tackled me in front of Dad. He started punishing me. I yelled out for Dad to help me, but he just kept watering the lawn. Finally after several minutes of watching the abuse I was receiving, he watered Butch, which caught him off guard. I tackled him and punished him until he began to cry. My tender heart prompted me to apologize for making him cry. That was the moment I started standing up for myself. I owed that one to my father, Alphonse.

One spring day, the olive tree in our front yard was in bloom. Dad didn't punish me often, but when he did, he used a switch he'd break off the olive tree. Jesus took thirty-nine lashes from a flagellum, a short whip. Being flogged by an olive tree switch was nothing in comparison to that, but it hurt and left marks.

Life continued at what seemed to be a slow pace. When I was eight, I was feeling pretty worn out. The bed-wetting continued, and so did the beatings—physical and mental. I did manage to keep praying to God but with little spiritual guidance. I managed to make something of God the best I could mostly from what I learned at church. He was my escape in many ways on many days.

One summer day, after Mother had tried everything she could to get me to stop wetting my bed, she took me to the store for extra-large diapers to absorb wetness. It ended up absorbing my spirit too. I assumed I'd wear them at night. She was dressing me in one of the diaper in the middle of our living room when some of my friends came over. They heard my wails and screams behind the closed door. Mother opened the door and nudged me outside. I met them in the front yard with nothing but my diaper on. They laughed at me. I fell to the ground and lay there with my face in the grass humiliated beyond belief. I was crucified that day. Jesus had been stripped, exposed, and beaten publicly. The word *excruciating* comes from the Latin word for crucifixion, death on a cross.

That was the day I lost my spirit. It didn't come back to me until Easter Sunday 2000. At moments in my young life back then, I felt twinges of a spiritual excitement, but my spirit quickly went into hiding again. I was broken. My heart was crushed, scarred, and worthless. I couldn't understand why my mom had allowed me to be crucified publicly. I couldn't understand the level of pain she must have felt.

Chapter 5

✑ ✑

Divorce

One fight led to the big D—divorce. I can't imagine how mother had stayed with Dad as long as she had. In the last two years of their marriage, I sensed their relationship would end. But Dad had one last opportunity to get it right.

He took me fishing at our favorite lake one summer morning. He must have started drinking right after he had gotten out of bed. Mom asked him about the wisdom of taking me, and as usual, that quickly turned into an argument. Dad spat a mouthful of egg sandwich at her. As my mother wiped her face, Dad grabbed the poles, tackle box, and bait, and off we went.

I was frightened. He drove erratically most of the way to the lake. That day, I caught fish and Dad got drunk. Dad drove drunk often. On an earlier fishing trip, he had put the whole family in danger when he almost drove off a cliff. Mother was screaming at him and crying, and we three kids were very scared. Another two feet and we would have driven over the edge. Mother got out of the car and made sure my sisters and I got out too. I was crying in fear. Dad was already upset from having lost the muffler after he had hit some big bumps in the dirt road. Dad finally retreated from the side of the cliff. All the way home, the little Plymouth Valiant sounded like a muscle car.

I think Mom mustered up the strength to divorce him after Dad and I got home from our fishing trip. Dad cried nonstop for two days and nights. He gathered us kids in the front yard and held us while crying a river for our neighbors to see. We were all crying and afraid. He cleaned the entire house. My sisters and I were forced to help. Dad promised Mom he would quit drinking. He begged and begged until mother caved in. She took him up on his commitment to quit and get help.

Dad went to AA and learned about alcoholism. He quit drinking but just for a year. During that time, he was more of a father to me than he had been in all the other years combined. It helped me understand that my real father was a fine man when sober. I loved that father I'd never known.

One day while we were visiting a small, southwestern, historic, and touristy town, we were in a rustic restaurant when my parents got into a big spat. Dad left and spent a couple of hours in a saloon while we visited the quaint stores up and down the streets. That was it. Mother was done. I can't say I blame her.

They divorced. Dad took what he could fit into his VW Rabbit and set off to New England to live with his mother. He took my sister Kristen with him for company, which deeply concerned me. She flew home after Dad got there. Grandpa Chip had passed away, and Grandmother Lori was a widow. Dad also wanted to get as far away from Meme Amelie as he could.

Mother, my sisters, and I lived in our home for a few more years. Dad sent letters and made calls threatening to kill us all. Mother was afraid enough that she sold the house and moved us in with Meme Amelia and Pepe. However, day by day, Mother's behavior began to change for the good; she was clearly recovering and maturing. I began to like who she was becoming.

The move to Meme's wasn't good for me, though. I didn't like her, but I felt guilty about that. I wondered where my dislike of her had come from. Partly from Dad's example of hate for her but mostly from my own ability to know that Meme didn't like men. My senses were way too heightened for a boy my age, but I was in survival mode.

We were at Meme's for about two years before we moved. I was around eleven, and by that time, Mom had dated several men and had met her future second husband, John. He walked into our lives ... well, more so into Mom's life. I don't feel he ever truly invested in our family. He had a son, Leon, and a daughter, Bernie, both sweet kids, but they really struggled to like their father.

Mother took me to a doctor after she had exhausted every way of getting me to stop wetting my bed. The doctor took me into a room without Mother and questioned me. He knew something wasn't right. My eyes must have been empty; he probably saw my dried-up soul and lack of spirit. This doctor knew all the right questions to ask, and my answers didn't reassure him. It wasn't his first rodeo with children with problems.

After our discussion, he spoke with my mother. I can only assume he told her about his concerns. After that visit, Mother backed way off. When her abuse stopped, so did my bed-wetting. I wet my bed because I would travel into another dimension, a deep sleep. I wouldn't stop wetting my bed until I had a reason to wake up. The doctor knew more about my condition than my mother or I.

Over the years, Leon became my best friend, my brother, my confidant. He was an angel sent by God who put a little taste of life back into my spirit. Each time I learned he was coming over, I would overflow with excitement. Never a dull moment when we were together. He lived with his birth mother, Regina, who had married Franco, Leon and Bernie's stepdad.

My experience in Meme's and Pepe's home had been creepy and uncomfortable. Pepe did everything Meme asked of him. I grew to love Pepe, a gentle man. I could feel his care for me. He had protected me the night of the bad fight years earlier. He didn't live long enough; he died because of a surgery that had caused him ten years of health issues.

Meme, on the other hand, was a hard woman who wanted everything her way. She threatened to send me to a boy's military school. In hindsight, I think that would have been a good opportunity for me to get out of the situation in Meme's home. I decided I'd be better off living with Dad even though he had threated us. Mom allowed me to go, and I did.

I wasn't with Dad long before I realized how poor my decision was. He was drinking more than ever. He had a live-in and -out girlfriend. I often spent days with my aunt and uncle. Grandma Lori was the grandmother I adored. I was so happy to be back with her again. But she had come down with Alzheimer's, and she barely remembered who I was.

After about eight months, I told Mom I wanted to come home. She said she didn't have room for me because she had just moved out of Meme and Pepe's home. I told her I'd live in a closet if I had to, and that's exactly what I did.

Back in the Southwest, Mom, Kristen, and Pamela had moved into a two-bedroom townhouse. I moved into the coat closet; I slept there and read my Bible. I was always embarrassed to let anyone know I was reading a Bible; to this day, I can't say why. I never even told my sisters. I hid my Bible reading the way some kids hide their smoking from their parents.

In the meantime, my relationship with Leon grew every time we were together. He was also in desperate need of a friend who could help him with his suffering relationship with his dad, John. I was in need of a friend I could share anything with, and he was that friend. He heard my story of abuse as a child but promised to never tell anyone. He never disliked Mother, which showed his rock-solid character. Leon was the first real, true friend I'd ever had and trusted. We did everything together; we were always up to no good in a cute way. We should have been killed many times over with the stunts we pulled. The crazy, fun moments we shared filled my mind with love and adoration for Leon.

John, Leon's dad, was very hard on Leon and me. I thought for a moment that I could have a genuine father figure in my life, but his performance as a father proved otherwise. Mom wanted me to call him Dad. Yeah, right! He smoked pot and drank. I'd already been down that road with my father. The two substances, one of them illegal, made John unattractive as a father. My bad memories of him trumped any good ones.

Once, we went on a family ski trip to the White Mountains. He was smoking weed while driving. His 1970s-something VW van had a terrible time starting; we always had to push-start it. I realized he would never be my father figure when we were on our way home from that ski trip. We had had such a great time as a family, but John was driving stoned and speeding around corners erratically. This ski trip went from being one of the most-fun trips to, well, let's say the most memorable trip we had as a family. Mom, Leon, Bernie, Kristen, Pamela, and I were scared stiff. Mom and we kids all had flashbacks

33

of Dad almost taking us over that cliff. Mom started crying and yelled at John to stop and let us out. He slammed on the brakes in the middle of a major winding highway. We all got out of the van as quickly as possible, not wanting to get struck by passing motorists. John was fuming. I'd seen that behavior before, and I refused submit to it again. We walked for what seemed miles. Leon and I were very upset; Leon was so embarrassed about his father.

My relationship with John went nowhere. Neither did Leon's with him. I yearned for a father in my life. I grew to feel the presence of God. I'd reach out my spiritual arm but could never seem to reach Him. Now, I know He had actually been fathering me all along. But back then, so much was still missing in my life. I continued to be a lost, desperate, confused, and spiritless young man rightly named Alter Pain.

Pamela had gravitated toward God by that time. She had started attending a Baptist church, and her life as a young girl was changed. The example she set for me was remarkable. I watched her closely for many years; that helped me grow with God. At that point, I still didn't know enough to surrender everything to God, but I had been reading the Word. I prayed often but remained confused about who God really was. I saw Him as a friend I could talk to. I had become socially awkward and just didn't trust men very well. The men who had been in my life had never cared about me. I had plenty of female friends in my life but few male friends. I was often teased by others. I learned that kids could be downright mean. My grades were slipping; I started getting Cs and Ds and even some Fs, and that lasted into high school. I felt dumber than a box of rocks. Peer pressure and encroaching adolescence were twin burdens.

I thank God for keeping an eye on me; no one else was. Mother was so into her new boyfriend John that she often went to his place and stayed the night while us kids were at home alone with little in the fridge. I thought nothing mattered to mother other than John, who showed little interest in me.

Chapter 6

❧ ❧

Molestation: The Beast

I started junior high; it was my sixth school. I went there from sixth through eighth grade. I was the odd child out there. I hated going there as much as I had hated my first day in first grade. I did manage, however, to experience my first kiss. I met a cute girl in English class. She was a popular girl, and I thought I was so cool to have her as a girlfriend. Soon after we met, we walked to McDonalds down the street from her home. We purchased a couple sodas and went to the playground; my first kiss happened inside the Officer Big Mac character there. He was supposed to catch the Hamburglar thief dressed in a striped prison uniform. I went home in love that night.

The next day, I couldn't find my sweetheart at school. I looked everywhere. I gave up my lunch hour to find her. I started to think I'd said or done something that had turned her off. I noticed her posse she hung out with every day. When I walked over to them, they started to giggle. I saw the girl of my dreams hiding in the huddle. One girl blurted out, "Hey, bubble butt!" Another said, "Where's shorty? I can't find him. Oh there you are!" as she looked at the ground, laughing. My girlfriend said, "Hey Alter, you really are the owner of the moon!" They all laughed as I walked away.

I was mortified. I did and still do have a somewhat disproportionate hind end. Ha! God has graced me with some padding. One of my friends told me my new girlfriend wasn't my girlfriend at all. She had been dared by her friends to lead me on and kiss me. That was a cruel joke. What a way to welcome a new kid to school. She and her friends on the student council ended up getting a comment printed in our yearbook. It mentioned where we would all end up, and I was supposed to become "the owner of the moon." I've gotten over that, but it was a painful day. It turns out they were partly right—I love a God who owns the moon as well as earth and the stars and has shared it all it with me. The laugh's on them.

I managed to make it through junior high by becoming the class clown well known to the principal and other administrators. Inside, I was lost, spiritless. It seemed I was crucified every time I turned around. I had no friends. I trusted no one except one boy, David. That was until he ended up stealing from me at home.

During the summer between sixth and seventh grades, I met Stan, a new kid on the block. He died in 2015 from unfortunate circumstances. I had just spoken with him after a thirty-three-year gap. We'd lost track of each other; our relationship was resurrected for a brief time thanks to Facebook. He was able to tell me he was saved when we talked about God, but I could tell he was still pretty messed up. He had lost his way. I did everything I could to get him reconnect to God. I didn't expect what would happen, though. He took his own life at age forty-nine. He told me he had gotten caught up along with another of our high school friends in a synthetic drug ring that had ended our other friend's life. He and his best friend had gone to prison for manufacturing and distributing synthetic substances, and the best friend had hanged himself. Stan died not long after. He loved his friend more than life and could no longer bear that loss on top of the pressure he was experiencing from his past. Stan and I had become good friends in school. He was a good kid, and I thought he would have a fair chance at life. He had good parents and seemed genuinely happy. What a giving soul he was. Though he did seem troubled back then.

He introduced me to this really cool guy down the street. His name was Daemon. He was about thirty-five and had a thin but strong build and dark hair. He looked like a beardless Abraham Lincoln. He was a Vietnam veteran who had received two Purple Hearts after having taken a bullet in the left arm and the right wrist as he piloted a Cobra gunship and a Huey transport recue ship in the army. He had worked as a police officer and later as a federal agent.

I loved his stories, but I could tell a lot of pain was associated with them. He was a very nice and approachable man. The inside of his townhouse was cool. He had a pool table, an Atari video gaming unit, and a bunch of cool guns—all things young men are attracted to. I began to hang out there quite a bit with Stan, and after getting to know Daemon better, Stan started getting a little jealous of me, and I started getting jealous of the other boys who hung out there. I never thought for a second that all the boys hanging around Daemon was a red flag; I was in desperate need of attention from a male figure.

Daemon realized how desperate I was and started giving me more and more attention. I knew I had arrived when he let me play with his pool cue on his pool table. It was a pricy stick with imbedded gold, a horsehair grip, and lots of ivory. He taught me how to play pool well. I started to win games against him and his pool shark cronies. It felt so good to be paid attention to. I ate well when around him. He kept me safe and out of trouble, and he was teaching me good, wholesome things.

One time, he took me into the desert to do some shooting, which I loved. He trained me on gun safety, target practice, and self-defense. He taught me how to fight well as shoot. He realized I was a pretty good marksman. He loved to hunt and camp, and of course I was excited to have those opportunities I'd never had before. Here was a man to teach me about life, the rugged outdoors, and survival skills. I learned how to boil water in cactus barrels, cook, hunt for fruit on cacti, kill game for food, and survive in the desert heat.

I was almost thirteen. Daemon was so good to me, and he had always wanted a son. I had always wanted a dad. We talked at length about my moving in. He was okay with it, so I talked with Mother about it. She was a little apprehensive at first, but she noticed how happy I was and that I was making great strides having a regular father figure in my life. I was becoming more normal, more socially interactive, and much more confident. I moved in with Daemon. I was so excited and couldn't wait till our next camping trip together.

Over the summer, we talked about which of his weapons we'd take on our camping trips. He had everything from pistols to rifles, semiautomatics, illegal automatics, silencers, shotguns, and more.

Daemon had a real liking for one gun in particular, the one he had used on the force and as a federal agent. He had actually killed bad guys with it. He was known on the federal force as being reckless, maybe a little like Jack Bower on *24*. I am a survivalist, a good shot, and someone who knows a great deal about guns and how to use them in self-defense thanks to Daemon.

I earned the next step of my training. We set up silhouettes of human targets and lined them up and down the creek beds in the desert. Daemon strategically placed them in tactical locations without my knowledge of where. We then "hunted" them through the twisting desert washes; we practiced drop-and-rolls, surprise attacks, swing fire, run and fire, all the time identifying our targets labeled as either dangerous or innocent. I would be wiped out after each exercise. Don't mess with Vietnam vets. He graded me at the end of each exercise. It took several outings before I could calm my adrenaline rushes and accurately assess my targets. I took it all very seriously.

I invited several friends with us on our camping and survival trips. They loved to go camping and shoot his guns; they really liked Daemon. We always had a ball in the desert. We'd hang out at an old gold mine that dated to the days of the Old West. According to legend, a pot of gold was hidden in the mine. This always intrigued me, and I did things in that mine that no boy should have been allowed to do. I'm alive today by the grace of God considering the cliffs I climbed. Many others ended up going missing out there in a land with mountains that went up to ten thousand feet and cliffs with nearly 1,000-foot drops as well as desert beauty.

Mountains have played a significant role in my life. I learned from Daemon to be a true survivalist in any situation. That on top of my mental and spiritual survival skills have made me the warrior I claim God has wanted me to be all along.

At the end of each day in the desert, my friends and I ate rabbit stew to celebrate our kills and skills. Besides rabbits, we hunted javelina, a type of wild pig that tastes good if you're hungry. We'd talk all night about how much fun we had shooting our BB gun pistols at camp while playing good cowboy bad cowboy. I still have two BBs in me that I know of. We did wear eye protection for whatever that was worth.

Our fun and games eventually turned into a business for Daemon. He entered me in sharpshooting competitions with his friends and invitees. I had no idea Daemon was making bets and cashing in on my marksmanship. I loved outshooting others. Ironically, I used my right eye, the wrong eye for a left-hander, but I managed to shoot pistols and rifles well.

My first year living with Daemon was perfect; the other boys were jealous of me. I was so excited and felt I had a purpose. I was as good a son to Daemon as he was a father to me.

I played little league baseball and Pop Warner football with my friends and was enjoying a normal life for the first time ever. That is if you can call living with a man you hardly know normal. Daemon did a good job making sure I saw doctors and dentists; he was concerned about my health as much as any father would be. During one of my dental checkups, the X-rays showed a large black spot on my lower left jaw. It turned out to be a large tumor. A maxillofacial surgeon look at it, and he was concerned as well.

Daemon hid the seriousness of it from Mother because he didn't want me to have to move back with her. He told me to keep it a secret, but I argued that Mother should know, so I told her.

The test on the mass was inconclusive, but the cyst-like tumor had eaten a large hole in my jaw. They wasted no time scheduling surgery, but Daemon continued to be very private about the results and wouldn't let the doctor tell me anything other than it was inconclusive.

Later in life, I realized something had stunk about that whole thing. Daemon had never told me what the true results were. Years later, after being troubled about the surgery, I decided I wanted to know the truth. By then, my surgeon had passed away, and it was too much of a hassle to track my records down. It's probably better that I didn't know what my diagnosis was. I remember my nurse telling Daemon and me that the surgeon had believed he'd gotten it all. I was told I should be checked every six months for the first two years then once per year every year after that. But that's all I ever learned about my surgery.

Just before school started, I met the Beast. I had come to know and love Daemon, but I met his counterpart, his other personality if you will. The father I had always wanted, the man I trusted with my heart and life, rocked me to the core. He purposefully gave me more painkillers than what was prescribed after my jaw surgery. While under a helpless dose of them, the darkest moment in my life unfolded. I started getting extremely dizzy. I remember talking out of my mind and trying to be funny. I got nauseous and fell in and out of consciousness. Daemon molested me for the first time and began his reign over my spirit. It was bad. The drugs rendered me completely powerless. I was drugged up and defenseless but awake enough most of the time to know what was happening. It happened just as my spirit had surfaced thinking the coast was clear after so many years. "Why?" I cried out. "Why are you doing this? I thought you were my father! Remember?" But he didn't care. I began passing in and out of consciousness.

When I came to, my spirit had hidden itself again but this time deeper than before. Just as I might have started to grow a spirit, it went into hiding for another twenty years. *This can't be Daemon*, I kept telling myself. *He wouldn't do this to me. That wasn't my father figure, Daemon.* The trauma and drugs made me throw up. My world was spinning out of control, my eyes were blurred, and I was emotionally crashed. I went back to that place and time when my mother had left me on the front lawn in a diaper in view of my friends. I felt I was in a black hole. Daemon told me something like, "If you tell anyone about this, you'll come up missing." I blacked out.

When I came to, he was pointing his prized pistol at me. I was staring down the barrel of a gun and into his yellowish, beady, sick eyes. I thought I was seeing a beast. I went out for a good while. When I came back to consciousness, Daemon was sitting in his chair where he always sat smoking his favorite cigars and acting as if nothing had happened. I began to wonder if it had all been a dream.

But reality set in. Things didn't feel right. I woke up in different clothes. I smelled as though I'd been bathed. I curled up for days and missed school. Daemon repeatedly reminded me that it was in my best interests to not say anything and go back to school as soon as possible. He said, "We don't need your mother to be suspicious."

I knew Daemon had seemed to be getting more and more overly friendly with me, but not knowing any better or having had any real experience of how a father and son act around each other, I had always just passed it off as this is how a father showed love for his son. Daemon had preyed on my desperate need for a father and my insecurities. He destroyed my innocence and all hope for the normal life I thought he and I would have together.

Now, I can recall subtleties that would have clued in an older, less-insecure child. I wished I had had a clue that things weren't right. That was the beginning of a long, dark road. I became deathly afraid of Daemon. I had lived for many years in fear of my mother, and suddenly, I started living in fear every day. I had no doubt he would kill me and perhaps my family if I told anyone. I had lived in mental prisons before; I couldn't understand why my friends lived normal lives but I didn't. I didn't know if this meant I was gay or that I had lost my innocence. So many questions. So much confusion. I had to act as though everything were okay around friends, my mom, John, and my sisters. Inside, I was screaming for help but was too afraid and embarrassed to show my emotions.

What's really frightening as I look back is how well I hid it. I felt it was a matter of survival. I didn't know God was my ally. I believed in God but didn't have a valid relationship with Jesus Christ. I also felt that John was so deep into his own life that he couldn't relate to mine. If he had cared, he would have made me come home where I belonged. If he had been interested in raising me, he would have noticed my brokenness and sensed my troubles. I wonder if he and my mother had ever thought my living with Daemon could have been a bad thing.

The fact was that John had sensed my troubles but didn't want to take them on. I was hoping John would step up to the plate and take me home to be a family. Instead, he'd make remarks that embarrassed me and made me feel I was a joke. But other times, he'd say things that made me feel good about myself. I could never tell what he would say next because he was stoned half the time. I learned to block him out.

He took on very little responsibility for us kids financially or otherwise, though Pamela and Kristen often told me John was good to them. I was jealous, but I was also relieved to know they were safe and well cared for. Looking back, I can see that John didn't want the whole package of our family, just Mom. John wasn't a good father even to his own kids. He and Mom lived together for well over ten years before they married.

I stayed home from school or ditched it for fear that my facial expressions and body language would give me away and put me in harm's way. Daemon knew when I did, but he'd act all surprised when school called him or when he spoke with Mother. She called me one day furious at me but I couldn't tell her what was happening. I was mentally imprisoned. If I had told her, I might have disappeared.

One day, I unloaded on her after hearing one too many bad words from her, something I had never done before and hung up on her. I felt a great weight lifting off my shoulders, but I felt horrible for having yelled at her. Thank you, God, for a good conscience.

Hiding my emotions at school was getting tougher. I became angrier each day. My educational career was tanking. I was brutally raped by Daemon a second time soon after the first. That time, I was not nearly as drugged up because I knew better and monitored my intake of painkillers. It wasn't going to be as easy for him this time, and he knew it. So he came to me with his companion, his gun. He cocked it. I immediately went into a dark hiding place.

I would just talk with God during those times. I went to school the next day because I didn't want to deal with mother yelling at me again. I arrived at school angry at the world. My jaw was still not healed, and I had stitches inside and outside of my jaw. A bully made fun of my swollen jaw. I told him to meet me in the alley after school. I told him we'd work it out there.

Everyone in school found out and showed up. It was quite an event. His first punch went directly to my jaw. I was still on painkillers and had no coordination. He dropped me flat. It was over as quickly as it started. I could tell the kids were disappointed. Makes me wonder if they had had money on me. I was an explosive young man at that point in my life. I had many more fights as a young man and won them all out of sheer anger.

I wished I could say the abuse stopped as suddenly as it started, but it went on for much longer than I care to think about. Yes, until I was sixteen. Daemon was getting mentally sicker and more demented each time he would violate me. I often went to a friend's house as an excuse to get away. Thank God for my brother Leon. Even though Mom and John weren't married yet, he was as close to a brother as anyone could ever ask for. God and Leon never let me down. I'd spend almost all my weekends with him at his mom and stepdad's home.

Daemon questioned me each time I came home to verify I hadn't talked about the bad stuff. My answer to him was always the same: "I wouldn't dare spill the beans." The truth is that I talked about it all the time with God. I was never home later than 8:00 p.m. unless it was a special event. I was so afraid of being late that I'd worry about someone's car breaking down and my not getting home on time. I never wanted to go home to Daemon's. My abuse had gone from bad to worse from hands and spoons to guns and sexual molestation. I was once again afraid every day of my life of what I had to come home to.

One of my worst moments was when I was sixteen. I borrowed a friend's car to take Pamela to a water park. She and I had so much fun that we stayed until 10:00 p.m., when the park closed. I knew there would be consequences. That evening, I crept in hoping I wouldn't wake the Beast. He often went to bed early because he went to work every morning at 3:00. I had to pass through the living room without any light. I walked down the hallway past his bedroom door. His bedroom essentially became mine; I avoided it at all costs, but that was where I was made to sleep every night. I had just made it past his door and inched mine open. Click. The sound of his weapon of choice being cocked. Ironically, I had become a better shot than he was with that gun. Don't think for a second I couldn't have used it on him. The click meant *Get in here now.* I did. He had his way with me. I went into a mental vacuum as I had before and spent the time with God. I often thought about how angry God must have been at that moment. I wondered why He was allowing this to happen to me. I chose not to count how many nights this happened.

That night was one of the worst. Daemon was so concerned that I might have told Pamela. I couldn't convince him otherwise. I became as concerned for her life as I was for my own. I had thought many times of killing him, but God had always stepped in. During the dark moments, I would visualize Emanuel—God with me. I knew I was safe even during the tremendous violations.

Unfortunately for Daemon, God will one day lay a heavy hand on him and he will pay the ultimate price. (Mark 9:42) "But if you cause one of these little ones who trusts in me to fall into sin, it would be better for you to be thrown into the sea with a large mill stone hung around your neck."

Things got even worse. Daemon started needing some extra help to boost his demented sickness. He introduced me to porn videos. He covered all the windows with aluminum foil and turned our living room pitch-black even in the day for maximum privacy. Daemon would tell everyone it was because he loved to watch movies so much. He had a huge collections of VHS tapes, a big-screen projector, and big speakers all around.

One early evening while I was doing homework in the kitchen counter, Daemon slipped on a porno film. He had told me we would watch a show called *Buck Rogers and the Twenty-Fifth Century*. I cried in disgust for what I knew was about to happen to me. None of it made any difference to Daemon. My first clue was always the look. His eyes would turn yellow and empty, he would get a terrible odor about him, and he basically went into another dimension. This time, however, I put up a fight. I resisted. I threatened to talk. He whipped out his pistol and cocked it. I went dark again in my vacuum to be with God again. That time and several times later, he took photos.

This horrific abuse went on until I was almost seventeen. I harbored the pain and masked my life with Daemon so I could stay alive, so my family would not be in danger, and so I could save my dignity. I eventually learned how to escape into my own world. I felt I had lost my soul forever. I kept trying to convince myself I could get through this. *It won't last forever.* I read my Bible after each incident. Oddly enough, I continued to hide the fact that I read the Bible from everyone.

The same God I prayed to as a little boy would become my Father, and my mind was made up—no other father would ever take His place. I've kept my word. If only He had protected me from the sexual abuse ... As crazy as it all sounds, God had a plan, and I needed to remain strong for Him.

Chapter 7

❧ ✦ ❧

Attempted Murder

Backing up a bit. I was thirteen and was starting to get braver. Daemon was sensing that I might talk to my girlfriend. He drove us on our first-ever date. I was surprised that he would let me go on a date with a girl considering how protective he was and worried I would talk. He clearly didn't like me having a girlfriend, but it made me feel normal; I felt attracted to girls, not men. I knew that things with Daemon wasn't normal, but I always tried to prove to myself that I was.

She and I enjoyed the matinee though I can't remember what it was. We left hand in hand. Daemon had not yet arrived to pick me up. As I was walking my girlfriend across the street, I felt a massive blow to my leg. Though I didn't know it then, I'd taken a bullet in what was not a very dangerous neighborhood. I spun around, limped a couple steps, and dropped into the far right lane of the double southbound lane. My girlfriend had made it safely to the sidewalk. I'd seen a cement truck coming and was sure it wouldn't stop in time. My quick thinking saved my life that day. Maybe it was God's quick thinking. It would have been a perfect exit for me. I didn't know at that point in my life if I wanted to live or die. There seemed to be a promise lodged in my brain that God wouldn't let me regret this pain. I'd often thought of ways to end my life, but somehow, I felt God would keep me safe.

The truck ran over me taking only a button off my Ocean Pacific golf-style shirt. The tires somehow missed me as well as the rear differential. Daemon arrived soon after the shooting and saw that I was bleeding. He took us to the ER rather than wait for the emergency vehicles to arrive. I thought it to be a bit odd that Daemon was panicked when he realized my girlfriend had already called the police from a nearby phone booth. Daemon questioned her as though she were either the victim or the shooter. I thought that was a bit weird. She was very shook up, and I was trying to sort things out in my head.

Once I arrived at the hospital, my girlfriend called her mother for a ride home. I'd lost blood but not a life-threatening amount. The X-rays revealed several pieces of lead. One was a nugget close to the surface of my knee, and another smaller piece, a bullet fragment, was lodged in the back of my knee. The doctor determined that taking it out could cause greater damage than leaving it in. Daemon insisted that the surgeon take it out and give it to me as a souvenir. The doctor explained to Daemon that if he took the bullet out, he'd be forced to give it to the police. Daemon was smooth. "Doctor, you won't let Alter have the bullet if you were to pull it out, but he can keep it in his leg? Doesn't make sense." The doctor agreed. He removed the fragments and gave Daemon the larger piece.

Later in life, I had the last fragment removed when I had surgery to remove a tumor the size of a golf ball caused by the irritation the fragment had created. Just as was the case with the tumor removed from my jaw, they couldn't determine if it was truly benign or not. Weird!

At the hospital, I almost did spill the beans about Daemon. I thought it was an opportunity to escape him, but I was worried about my family's lives as well as my own. I was so close to talking, but I noticed Daemon watching me closely with his stressed out yellowish eyes.

Daemon and I left the hospital the same day. I was told I had been very lucky. It was guesstimated that the bullet hit the blacktop first, which made sense based on the angle and trajectory as well as other particulates that were imbedded in my knee bone.

Here's how gullible I was at the time. On our way home, Daemon made a call on his walkie-talkie or military phone or whatever it was. All I knew was that he talked on it occasionally. It was a big military box with a phone-like thing in it. He told me he talked with a few friends on it; it was just a hobby. He said three words: "It didn't work."

When we got home that evening, Daemon asked me for the bullet which the doctor had given me. I gave it to him, but I wanted to keep it as a souvenir as he had promised me. Once he got the bullet in his hand, he told me to tell my mom, sisters, or anyone else that I was not shot by a large-caliber gun. I was to tell everyone that it was a .22 magnum or even a BB gun. *That's weird. Why?* I asked myself. Daemon knew I recognized the bullet type. I was told that the bullet would no longer exist because he didn't want to worry my family.

That evening, the police showed up looking for the evidence. Daemon eventually turned the evidence over to the police, and I was heavily interviewed. The doctor should never have turned over the evidence to Daemon, but Daemon was good at manipulating people. I had my chance to escape, but I couldn't get past the fear for my life and my family's. I did a remarkable job staying poised and on point with my lies. I was willing to save Daemon out of fear because I believed he was the devil and would find me even in my sleep.

It eventually dawned on me that Daemon had tried to kill me. Could he have hired someone to try to kill me? Who had he talked to on the walkie-talkie? As far as I know the police never asked to interview Daemon.

I waited until he was asleep that night and checked his guns to see if one had been discharged. I discovered his prized possession had just been completely cleaned. I asked him the next morning if he had taken that shot at me. I was crying and afraid I'd end up dead right then, but he said no and offered no explanation.

The molestations stopped around when I turned seventeen. Daemon had a couple of health issues—he'd have dizzy spells and almost fainted several times. He ended up in the hospital and had surgery but hid from me what had been found. I believe he lost his sex drive; that was my saving grace.

God is allowing me to remember more and more. He purposely gave me more than I could handle so I would keep focused on Him and get through this alive. I struggled for years getting up the nerve to allow God to use my story. He has been so patient with me. I must say that it hasn't all been easy, but my wife has been my rock, and my pastors, friends, family, and home life group have been my prayer warriors and support structures.

But back then, I wondered how I could escape Daemon's clutches. How could I save myself and not look suspicious?

When I was sixteen, my best friend in high school was having a rough time with his mother, and he was without a father. He needed a place to live, so I offered my room to him. I thought about it long and hard. I was worried he'd become a statistic like me. I was afraid for his life, but I never told him that. I've felt guilty to this day that I put my buddy's life in jeopardy and he never knew it.

Daemon let him come stay with us. Why not? He was another boy. He was much bigger than me and was much less needy of a father than I was. I thought he might help me escape. He was with Daemon and me until I turned seventeen. Daemon was so good at hiding the real him that my buddy never knew what went on. The one thing I didn't think through very well was that my buddy needed a room and took mine. Though I wasn't in it often, it was my only refuge. How could I have been so stupid? I had assumed he and I would get two single beds and share my room. Daemon told my buddy that I could just stay with him in his room instead. My buddy thought nothing of it. My plan backfired and caused me more grief and pain.

If I told my friend about Daemon, could he rescue me? No. He had no place to go either and wasn't trained with weapons. His life could have been in danger if he had tried to help me out of there. While he lived there, I was able to stay out later with my friends. Daemon had to loosen his grip on me a little to keep things looking as normal as possible. I was comforted having my buddy there with me. He's my best friend to this day. He doesn't yet know about my secrets with Daemon. He will learn as will so many others when he reads this book.

I was sure that if my buddy and I ran off, Daemon would find us. He had been trained to track down people. How ironic. He'd been trained to put people away but had gotten away with molesting children for so many years.

Chapter 8

❧

The Exodus

When I was seventeen, I was working two jobs—one at Sears in the catalogue department weekday evenings and the other at a printing company on the weekends to support Daemon and myself while going to school. Though Daemon hadn't violated me for well over a year, I knew he didn't want to let me out of his sight. I had an old '77 Camaro I drove illegally with no insurance. I had saved up $500 for it. And I scripted a cunning escape from Daemon.

I came to him trembling one day knowing that I might end up dead for what I was ready to do. I still don't know how I dreamed this up myself. It was another God moment. I had spent a weekend with Leon. I had told him my life story and escape plans. Leon also wanted Daemon to go away. I insisted that we let God have him. Leon, my rock-solid friend and brother, was devastated. He was willing to do anything to help me. He asked me to come live with him. I couldn't do that because if I didn't finish high school, my family would start figuring things out. I didn't want to reveal the many embarrassing events of my life to anyone else, at least not then.

This is how my plan developed. I was watching the news in the living room one day. In the mid-1980s, we all started hearing more about DNA for forensics purposes; DNA matching was becoming a threat to criminals. I made sure Daemon and I watched one part of the series before I said anything to him.

About two weeks later, I told him I'd saved strands of his hair and other types of specimens hoping that one day the DNA would be of

49

use. I explained that friends of mine had hidden it. I didn't have any specimens, but he didn't know that. I told Daemon that if he didn't let me leave peacefully, I'd expose him. If I ended up dead or missing, my confidants would go to my family, friends, and the police to expose him. I told him I had copies of some of the pictures he had taken during the molestations. That was another lie.

He became extremely uncomfortable and agitated. I'd gotten deep into his head. Fire was coming out of his eyes. He never touched me. I told him that if I ever heard another click of a gun again, I would end his perfect little fantasy world. I told him to not say a word to anyone about my moving out. I told him to cover for me at all costs. I told him he could walk free and never worry again. I left a portion of my clothes, old toys, and other things in my room to make it look as if I were still living there. I told him not to follow me. He didn't.

It was over. I was out. Praise God. I was free. I was only seventeen. My mom and John had no clue. Daemon clearly covered for me until I finished high school. I was able to get an apartment by lying about my age. It was a rundown unit with lots of roaches. But I slept better with all those roaches than I had a single night with Daemon. I had to pull this off until I graduated. I did. My mom thought I was living with Daemon while I finished up school; she never knew because she never checked up on me that I know of. If she had, I'm sure Daemon covered it well. He was a master liar.

One day after school, Daemon followed me to my apartment. I was visibly shaken. He looked remorseful. I told him that if I saw him again his life would be over. I threatened to call the police. He left. But I realized he knew where I lived. I called Regina and Franco, Leon's mom and stepdad. After my mom's boyfriend John had divorced Regina, she had married one of the greatest men I've ever met—Franco. My soon-to-be new parents were a godsend. With Leon's blessing, I called Regina and Franco and told them about Daemon. Leon swore to me that if I didn't, he would.

They picked me up. I left my car behind so Daemon couldn't track me. He had friends in the police force and the FBI. I never knew what happened to that car. I moved in with my brother Leon, Regina, and Franco, who protected me. Regina and Franco lent me $3,500 for a car, a generous loan I eventually paid off. They taught me how to budget and how to hold down a job. Leon was gracious; he invited me to share his room and even his clothes. He and I were about the same size and build. It wasn't always easy for him, but he loved me and made sure I was well cared for.

While living with Leon, I was able to relax for just enough time to gain my composure and breathe again. Leon and I would do chores around the house and yard and earn money from Franco so Leon and I could enjoy a nice breakfast on occasion. Franco owned a successful specialty coatings company. Leon worked for Franco for a number of years. Leon also enjoyed his career as an actor. He was in a number of commercials such as "Got Milk?" and "Wells Fargo Bank" where he was a cowboy riding hard on a horse to intersect the stagecoach that delivered the mail. He also did a roofing company commercial and had a small role in a production with Kirsty Alley, *Look Who's Talking*, as well as a couple of parts in the *Young Riders* TV series. He was really starting to find himself and his career. He was a member of the Screen Actors' Guild and had a quite a portfolio.

Leon was a handsome, talented young man with a heart of gold. He despised cussing, smoking, and drugs, and he didn't hang around people who would do any of those things. He was very dedicated to his friends and family. He didn't have many girlfriends, but he was all in with those he had. He was always there for me as a good listener, friend, brother, and confidant. He and I were inseparable. He loved his dog, a large Doberman pinscher.

He and I enjoyed camping, action, adventure, and risk. I want to give you a sense of the passion we shared. I owned a yellow Toyota SR-5 four-wheel drive with thirty-five-inch Mickey Thompson tires. We'd let a little air out of them and hop on the railroad tracks and drive on the rails. The tires would cup the tracks and hold the truck center to the tracks. We'd get up to sixty miles per hour, and by the grace of God, we never met a train. We did get chased by railroad security however.

One day, Leon and I decided to set fire to a haystack that was about three stories high. It was in the middle of a large hay field a few miles from his house. We didn't like the farmer and for good reason. But we knew the farmer well enough because of his cute daughter; she had taken us on tours of the mazes formed by haystacks many times when we were kids. The hay was old and unusable or we would never have set it on fire. We actually did the farmer a favor; he wasn't allowed by law to burn it themselves.

The haystack looked pretty much like a high rise with windows of sorts due to poor stacking habits and the tendency of farmers to pull out individual bales here and there. The stack would have these holes in it that led to rooms of sorts inside. We got inside to make sure no one else was there. Leon lit a string of firecrackers, and my ears were ringing in the tight quarters. That started a smoky fire. Leon and I started on our way out followed by flames and smoke. We could feel the heat, and we began to gag and choke, but we made it out. We kept our distance from the stack and watched it being engulfed in flames that I'm sure could be seen for miles.

We argued about who saved whose life all the way home. Shortly after making it home, the cops came knocking. Okay, so maybe I shouldn't have told them, "Officers, well … I don't really know why we did that except that we were trying to prove who would save whose life." Of course we had both practically climbed over one another on our way out. Yeah, we got into heaps of trouble over that one.

We once hiked the desert to hunt rattlesnakes. Leon was a cowboy with his late-1800s design Winchester and a .357 Ruger Blackhawk. I planned to sell the heads and tails, the rattlers, to gift shops that would put them under glass and sell them as souvenirs. Leon was doing more talking than looking and completely overlooked a javelina about thirty feet from him that was cornered in a crevice. I had long since learned never to corner a javelina. I told Leon to stop. My heart was pounding while Leon thought it was some kind of fun. He fired his rifle above the javelina's head, and two baby javelinas came running out. Leon was so enamored with the little critters that he didn't see their mother charging at him to protect them. Javelina teeth are long, sharp, and can cut through flesh and bone. She made it to about two feet from his leg before I shot from the hip and tagged her behind the ear at about eight feet.

Leon never said thank you; he simply murmured, "Lucky shot." Then he ranted about how I had killed the babies' mother. He wanted to take the babies home and raise them. Thanks to my common sense and long-winded dissertation as to why we couldn't raise the piglets, we went home emptyhanded, not even a snake. A mountain ranger patrol officer followed us home. We tried to ignore him and were sure we had lost him after a few miles. Again, we had some explaining to do.

In short, Leon and I were certainly mischievous, but we never did drugs, steal, cuss, or look for trouble. It always seemed trouble found us, though. We were good kids who just happened to take risks. Many risks.

Because of my pent-up anger due to my difficult life and the emotional baggage I carried, I became a fighter. I never started them, but I was always eager to finish them. Leon and I would chase the bad kids around the streets one by one when they started trouble. As a group, they often teased the cowboys at school like Leon and me, but when they were alone, they weren't that tough.

Leon and I had walkie-talkies in our vehicles. When bored, we went out on revenge campaigns. One of us would spot a bad guy and radio the other. We'd stalk our prey. When I gave the cue, Leon and I would jump out of the trucks and tackle the mean guy, blindfold him, and shave his head with the electric clippers we kept in our trucks. We wore masks so they wouldn't know who we were. One by one, the bad guys showed up at school bald. I'm not proud of that, but it was my way of saying I wouldn't tolerate mean people any longer. I look back at my anger and how immature, scared and mentally wrung out I was. I'm so lucky to not have ended up on drugs or in prison. Thank you, Jesus.

Chapter 9

❧ ❦

Marriage Number One: Lust

Sometime after I moved in with Leon, I met Bobbie, a beautiful seventeen-year-old. She had me at her first smile. It didn't take long before she and I were head over heels for one another. She was a fit, trim gymnast with an eye on the Olympics who had to quit gymnastics after she was discovered to have a dangerous heart murmur. I caught her on the downward spiral from that sad news. She was a confused young woman who had experienced poor parenting. Many of her brothers and sisters had different fathers. Bobbie was angry much as I was about certain things; we shared some similar pains.

Less than a year after we had met, we were married by a justice of the peace. Bobbie had just turned eighteen and I was nineteen. It was held in the backyard of Mother's home. The ceremony went very well, and Franco, Leon's stepfather, gave her away since she didn't know who her father was. Leon was my best man. Meme Amelie and one of her friends created chaos at our wedding. Several of Leon's and my friends didn't see eye to eye with Meme's friend. A cousin of mine was a female boxer who also didn't like Meme at all. Throw in some alcohol and what we ended up with was mayhem. My cousin used her boxing skills on the house door while Meme hid behind it. That happened after Meme had pushed her into the pool. Several others ended up in the pool as well.

I moved out of Mama Regina's and Franco's to live with my bride in a small trailer at a dude ranch. We were broke. I began breaking some of the Indian paints that had come from Indian reservations. They made great trail horses. I had two options to break these horses—the hard way or the long way. At fifty bucks a head, I couldn't afford the long way, so I chose the fast way, bronc riding.

Bobbie and I had a deteriorating relationship from the start; we never stood a chance. God clearly was not at the forefront of our relationship. I had married her solely out of lust, and I paid the price for years to come. I hadn't learned to trust. I was no better for her than she was for me. She cheated on me right out of the gates by going back to her old boyfriend. I tried to see it through with her. I believed I loved her.

Chapter 10

❦

The Arrest

I was twenty in 1986. I worked hard at a pipeline company installing natural gas lines as my main source of income, and I broke horses for some extra cash. I bought a white, 1979 F-250 Ford pickup I was so proud of.

I was coming home from work one day and was pulled over for a missing tail light. The officer said, "Mr. Pain, this truck matches the description of a similar truck that has been reported stolen."

"Why yes, officer," I replied sarcastically. "I stole it all right. The man who sold it to me was upside down on it. I paid next to nothing for it. I didn't realize it was illegal to get a bargain by capitalizing on another's woes."

He didn't appreciate my quick-witted response. He took his time running my registration. He came back with the news my registration was clean, my truck wasn't the one he was looking for. "Phew!" I replied with a show of some angst. He apologized and sent me on my way. I drove off.

But shortly after, I saw the flashing blue and whites in my rearview mirror again. I came to a full stop in the middle of the road just to irritate the same officer who had just pulled me over. This time he was walking toward me with different body language. I was worried he had taken my disrespect for him personally. He had one hand on his gun grip and the other hand on his radio. He asked me about some unpaid tickets and said he had warrants for my arrest.

Within minutes, three other police cars arrived. I felt like a criminal.

I'd never been in trouble with the law. I must have been one mean bean in my previous life because I had apparently left a bad taste in the police officer's mouth a mile back. I didn't think making a deal with God right then would save me from whatever was about to happen.

"Mr. Pain, you have the right to remain silent ... any ..."

I started crying not because I was a big baby or scared but because I knew something was terribly wrong and I was already worn out from life in general. My reaction took the six officers by surprise; I think they were worried I'd pull a Houdini disappearing trick or pull a gun.

I put my hands behind my back for the handcuffs and was put in the back of a squad car. "How cool is this?" I said to the officer. "My first police escort."

The officer asked if I was okay on the way to the jail. All I could mutter was, "And you thought I was a criminal, didn't you?" The officer replied, "I'm just doing my job, sir."

I was in a holding cell for what seemed an eternity. I was able to make a call just like in the movies, but Leon didn't answer. I called Mom. I don't know why, but I thought she'd believe my story. I told her that I'd been arrested but didn't know why. I knew she would think that was just another lie. "You got yourself into this mess, so get yourself out."

In mother's defense, I had become quite a good liar due to my life with Daemon. I had lied all my life to protect her and my reputations. I lied to stay alive. I lied to get my apartment when I was underage. I lied to simply stay alive; it was my defense mechanism.

Sixteen hours later, a judge asked me if I wanted to plead guilty. I asked for what. He said for failure to pay my tickets. Nothing was making sense; no one was willing to hear me. I knew I had one expired ticket but no more than that, and it was for a nonmoving violation. I had intended to pay it, but I had to eat first. I went into a black hole as I had when being violated by Daemon. I was shaking so hard I couldn't control my arms. The judge sentenced me to ten days. I must have looked like an idiot crying and sniveling and promising to pay the ticket. I was a broken man becoming more broken.

I was fingerprinted and photographed. I was thrown into a cell with ten or so other men. I underwent a full-body search with other inmates around. It was a violation if you know what I mean. I had a flashback to the time I was in the front yard in diapers and times when Daemon had violated me.

I was then escorted to a cell I shared with one other prisoner. I read books, mopped floors, and served food. I was well behaved. On day ten, the sheriff came into my cell. A guard hollered, "Roll it up." I began to roll up my pant legs thinking maybe I was going to be searched again. "Have a seat, Mr. Pain," the sheriff said. He handed me a driver's license and asked me to look at it closely. It was my name all right, but the picture wasn't mine, it was of Peter, my wife's little brother. He had apparently run up many tickets under my name but with false ID in two states. I received a heartfelt apology from the sheriff, who put his arm around me when I broke down. I believe I could have sued the city, but I never did. I'm just not built that way.

I called Bobbie to pick me up. I never told her about Peter. He had put me in the slammer, and I wanted to clean his clock. My gentle soul was about to go Satan on him. I couldn't find him, and I never saw him again. I was filled with thoughts of revenge, but I had no money and had lost my job. I was once again completely spiritually broken. I never told my mother the truth about my innocence; I was sure she wouldn't have believed me.

Several months later, I was pulled over again. I was as nervous as could be, but I had all the paperwork from the former investigation in my glove compartment; it would prove my innocence. That time, the police officers treaded lightly. I'd been pulled over because I had allegedly collected and kept some tenants' rent as a manager of an apartment complex. I was able to prove it wasn't me. It turned out that my mother-in-law's boyfriend had impersonated me by using my birth certificate to get a job as a manager of an apartment complex and had skipped town with the rent money. Apparently my birth certificate has make its rounds to this whole family.

I was able to wiggle out of that one, but I was getting angrier with each incident. I was a walking nuclear bomb. After that, I carried my documents with me everywhere I went. I didn't know how I would react if a next time were to come.

Chapter 11

❧ ⚜ ☙

The Affairs

My older sister Kristen moved with her husband to Utah. She never judged me; she always believed in me. I had a great deal of trust in my sisters, but I could relate better to Kristen at that time in my life. She knew me better than anyone in my immediate family did. I wanted to be near her. I also thought Bobbie and I needed a fresh start.

It wasn't long before Bobbie and I moved closer to Kristen and her husband. I quickly got a job at a car repair place and then soon after, took a better-paying job at a tire shop. We purchased a plot of land with a trailer with a lease-to-own agreement. It was near a river. The trailer needed lots of work; it didn't have a living room floor for one thing.

A few weeks later, Bobbie asked me if she could see her family in California. I encouraged her to go because our trailer was no place for a woman. I planned to get a floor installed while she was gone. Creatures often entered our place through the missing floor. One morning, I literally shared breakfast with a raccoon.

During the first week of Bobbie's two weeks away, I took measurements and bought all I needed to fix the floor. I realized something was wrong when Bobbie wasn't answering my calls and her mother and sisters weren't talking either. Her two-week vacation went to three and then four weeks. Bobbie's sister finally told me she had taken up with someone else. I went out of my mind. I couldn't take it any longer. I decided that if she wouldn't divorce me, I'd divorce her. I was a walking stick of dynamite.

I told my boss I wanted to go to California with a purpose that wasn't a good purpose. He talked some sense into me, and I stayed. I tried to work on the trailer, but I fell into a deep depression. Kristen visited me daily; she was deeply worried for me. I was losing what little weight I had, but my psychological burdens were getting heavier. I slept for days on the living room couch close to the hole in the floor. It was cold at night. I had to stay awake the best I could by candlelight to keep the critters and wild animals at bay. My shotgun gave me some comfort.

I wasn't eating or talking to anyone, and I missed a lot of work, but I never stopped praying to God even with my damaged soul, missing spirit, and broken heart. Though my wife had a number of her own issues, I wasn't helping her with them. I didn't know how. I was never taught how to be a man. If Kristen hadn't been there, I would have probably died from starvation and lack of sleep. I looked like death.

Bobbie came home. She told me she had met a man from the Middle East, a prince or something. That was the third time she had cheated on me in less than two years. Her relationship with the prince had come to an end; I suspected it was because she was worried she was pregnant. Once most of my anger subsided, I wanted to fight for her and keep our marriage alive.

I was promoted to assistant manager at the tire shop. My boss asked me to come up with a slogan for the business, and I did: "Welcome to Simeon Tire. We hope you've enjoyed your experience with our company and crew. We Guarantee to Tire, Shock, Brake, and Exhaust You!" I thought it was great, as did the employees and customers.

I had a bad moment at the place. We repaired huge truck and farm equipment tires, and it could get dangerous. The rims were not solid; they were split ringed in two parts, and they could separate as you aired up a tire if they weren't connected properly. We'd air them up in a cage to protect ourselves; rims coming apart under air pressure could kill someone.

I wanted to blow up a tire tube to show the employees how dangerous it could be if aired up outside the cage. Actually, I just wanted to blow up a tube. I grabbed one that you could have driven a Prius through. I knew it would take about twenty minutes to pump enough air into it to make it go boom. Well, I got distracted. I proved the big bang theory with that one. When the tube blew, the building shook and the windows shattered. All of them. Even some windows across the street and some windshields of vehicles in the parking lot. The noise was deafening. The explosion was something I had never experienced. One of the tire techs watching my experiment was blown twenty feet back. *Uh, I'm in deep doo-doo.* Thank goodness no one had been seriously hurt.

I calmly went to my trailer and started packing. My boss called and told me that I wasn't fired but that I'd have to pay for the damages out of my pay. That amounted to $23,000. I couldn't afford that. What a loser I was! I couldn't face up to my own problems. I didn't know how to.

On top of that, Bobbie told me, "I'm pregnant!" She was smiling, but I suspected I wasn't the father. Bobbie wanted to move close to her mother, who had moved to Los Angeles. I had no money and was deeply in debt. Though her mother had caused me so many problems, I knew I wouldn't be the best husband for her because of all my baggage. I thought the best thing to do was get her close to her mom as we awaited the baby. We picked up and moved to California. *God, what am I doing? I don't suppose you approve of this? Even a little?*

It was mid-December 1989, and things were getting worse. Bobbie was eight months pregnant. We were broke. We were living with her grandmother. Bobbie suffered from a heart condition, and the baby was also suffering from an overdeveloped placenta and something wrong with the umbilical cord. Their heartbeats were abnormal; their blood pressure was dropping. I got her to the hospital, where Bobbie's and the baby's blood pressures and heartbeats were brought under control. They were thinking about taking the baby that night but decided to let it go to term.

I was so concerned for them and prayed for them. I loved her and our unborn child as best I could. I invited God into my marriage out of desperation. I was afraid of losing them both. When Bobbie and I got home from the hospital that evening, I dropped to my knees and prayed to God. I knew He was with me; He had proven that so many times in my past, but I didn't know God intimately. I still read the Bible, and I was slowly figuring out that my not having accepted Christ was hindering my ability to have a real relationship with Him. So I made a deal with God, one I fully intended on keeping. "Dear God, give me a healthy baby and keep Bobbie healthy, and I'll learn more about you and will follow you all my remaining days." That was it. Oh, I almost forgot. "And God, I want a boy."

I didn't say please or thank you; I said "You give me" and "I want you to …" I had been talking to God like that for more than fifteen years. I knew no better, but He knew that and nonetheless extended me grace upon grace. God smiled down on me that day regardless of my spiritual state. I think He believed me.

Bobbie went through a flawless delivery that Christmas Day, and Jason Daniel, JD as we called him, was a healthy eight and a half pounds and nineteen and a half inches. God had shown His mighty power to me that day.

And the selfish deal I had made with Him changed my life. I wasn't all in yet, but I knew it was coming. I could feel it. Since the day I made my deal with God, I've read the Bible cover to cover eighteen times, not counting hearing it at church and in Bible study. I'm implying I kept my promise to Him.

Not long after JD was born, Bobbie needed to find a job. We were in a tough state financially; my pay wasn't enough to cover our living and medical expenses. Bobbie's mother watched Jason while we worked.

Bobbie found a job at a company that made food trays for the airlines. She wasn't there long before she started coming home late. It became clear she was having another affair, this time with Payton, her boss. They were both fired for violating company regulations. Payton studied law, and I heard he would represent and help Bobbie through the divorce.

Technically, I should have been the one to divorce her, but God kept me grounded at least in that regard. I couldn't imagine not fathering Jason. I was growing weak, weary, and sick from stress and lack of nutrition again. I felt I was such a loser and a weakling. *God, do I have to make another deal with you to get some results here?*

I called my faithful sister Kristen, who was always there for me. She was also struggling in her marriage and wanted a divorce. She left him, came to California, and took me back to my old stomping grounds even though she had a baby and was scared. She always rescued me whenever I wrecked the train. I was selfish then. I was all about poor me. I had to pay her back. Thank you, Kristen, for always loving me and being there for me. I'll always love you, sister.

Chapter 12

❦

The Big Save: Born Again

I was back home with a chip on my shoulder. I'd come full circle. I was wifeless, lifeless, spiritless, and 800 miles from my son, whom I missed terribly. But I was happy to be back in familiar surroundings.

I was a few months into reading the Bible every day. I realized God had had my back and had followed me. He had plans for me, and He had answered my prayers even when I was unsure whom I was praying to. He had accepted my deal. I wanted to know more about Him, but I knew that would come in His timing.

I was homeless for the first time in my life. I had no one to go to but Mom. I was afraid to ask her to take me in; I was sure she and John would say no. Much to my surprise, they said yes. That was the beginning of a very slow rekindling of our relationship. God certainly had something to do with her taking me in. I began to feel mother was there for me as a dedicated Mother for the first time in my life.

While I was living with them, they came home one evening after John had been drinking heavily. He and mom had been playing horseshoes at a party. As Mom had drawn back to pitch a horseshoe, she had hit John on the cheek. He had a big bruise and was in a foul mood. At home, he went on a rant as drunk people tend to do. I'd lived through my father's drunken rants. John was telling me I wouldn't amount to anything. I didn't say a word. I'd seen enough lives ruined by alcohol. I did continue to respect him, and I treated him fairly, but I never got close to him again.

At times, God intervenes in relationships, but this wasn't one of those times. It's okay to stay away from people who will bring you down. I knew we'd never be like father and son. I believed I wasn't fatherable after having lived with Daemon. In all fairness to John, perhaps he didn't have a chance either way you looked at it.

I once again turned to God and learned more about how God was my Father. Each new letdown in my life became less and less painful. My skin had toughened up, but also, God was comforting me through this pain. Still, I didn't understand what our relationship was supposed to look like. I had only a childlike faith, but that was enough to keep me connected to Him. It was a foundation I built on that led me to Jesus. More and more, the Bible was speaking to me.

I was at Mom's only briefly, but it was long enough to know she had some soft spots in her heart for me. I realized she loved me, but we had some work to do. We danced around each other for a couple of months pretending our relationship was hunky-dory. We had some good moments. She'd tell me she had always loved me and was proud of me, and I loved her, but I needed more than what she was capable of giving me at that point in our lives.

May 19, 1999, was the eve of the seed. I had a nervous breakdown. I couldn't think. I couldn't talk. I couldn't breathe. I felt as though I were dying. I couldn't take one more bad thing in my life. I prayed to God, but no matter how hard I prayed and even though I felt His presence, I couldn't get my spirit filled. I was empty, depressed. I never thought of suicide—I was too much of a warrior—but I think God had me under a spiritual suicide watch. He heard me. He told me through prayer to call Ron, my sister Pam's husband.

Ron was a good Christian, husband, and father, a great example of who I wanted to be. Pamela had a strong relationship with Ron and God. I called up Ron late on the eve of the seed. I could barely speak. He knew something was up. "Alter, why don't we meet at Goose Park tomorrow?"

"See you there," I said. "Goodnight, and thank you, Ron." I slept surprisingly well that night. I had a twinge of excitement that I would lose the empty feeling in my heart.

May 20, 1999, was the day God planted a seed in my heart. Ron and I sat on a park bench for what seemed eight hours. When I told him about the deal I had made with God, he laughed so hard that he was crying because of the ridiculousness of my deal. We talked about so many questions I had having read the Word more consistently. With grace and love, he helped me understand the importance that Jesus plays in my relationship with God. He told me Christ had died on the cross for me. I sort of knew that, but I was blind to the significance of His death.

Ron said God had been with me since I was born. He'd been present with each step I'd taken. He had never stopped loving me. Ron told me God had been trying to get my attention in all the dreams I'd had in which I felt His presence. He said my eyes weren't fixed on Jesus. Ron was right. I knew I had to come to the Lord through Jesus so we could complete our relationship and I could experience eternity with Him. Ron explained that His death and resurrection had freed me from my sins and that my spirit would become whole again. Ron asked me if I was ready to take this journey with Christ. I said yes. Ron had me say a simple prayer with him.

"God, I need your Son Jesus to come into my heart. I want a complete relationship with you. Jesus, I believe with all my heart that you were given to me as a gift from God. I believe you died for me on the cross and your blood was shed to erase my sins and allow me to live forever more in your kingdom. I believe you were raised from the dead so I would no longer be bound by my sins. God, thank you for giving me this gift of life. I do love you, amen."

Ron and I parted ways, and I felt as though the weight of the world was off my shoulders. I didn't change my ways overnight. The seed would grow slowly in my heart, but it grew deep roots. I was so tightly wound with energy after that day. I had to expend my energy by running every evening for miles and miles, and even that wasn't enough, so I started to do sprints. I had energy I couldn't account for. This was the day I began a gradual turn toward God's desires for me. Some people who are saved jump right in and have this amazing experience and go gangbusters with God. Not me. I wasn't the trusting type. I planned on asking Jesus to be my Daddy, but I'd known Him for only one day. Even though Jesus proved himself to me by dying on the cross for me, I had to experience a trusting relationship for a while. Every father figure

I had ever had had wronged me or left me. I had to be able to count on Jesus, but I thought trusting Him would take some doing.

I moved out of my mother's home when I got a job working on cars. I worked hard and landed a management position. I was assigned to a store. I formed good relationships with several mechanics; we had each other's backs. I was best man at a couple of their weddings. I felt respected, trusted, and a part of the team. I won manager of the year awards twice, but I felt the techs had made that possible. These achievements were huge for me. I started to feel I had some value.

It was a quiet time in my life. I spent a lot of time with Leon. I lived in a small apartment in Chandler; I wasn't rich, but for the first time I felt secure. Jesus was with me, but I was still standoffish with Him. I tried my luck at dating. I met a woman through work, but I found out she was married. That was all I needed to cancel my pursuit. Nothing good comes from an affair. I felt terrible for the pain I caused her, but I realized I wasn't ready for a relationship. I was way too broken though I did a good job hiding that. Or so I thought.

One evening, Kristen called. She was in desperate need of a home for her baby and herself. I let her move in with me and eventually ended up in another place to give her some space. I made just enough money to help her out, but I was strapped after each paycheck. I loved having the opportunity to be there for my older sister as she'd been there for me through many dark moments. I trusted her. I hated how hard life was for us. I actually felt a little Christlike for the first time in my life. I felt I was showing love, grace, and compassion.

I went to California to finalize my divorce with Bobbie. That was the last time I saw Jason, my son, for many years. I lost track of them. They moved about quite often. I was told to keep sending child support to them, but I was sending it to a post office box. I'd catch up on child support every time I fell behind. The system is tough on fathers. I paid and paid, but no matter how many times I tried to get the government to offer up information on their whereabouts, they simply wouldn't. When I complained that the divorce decree gave me visitation rights, I was treated like a bad guy. Every Christmas, Jason's birthday, depressed me. I wondered where he was.

I yearned for the chance to get to know my son. I was consumed with finding him, but I needed money for that. I learned that a big tire company was trying to develop a brake and front-end business, and I had some mechanical experience to offer. I interviewed for the job, which involved mentoring the techs. I made a decent wage, and this class-act company took good care of me. I was excited to be in on the ground floor level of this test project. I worked there for four years, but I never gave up my search for Jason.

I was taking care of myself well enough, but after child support, I had little money left over to find out where he was. Even if I had found him, I would have had to fight to see him. I hired private investigators twice. I quickly gave up on the first one. The second one, Lefty, was the answer to my prayers. He had lost his right arm in a hit-and-run auto accident and had had to endure a lengthy recovery. After Dan (which I'll use as his real name) got out of the hospital, he started checking in with the police to see if they had learned anything new about his hit-and-run, and that had led to his becoming a private investigator.

He and I hit it off immediately. He charged me only half his normal price because he loved my story. He dedicated himself to finding my son. I asked him, "Why are you so locked onto my case? You're losing money on it." He told me that some time ago, he had discovered the police hadn't been working on his case at all; they'd just been giving him lip service. He took on the case himself and found the woman who had injured him so severely. Her name was Dani. She had told him she had promised her husband she'd quit drinking. Her husband had promised to divorce her if she didn't. She had told Dan she couldn't admit to the accident. She had said, "Every day I've struggled with my decision to run from the scene. I can't live with my guilt any longer." He had thought she was suicidal. He had planned on taking her into the police station, but after learning she had lost her job, husband, and dignity, Dan hadn't had the heart to turn her in.

He told her he was a Christian. He helped her get sober, and he fell in love with her after she gave herself to Jesus. They got married. He realized he was pretty good at private investigations. He hired her as his secretary.

Dan and Dani found Jason at an elementary school under a false last name. That explained why I hadn't been able to find him for years. Dan took some pictures of him, but it had been a while; I couldn't recognize that it was him.

I immediately flew to where Dan and Dani said they had found Jason though the last-minute ticket took my last dollar. Dan and Dani picked me up at the airport and put me up at their home. The next morning, Dan and I set off on our mission together. We parked within eyesight of the school playground fence. Kids poured out with all their pent-up energy, but Jason never showed. I had vowed to not go back home until I had seen him. Dan and I went back two more times. On the third day, I saw my boy playing and cried. I didn't know if I should talk to him. I took Dan's advice and didn't rock this little seven-year-old boy's world just then. What a handsome kid he was. He looked just like me. I had little doubt he was mine, but I wasn't worried about being wrong. I decided I never needed to know the truth. God had planted this paternal desire in my heart.

I had to figure out how to meet him in a way that would be in his best interests. I was filled with hope. I was sure that one day, Jason would learn who his real father was and that I would enjoy a relationship with him. Dan had learned Bobbie and Payton were married, and we found her address through court records.

I went home and worked at my job with a renewed passion. I hoped that one day I'd be fathering my son again. I continued to reach out to Bobbie to initiate a dialogue, but they moved around so much I could hardly keep track. I tried to be respectful about breaking the news to Jason; Bobbie had admitted to hiding that fact from him. She knew I didn't have the money to fight it in court. At least I knew where they lived and that my child support was getting to him.

I started to learn something neat about being a Christian—other people were praying for me, some I didn't even know. My younger sister Pamela and Ron had set up prayer chains everywhere I turned. And so did Dan and Dani. What a powerful and hopeful feeling this was. I knew God would answer the prayers in His time.

Chapter 13

❧ ❧

God's Wrath

I normally spent weekends with Leon; that took my mind off my troubles. We ran around like a couple of nut jobs and had fun together. We'd go to our favorite pizza place and work out at the gym often. After one action-packed weekend, I got a call from Mom. She was devastated and regretted to tell me Daemon was dead.

A boy had shot him with his favorite gun out in the desert where we used to go. It made me sick that my mom was crying. I was crying not because he was dead but because she had no idea he'd been a sick child molester. I was crying because I had never felt I could tell her the truth. I was crying for all the times I had had to retreat into that dark place when I was being molested. During those times, Jesus would continue to whisper to me in my head something I hadn't heard or read elsewhere until I started reading the Bible to keep my deal with God. "But if you cause one of these little ones who trusts in me to fall into sin, it would better for you to be thrown into the sea with a large millstone hung around your neck." (Mark 9:42) It was a major spiritual moment for me. I couldn't stop crying for so many reasons. I replayed the molestations and Mark 9:42 over and over in my head. The pain was nearly paralyzing but I had always known that knew that it would come to an ugly end for Daemon. This is a very powerful verse. "But if you cause one of these little ones who trusts in me to fall into sin, it would better for you to be thrown into the sea with a large millstone hung around your neck." This clearly says don't mess with His word, especially because He keeps it. While crying with my mother, I realized it wasn't about Daemon's death. Jesus was once again whispering to me, and that trumped my mother's words and tears. The Beast was dead. I believe it was by the hand of God, not that little boy who had shot him. You would have had to have lived in my shoes to know that. Being a tenderhearted, forgiving Christian, I managed to squeeze out some tears for Daemon, who I was sure was bound for hell. This was the moment I learned forgiveness, a major sign of spiritual maturity for me. I took a deep mental breath and said, "I forgive you, Daemon."

"Alter," my mother said, "repeat what you just said."

"What? Nothing, Mother."

It was an awkward moment. Mom had no clue what I had been through. I didn't want to explain why I had said that. I was sure she had heard me, but I diverted the conversation. I had covered my tracks with Daemon for so long, but it was getting harder to do that. I badly needed to tell someone about my excruciatingly painful memories of Daemon, but I had little trust in anyone, including my mother. I wondered if I could say those words and mean them. But I was learning that the power of God was amazing and that when He lives in me, I experience it firsthand. Jesus had been my Savior for only a short time, but He demonstrated His power at that moment. I had so many times in the past wanted to kill Daemon. Was my heart being transformed?

After hearing of Daemon's murder, I couldn't sleep a wink for several days. I wanted to learn all the details of his murder. Who had shot him? Why? I called the police station and asked for the detective on the case. I froze when he answered. That happened a few times. My mind would spin, I'd break out in sweat, my heart would race, and I'd lock up. I was afraid that if I talked to the detective, the whole story might even make the papers. I wasn't ready for that. But the Holy Spirit played on my conscience. I could only imagine that whoever had shot Daemon had been protecting himself or was emotionally distraught and had snapped in disgust and fear. I could have snapped back then a number of times myself. Daemon had drawn in boys like a magnet and knew how to prey on them. I was sure whoever had killed him did so out either out of disgust or his instinct for survival.

I gave into the Holy Spirit and called the detective. "This is Alter Pain. I'm calling about the murder of Daemon." I asked him for information; he was reluctant to give me any until I told him I had lived with Daemon for many years. I told him my story. I was disappointed with the detective because he acted as though the bad things that had happened to me were insignificant compared to the murder. He had no idea how difficult it was to relive my story for him. I'm sure he'd been hardened by all the stories he'd heard in his career.

He told me Daemon had been shot with a .357. More than likely it was his own Colt Python. The detective said that the murder was clearly intentional due to the fact that he'd been shot with all six rounds in the gun. I told him I was sure it was intentional. I told him I had wanted to kill Daemon many times and would have put six rounds into him myself. I asked the detective if he would entertain the idea that the boy might have a story to tell about Daemon as I did but was too embarrassed about it to tell it. I was sure that was the case. He was a minor but would probably be charged as an adult. My story would be another example of what Daemon had been capable of and could help the boy who had shot him.

I prayed like crazy that the boy would be relieved of some emotional pain. If he had killed Daemon to steal his guns, as the investigator had suggested, he was in a lot of trouble. If he did it out of self-defense or insanity due to stress, he'd still be in trouble and in self-imprisonment because of the guilt, fear, embarrassment, and nakedness he felt for having been violated if he indeed had been. I was sure he had; I had to get that possibility across to the detective. I knew what it was like to be imprisoned in one's own jail. I was hoping the boy would not suffer if this had been God's way of getting rid of Daemon. Once again, spinning in my head is this verse, "But if you cause one of these little ones who trusts in me to fall into sin, it would better for you to be thrown into the sea with a large millstone hung around your neck." (Mark 9:42) God has this, but the boy had to get right with God if he wasn't already. Jeremiah says this in 1:8, "I promise to be with you and keep you safe, so don't be afraid." God put these words in Jeremiah's mouth. I prayed that these calming words would be laid upon the heart of this young boy.

At that time, I wasn't outwardly promoting Jesus; that would have been too much of a stretch for my new faith. I knew God was working in me, but I couldn't get a handle on the spiritual stirrings I was feeling. I was, however, ready to let the world know what had happened to me all in the name of Jesus. Up to then, many had crucified me, hurt me, stepped on me, yet there I was willing to dive into deep chaos, pain, and confusion as if I were craving it. I wanted to help this boy, but I wondered what I would gain by putting myself out there like that. My heart hadn't healed enough to open itself to someone who had killed another. I felt I had to get into the boy's mind.

I eventually met with this young boy. I told him who I was and explained my story and why I was there to talk with him. He started crying. I knew he felt an instant warmth come over him. I knew that look; it expressed the relief I felt the day I escaped Daemon. I knew his and my stories were the same. I said, "I'm sorry, young man."

"No one will believe me!"

"Young man, I do. You need to tell your story," I said though he hadn't told me anything. I thanked God that our conversation was being recorded and could help him. My pleas had fallen on the detective's deaf ears. I did all I could until I felt too mentally drained to continue.

I knew my story would get out. I wanted to break it to my family and friends first. I told them, and I told my brother-in-law Ron and his older brother. By testifying to Ron's older brother, I was able to pay the debt I felt I owed Ron for bringing me to Christ. As it turned out, Ron's brother, who was a special-needs person, had been sexually abused by a predator. I mentored him a few times. I told my story in a constructive way, and that helped relieve some of his pain and embarrassment.

My family is now learning of the details. I never learned for sure what happened to this young boy. I heard from one source that he spent some time in juvenile detention, was let out on probation and later became an attorney. I also heard from another source that he had become a pastor. That wouldn't have surprised me; that would be how God would have worked this out.

I ended up feeling wiped out, embarrassed, and humiliated. This was when I was trying to reconnect with my son. I dreamed of having a father-son relationship with him. Ironically, I had tried to rescue a young boy who had killed the man I had hoped would be my father but had become my worst nightmare. I felt God had given me more than my fair share of chaos, but I felt braver and stronger. I thought I was beginning to trust God and Jesus to guide me and light up the path I was supposed to take. (Psalm 119:105) "Your word is a lamp to guide my feet and a light for my path."

I'm beginning to understand that God works miracles in the midst of chaos. He takes our weaknesses and turns them into strengths. It's a lot to learn, but it's all worth learning.

Chapter 14

ᴑᴗ ᴔᴑ

The Search

I again got in touch with Dan, the private investigator, to find out where Jason had moved to after I had seen him last, and Dan went to work right away for me. He caught some leads, and I gave him my approval to continue. I didn't have the money to look for Jason myself, and the courts were useless in helping with my efforts. Lefty came up with their new address.

I called Bobbie. "How did you find me?" she asked. I never told her about Lefty, the best investigator this side of the Rio Grande. Bingo, this phone call was being recorded. That evidence was not helpful to her because it indicated she had been trying to hide from me. I took it to court. The judge sided with me. It scared Bobbie into allowing me to visit.

I visited her and Payton, her husband. He was the fourth person she had had affairs with when we were married. They looked as if they'd been through a tornado. She admitted they had partied the night before. Based on her mannerisms, I thought she could be on drugs.

Jason had no idea who I was or what I was doing there. It was clear that Bobbie had no intention of letting me be part of his life. Bobbie, Payton, and I negotiated when Jason was out of the room. Bobbie told me I could meet Jason and her at a park, neutral territory, the next time I came. Payton wanted to be there, but I rejected that idea. It was hard enough for me to hear Jason call him Daddy. I prayed to God about how to let Jason know I was his father. I was worried they might move again and hide. I hoped they realized they couldn't stay on the run as they had been and keep putting Jason in different schools. I figured financial pressure would trump their deceitful motives.

I flew home. I called Bobbie often to make sure we didn't lose contact. She knew I was on to her. After much negotiation and threatening her that we would go to court again, she finally coughed up a date for me to visit Jason.

My younger sister Pamela went with me for that visit to see Jason. I was nervous as we got to the park. I didn't want to tell him I was his father; I didn't want to confuse him. Bobbie met Pamela and me at a picnic area. Jason and his half brother were busy on the playground. Bobbie called Jason over to meet me. I was overwhelmed by my emotions. *Would I ever see Jason again? A good chance no. Would Jason ever learn I was his real father? A good chance no.* I couldn't take any more chances or spend any more money. I knelt down to meet his eyes and I held his hands. "Jason, I'm your father. Your mom hasn't been honest with you. Payton is your stepdad, not your real dad."

He didn't react as I'd thought he would. He was processing everything I'd said. I thought Jason had heard enough and would spur him on to question his mother and Payton. I'd done it! I'd told him. Bobbie went ballistic. "Alter is not your father! He's just a friend from a long time ago!" She grabbed his hand and took him and his stepbrother to the car. I saw that she was crying as she drove by us. She called me later. "You'll never, ever see Jason again!" she defiantly told me.

Pamela was perplexed and furious. We cried on the way home. She was my rock on that trip. How blessed I was to have grown up with two incredible sisters. We both believed Jason was my son. He was clearly introverted. That made me worry about what was going on behind closed doors at home.

Chapter 15

❧ ❧

Brothers for Life

Back home, I was brokenhearted. I was afraid I had seen Jason for the last time. I couldn't afford to continue my searches for him, and the legal system was no help at all. And Leon was down in the dumps because his girlfriend of many years had broken up with him. We were two peas in a wilted pod.

He and I spoke about my moving back home and living with him until I got my financial feet under me again. He was still living at home with his mom and Franco. I moved in, and we worked hard to save money so we could rent a home together. It was his first stint away from home, and we enjoyed every minute of it. We supported each other; we kept each other from giving in to depression. We did everything together.

Then came April 1, 1993. I came home from work and saw that all our furniture was gone. Everything Leon and I ever worked for had vanished. I was freaking out. Leon came downstairs and hugged me. "Alter! We've been completely robbed!" I'd been through too much. I didn't need that. He dragged me into the backyard. He said we needed fresh air. Outside, I saw all our belongings. "April fools, brother!" he yelled at the top of his lungs and laughed his Burt Reynolds *Smokey and the Bandit* laugh. It was a legendary prank he had pulled on me. It had taken him an hour and a half right after work to move everything out—kitchen table, chairs, sofa, microwave—everything. His antics make my life a better place.

The next week, he decided to hit the town for the first time since his breakup. I was happy he was trying to get over her. He invited me to come along, but I was feeling sick. As he always did, he came upstairs to my room, hugged me, and told me he loved me. I always did the same. That time, he gave me a Whitney Houston CD and some cold medicine. She was our favorite female artist especially when we were depressed. He left. The medicine knocked me out.

The phone rang. I was in a daze. My clock said it was 2:21 a.m. "Hello?"

The caller paused before saying, "Leon is dead."

"What?"

"Leon is dead, Alter."

It was Franco. He asked me to come over immediately. I dropped the phone and turned white as a ghost. I somehow managed to make it to Momma Regina and Franco's home. Franco met me at the door and hugged me. We held each other for a long time. The siblings started showing up. Regina was away at their cabin in the mountains, her retreat.

It didn't seem real. I couldn't imagine life without him. He had helped me keep my sanity. *God, what are you doing to me? Take me now so I don't have to endure any more crushing blows! Why, why, why?* For the first time in my life, I thought about wanting to die. I didn't want to kill myself; I hoped a train would come through my home and take me out.

I was suddenly reminded of a verse that said God has been faithful forever and we had to keep loving Him. I had to get out of their house. I was worried my emotions would provoke the others there. I found my Bible in my glove compartment of my car and searched for that verse. One minute I wanted to just die and couldn't stop crying, and the next minute God had dried my tears. Even if for that moment in time, I had forgotten my pain.

I found this verse. (Deuteronomy 7:9) "Understand therefore, that the Lord your God is indeed God. He is the faithful God who keeps His covenant for a thousand generations. And lavishes His unfailing love on those who love him and obey His commands." I was sick and heartbroken. My eyes were dry, red, and nearly swollen shut. But as this verse said, I looked to God and obeyed His commands. He had led me to His Word and had dried my eyes. At least for that moment. He is faithful, and He loves me. I knew I could get through this.

Looking back at the signs Leon had given me over the previous months, I believed God had something to do with it. He had made a pact with me that he and I would try to secure our relationships—he with his father and me with my mother. Leon was a believer; we had that in common. Now, I can see how God was slowly moving me to where He wanted me to be. I didn't see it then, though.

Leon went through with his desire to reestablish his connection with his father. He had called his dad a few months prior to his death. To please his father, he had cut his hair, which he had always kept long in case a movie role called for that. He started calling his dad frequently, and he also called some relatives he hadn't spoken to in a long time.

Over several months prior to his death, Leon kept saying, "I want to be buried in a pine box standing up." I grew to like that idea. We'd promised to ride off together on Harleys into the sunset of life, but I don't want to ride without him. I did keep my other commitment though; my mother and I began to work on our relationship.

Prior to Leon's death, my mother and John got married in Vegas. Leon and I had stayed out of trouble when we were in Vegas, but we had lots of fun together. Other than that, I had nothing but bad visions of people's lives being destroyed in that environment of sex, drugs, and gambling addictions. Nonetheless, I went and participated by giving mother away. That was a huge step for us considering I had a hard time trying to like John. I did keep peace with him out of respect.

Some months later, to keep my pact with Leon, I invited my mother to a therapy session called the Forum. It had no religious value, but I thought it would help us get to know each other better and understand each other's battles, stories, and concerns. I learned that we didn't know each other as well as we had pretended to. We spent twenty-four hours together in a room and did a lot of forgiving. True forgiveness didn't happen until later in our lives; that was on the surface. But what we had at the time sufficed; it was a start.

But back in the car right after Leon's death, I was praying. Franco came over to see if I was okay and startled me. I never finished my prayer. I was surprised at how much time I had spent with God and reminiscing about Leon. I walked back inside with Franco, much calmer after having spent some time with Jesus.

We drove to the mountains to tell Momma Regina that Leon had died. Franco drove. It was the longest ride of my life. Bernie, who was Leon's sister, Franco, and I tried to come up with the best way to tell Regina. We saw Regina working in the front yard. Bernie jumped out of the car when it was still moving. She ran to her mother screaming and crying. Regina realized something terrible had happened to Leon and started wailing. They embraced. The pain they felt and shared settled in my soul, mind, and heart forever. I cry every time I remember that moment. I'll always love Momma Regina.

Though it seemed to me we had gotten through the most difficult moments of this loss, it became clear we'd experience much more pain. We dropped Momma off at home and went to get Leon's truck out of impound.

Leon had died on April 10, 1993, at age twenty-five. He had been drinking that night, so he let a friend drive. He rode in the bed standing up and holding on to the roll bars, which at the time was legal. A witness thought he was reaching for his hat, which had blown off his head, and lost his balance. The driver, his buddy, stopped at a light, looked in his review mirror, and didn't see Leon. Since Leon was always playing tricks on his friends, the driver thought Leon had jumped out to play a game on him. The driver made a U-turn and was scanning the sidewalks and the streets on his way back. He noticed an object in the middle of the road. It was Leon, contorted and lifeless. He had been dragged for about a quarter-mile by a lowrider that had hit him according to the witness.

I wished I'd gone with him. I might have been able to prevent his death. He and I were each other's accountability partners, and we kept each other safe.

Leon was buried in a nice coffin, not the pine box he had wanted. I was in bad shape at the wake, which was closed casket due to what had happened to him. I went to the ground in front of his casket and wasn't able to regain my composure for a very long time. Momma Regina signaled for my mother to help me up. She did, and it was another event that went down in our healing book. We were inching toward a real mother-and-son relationship. I had to keep my pact with Leon; I would search for my mother's heart and reestablish a stronger relationship. God was slowly getting below my thickened skin.

We all worked up enough courage to go back to my and Leon's home. I hadn't been there for several days. I wasn't sure I was ready. Momma Regina, my stepsister Bernie, and I went through Leon's things. Bernie was a mess. Other than a pit in my stomach, I was holding up better than I thought I would. That was until I saw Whitney Houston CD he had given me the night he had died. I picked it up and saw a note taped to the outside that read, "Take two Alka-Seltzers and listen to this CD. Love you, brother." I had another meltdown. I prayed for sleep because I was running on empty. I had a dream. But I want to set it up first. Leon and I were cowboys known for sunbathing in the pool on an inner tube with nothing more than our bathing shorts, cowboy boots, and cowboy hats. That's how we rolled.

I dreamed I was on a beach by myself around sunset. I was looking out yonder and saw a speck moving closer to me with each wave. The remarkable sunset was backlighting whatever was coming toward me. I soon realized it was Leon in Hawaiian shorts, cowboy boots, and cowboy hat riding the waves on an inner tube. He had the biggest smile on his face. He said, "Alter, it's okay, buddy. I'm livin' the dream." I then heard a poem I had written and recited in seventh grade spoken by a familiar voice: "Eclipse of the Sun all fired up is greater than the distant horizon as my eyes grew darker and darker and darker." My eyes grew darker as the dream faded.

I awoke with a new calm. I was convinced Leon was in heaven. Though I was such a newbie to Christianity with many questions and doubts, I could make sense of my dream. God had allowed Leon into my life, and then He closed the chapter. It was sort of like how Jesus had come back for His apostles to reassure them His place was in heaven at the right hand of His Father. That was just the first remarkable chapter that God would close for me.

Enough questions came to my mind that I called Ron, my brother-in-law. I latched onto him because of the void Leon's absence had left in my heart. We spoke about his business a lot. He built iron ornamental fences, and he needed someone to handle the books, sales, and fabricating. We worked together for several years and grew the business. At one point, we had twelve employees, good contractors, and plenty of customers thanks to God.

What Ron taught me set me on a career path. Partnering up with him was a fantastic experience. He was a brother-in-law, a brother in Christ, a brother I had yearned for, and an accountability partner. We spoke a lot about God and Jesus and prayed a lot for each other. We had our share of difficulties, temptations, sins, and struggles same as everyone else. Some of us get caught sinning while others don't, but I've learned that God knows us all. Ron taught me that our being Christians was not an announcement to the secular world that we were perfect. He taught me that Christianity was a walk with Christ, that it was about our consciences and how the Holy Spirit communicated with our consciences. The Holy Spirit gives me a burning desire to do what's right, but that's not always easy. None of us is perfect; God sent His Son to die for us to be freed from our imperfectness. (John 3:16) says it best "For this is how much God loved the world: He gave His one and only Son, so that everyone who believes in Him will not parish but have eternal life."

I had more hope each day due to my deepening love for and relationship with Jesus. I was starting to understand the Holy Spirit thanks to Ron. The Holy Spirit is wired into my conscience directly. He is our helper. He fills our hearts, souls, and minds with Christ. (John 16:5-9) says... "But now I am going away to the one who sent me, and not one of you is asking where I am going. Instead you grieve because of what I have told you. But in fact, it is best for you that I go away, because if I don't, the Advocate won't come" (notice that Advocate is capitalized. It is the Holy Spirit, one of three parts of the trinity, the 1. Father, 2. Son and 3. Holy Spirit). "If I do go away, then I will send Him to you." (Him being the Holy Spirit). "And when He comes He will convict the world of its sin, and of Gods righteousness, and of the coming judgement. The worlds sin is that it refuses to believe in me."

Jesus is not focused as much on our day-to-day sins as He is on our biggest possible sin— not believing in Him. He died for our daily sins, but He won't forgive us for not believing in Him. That's a very clear message. For a while, He breathed oxygen and had a heart that pumped blood just as ours do. He traveled not too far while on earth, but His story has spread across the globe and is believed even 2,000-plus years later due to His believers. The Spirit is everywhere and offers us all God's promises. He doesn't promise we'll always be happy, but he does promise us we can experience joy. Praise Jesus, and thank you, God!

I'm learning how to be a better warrior against the sadness and darkness in my life, but I still have a long way to go. I'm alive and healthy, and I have Jesus and the Holy Spirit to get me through life. Thank you, Ron for the wonderful things you've taught me, brother. I love you like blood. I learned sales and accounting from you, and more important, I learned grace and how to be a humble leader. God surely placed you in my life with great intentions.

Chapter 16

❧ ❧

Marriage Number Two: Lonely and Codependent

While I was working with Ron, I met Corrine. I had no business falling in love again. I was far from healed, but my sexual drive was stronger than my ability to think clearly. Most people would say I was lustful, but actually, I was lonely. She was very pretty and had a personality greater than life. Her smile was compelling and attractive.

Just before Leon died, we were all standing in line for a Clint Black concert. She and I met, and that led to our marriage though I think we both knew we shouldn't have married. I should have let my skeletons out of the closet during our courtship; she hardly knew me, but she spotted my huge insecurity complex and propensity to jealousy. I can't sell myself short all the way; she had her own baggage. She clearly had her eyes on other men.

I left Ron's employ after having seen an ad for a sales position with a small company that wanted a rep for the Southwest. It sold industrial pumps, mechanical seals, packing and gaskets for industrial systems, controls, and so on. I traveled extensively. My neighbor kept in touch with me and told me what was going on around the house. He looked out for my wife and made sure she was okay. There were signs that concerned me. I became jealous of everything she did, everywhere she went, and everyone she talked to. I was still carrying emotional baggage and had lost my way with Christ. I started to drink. I liked my beer. I never became an alcoholic, but I could have. She and I became oil and vinegar. In hindsight, I realize now that I needed three things: God, a partner, and security. I lost all of those things by making poor choices. Another divorce. I was embarrassed by my poor choices. Can anyone relate?

With God absent from my life, I started to cave. I immediately hopped into another relationship. It was not a long-lived relationship, but it changed my life. She and I had fun, but not healthy fun. I ended up in jail twice while dating her. Once, I was pulled over for crossing the yellow line as I reached for a water bottle. I was driving buzzed. An officer had followed us out of the parking lot of the pub we'd been in. I ended up in jail. I accepted full responsibility, and that night, my relationship with Jesus grew.

I ended up in jail again. My girlfriend had been out drinking with her friend and had mouthed off to her mother in her front yard. I was disgusted with her behavior. She poked me in the chest, and I pushed her away just hard enough to make her take a step backward and trip over her purse, which was on the ground behind her. I told her, "Don't ever talk to your mother that way again." Her friend called the police. I waited for them to arrive. An officer asked me if I had pushed her. All I could say was yes. Her mother was crying. Rather than trying to explain my case, I let the officer cuff me. Again, I accepted full responsibility and went to jail. I wasn't a violent man. I didn't push woman around. I had stood for what I thought was right, but that caused me some anguish. I wasn't mature enough to deal with some volatile situations.

I loved her stepfather. He and I had often fished for bass and cat fish. He taught me a lot, and in some ways, he was like a dad. God was watching over me; I could feel Him. But He let me trip all by myself on occasion. I'm happy to say that my second misdemeanor was my last. At least, that was my commitment to myself.

She and I parted ways. We needed time to grow and learn. I had made a commitment to God to come back home to Him. I promised to heal in a safe place, church. The day I made the choice to come back home to Jesus reminds me of the parable of the prodigal son in Luke 15:11–32. I had no father who could be proud of me or with whom I could celebrate my return to Christ. I assumed Jesus was smiling from ear to ear. I felt a celebration in my heart. I would never run away from

Jesus again. I have remained to this day in a relationship with my Father. Being away from that was lonely and dangerous. It didn't take long for my life to spiral out of control. You could see a turn for the bad in my life. I had no lamp to light my path. I was as good as blind, but then, I was found. I could again see.

> Amazing Grace, how sweet the sound
> That saved a wretch like me
> I once was lost but now am found
> Twas blind but now I see.

Chapter 17

❦

The Transformation

When I became once again unemployed, I had to live with Ron and Pamela. Again. I was so embarrassed. I felt such a loser, but praise God, I had a sister and brother in law who loved the Lord and me. I started attending church again; the Lord was reaching out to me. I became close to my Daddy. Would I let go and follow Him?

Several months into my stay with Ron and Pamela, I had grown significantly with Christ. My first six years of walking with the Lord had been slow but steady; I had experienced some hits and misses, but God never let me out of His sight. He had allowed me to fall until I had finally had enough.

After my last meltdown with Christ, I had prayed for hours in my room at Ron and Pamela's home. I cried myself to sleep. I was looking for a future. I realized once again that God would be my only Father. I had finally given into that mind-set. I was ready to make another deal with God. Remember my first deal about reading His Word? This newest deal was that I would follow it and do exactly as He said if He would direct me. *God, I need you. I'm 100 percent yours. Let's go do this!*

I was finally asleep after making another ridiculous deal. But was it really ridiculous? A voice came to me in my dream asking me to make a certain phone call. I felt God was with me planning out my life in my dream. The voice told me to keep my eyes on Him always. This voice was a promise to me that God would always keep His. This was my chance.

I awoke. It was 9:00 in the morning. My dream seemed more of a vision; I think that was why I had a hard time separating my conscious self from what I had experienced. I consider it a divine event that marked the beginning of my new life. It was the second of several dream-like visions with the same loud, clear voice. I yearn to hear it again. I didn't know if it was an angel or God, but it was authoritative though not scary. I was trembling when I remembered the verse I had read in the car the morning after Leon had died. (Deuteronomy 7:9) "Understand therefore, that the Lord your God is indeed God. He is the faithful God who keeps His covenant for a thousand generations. And lavishes His unfailing love on those who love him and obey His commands."

For the first time in my life, I did not doubt what He told me to do: "Call Justin!" Justin was the president of Triple D Industries, an eight- or nine-million-dollar company. I doubted I could get him on the phone, but I called the 800 number anyway.

"Thank you for calling Triple D Industries. This is Justin." I was speechless. I hadn't expected Justin himself to answer the phone. I didn't know what to say. "Hello?" Justin asked.

I finally got my brain in gear. "Justin, this is Alter Pain."

"Alter! How are you, my friend?"

"Good, thanks. Sorry for my delay in responding to your greeting. I didn't think you ever answered the phone."

"I don't," Justin said with a snicker. "Ha ha! I try not to, but I felt compelled for some reason, and I'm happy I did. I was setting up some interviews. Funny you called now. I have my eye on a guy …"

"That's great, Justin. Speaking about interviews, Justin, you know I've been trying to walk in the Lord's light." Justin was a Christian too. "God or an angel told me to call you this morning. I can't explain it, but here I am. Justin, would you give me a quick interview?"

"Alter, I need a salesman in the Midwest. I'll hire you today if you're willing to move there."

"I'm embarrassed to tell you this, but I'm broke. I have no way of getting there."

"No worries, Alter. I'll pay for your move and set you up at a hotel until you get a place. I want to send you to the Chesterfield Global Training Center for your training and credentials."

I was speechless. Justin stopped all interviews and awaited my arrival in the Midwest. Wow! I'd listened to God in a dream and next thing, I was employed. *Seriously, God?* I can still hear His voice in my head from that dream or vision. I just needed to follow God. I was assured enough to tell Ron and Pamela about my dream and my call to Justin. Pam's eyes were spinning like a casino slot machine. Ron, a thinker, just listened. I knew they were thinking I was making a poor choice again. I had no one to raise me in the most important years of my life, no one to give me advice I trusted. Most of my life, I was a wanderer who had tended to make believe everything was great. But at that point, I was confident God was with me. I knew right from wrong, I didn't ever want to hurt anybody, and I was a nice guy. I didn't have much else to brag about though.

Ron and Pamela prayed with me. I knew they thought I was making a mistake, but the voice had told me not to let anyone get in my way and keep my eyes on Him. That's exactly what I did. I set out on my mission. At this time, I was upside down on my four-wheel drive truck. I planned to drive it to my new job and once on my feet, I would call the bank and turn the truck in. I hoped one day to pay off all my other debts, which totaled $70,000, and in 1998, that was big bucks. I had debt collectors and courts hounding me. I felt like a real loser with no life skills, but I was determined to change that.

I rented a trailer big enough for my possessions. I kissed Pamela good-bye, gave Ron a big hug, and left my debts, problems, family, messes, friends, and relationships behind. The pastor of the church I had been attending gave me an encouraging word. Pamela and Ron were perplexed. I had packed up and left within thirty-six hours after my dream.

Two straight days of driving made my head foggy. My confidence was shaken by the fact that I had undertaken this journey because of a voice in a dream. I had way too much time to think about what I was doing. During a moment of trepidation, I nearly fell asleep at the wheel. In His humorous way, God decided to wake me up and test my faith. I was scared awake when my trailer detached from my truck. I was pulling the trailer down the road at sixty-five with nothing but the safety chains. I pulled over as soon as I could, but it was a narrow spot that offered little room for driver error.

I turned on my hazard lights and ducked out of my car in a break in traffic. I walked to the hitch and saw that the ball was off the truck and lodged in the tongue of the trailer. Then I noticed that my truck had a flat, and I had no spare. I was way too close to the fast-moving freeway traffic. I didn't have a cell phone then. The ball had come off when the nut, which was long gone, had come unscrewed. The threads on the ball were badly ripped up. I needed a new ball, and the tongue of the trailer had gotten distorted. Two state troopers just drove by me and kept on going.

After about three hours of waiting, I realized I hadn't prayed for help. I got back in my truck, a dangerous move, and prayed for about five minutes. I heard a vehicle slowing pulling in behind me; it looked like a construction field service vehicle. The driver came over. He was a large man, and he smelled bad. His belly was hanging way over his belt and his shirt did not cover it well. He hadn't shaved in weeks. He looked menacing. He assessed my situation and said, "You certainly have a problem here."

I felt like saying something sarcastic, but I bit my tongue. He said, "You're in a bad neighborhood. We need to get you off the highway." I got nervous when he said we needed to unhook the trailer and move the truck. He connected the trailer to his truck and pulled it out of the road. "There's a Walmart up the road. I'll take your trailer and your tire with me to see if we can get it repaired. I'll look for a new ball for you as well. You can't leave it here."

"The heck I can't!" I blurted out. "It'll stay right here with me."

The man shook my hand and introduced himself as Bear. "I have three kids at home. They need me to cook them dinner before midnight. If you're here till morning, you'll be robbed. Do you want my help or not?"

I pondered on the fact that he had kids and was actually going to feed them. "Yes, Bear. Good to meet you. I could certainly use your help."

"Okay. I'll be right back," Bear mumbled. He drove off with everything I owned.

A half hour later, I was in my truck again and praying. A police officer pulled up behind me. My luck with the police officers had never been good.

"Everything okay?" he asked.

"No, it isn't. I trusted a man to help me. I think he drove off with my trailer." I began to shed some tears. "I'm pretty sure I've been robbed."

"Did you catch his name? Was it Bear?"

"Yes, that's his name."

"Bear's a good friend of mine. He goes to my church. He called me to come and stay with you while he was finding you some parts. He'll be back."

The policeman stayed with me until Bear returned. He and the policeman shook hands and hugged. The policeman asked Bear, "Why did you leave with this man's trailer?"

Bear chuckled. "It was safer with me than with him. I figured he probably had everything he owned in it."

I wondered how he had known that.

Bear unwound his welder leads and fired his welder up. He welded up the hole in the receiver to save me from having to buying a new one. He drilled out a new hole, grinded it flat, and repainted it. *What? Seriously?* It looked like new when he was done with it. He installed a new ball, and he and the officer put my repaired tire back on my truck. I tried to help, but they didn't let me. I couldn't hold back my tears of gratitude. Bear even connected the trailer to my truck.

"How much do I owe you, Bear?"

"Nothing, Brother. Pay it forward someday and we'll be even. God bless you. My kids are hungry. I gotta git." He told the officer, "See you at church."

He was gone as fast as he had come. I was speechless and wide awake for the remainder of the trip. I'd never experienced such an act of kindness. All I could do was cry. God had heard my prayer and sent Bear because He loved me and had a plan for me. God was keeping His word about leading me. I had learned what it was like to fear God.

I arrived at the Hummingbird Hotel, the place Justin was kind enough to set up for me. It was comfortable and all I needed. I wondered what I had done to deserve all this. The spiritual road in front of me was fuzzy but lit up. I didn't look back. I drove around Grand Rapids for a couple of days getting acclimated. I stored my belongings in a Triple D warehouse. Justin called to see if I wanted to go to church with his parents, his wife, and him on Sunday. Of course I said yes.

I was reading my Bible every night as I had promised God I would. I wondered what Justin was really like and what church they went to. *Why did Justin ask me to go to church with him? My new boss must be a Christian.* I mentally listed all the signs God had been actively laying on me. A healthy son Jason after a troubled pregnancy. Ron leading me to Christ. His voice getting me to call Justin. Bear's great assistance. Justin inviting me to church. *God, is this what you mean when you say, "Follow me?"* I'd gotten a taste of the results. But I wondered if it had all been by chance. There I was challenging God's will with my lack of faith. I read Psalm 91:1: "Those who live in the shelter of the Most High (God) will find rest in the shadow of the Almighty (God)." That verse resonated in me. God had used Bear in a big, big way. I understood I couldn't live life alone. I needed God, people, and faith. I was ashamed to have prejudged Bear; I learned a good lesson from it: God never wavers from His promises. I wished I could thank Bear again.

On Sunday at church, I realized I was in good hands with Justin and his family. I felt I had known them forever. I went back to my hotel room with a joy and peace I couldn't explain. I wasn't there spiritually yet; I still had my share of doubts. *What does Justin see in me?*

I looked up the verses I had heard in church that morning that dealt with marriage, a weak area for me. I wanted to learn where I had gone wrong. Yes, I'd been cheated on, hurt, blah, blah, blah, but I wondered when I'd take responsibility for my failed marriages. I hadn't been a great husband; I was a broken individual and had had no business dumping my painful baggage on anyone. I hadn't been equally yoked with my exes. I had slipped away from God and had made bad decisions. I knew I had to accept responsibility for them and let my Father teach me how to turn chaos into opportunity.

I noticed a little ribbon in my Bible that appeared to be a page marker. It wasn't mine; I figured it was the cleaning woman's. It was strategically placed under a verse that read. "Even when we are weighed down with troubles, it is for your troubles and salvation! For when we ourselves are comforted, we will certainly comfort you." (2 Corinthians 1:6) Then I saw a note: "Dear Sir, I am sorry to tell you that a wrecking company came in our office today and requested access to your truck. It was taken away. I thought it would be better for someone to tell you now than to go to use it and find it gone." I was embarrassed and humbled. My truck had been repossessed. I'd called the bank while on my way and had let them know I'd give up my truck and find a way to pay for every penny I owed on it. I had told them I'd be at the Hummingbird Inn.

I dreaded calling Justin with the news I wouldn't be able to make it to work the next day because I had lost my vehicle. I'd done the right thing by giving it back to the bank, but I'd have to pay for my upright decision earlier than I had anticipated. I was emotionally drained. *What now, God?*

The phone rang. A secretary at Triple D offered to take me to the office so I could see the place and meet the other employees. I guess God provided me a ride to work Monday. I thought I might not have to spill the beans about losing my ride.

On Monday, my first day at Triple D, I was excited and nervous. The very nice secretary introduced me around and took me to Justin's office. He handed me the keys to a Ford Taurus that I could use for business as well as personally. Once again, I gave the glory to God. It was as if Justin had asked God what I needed. God must have told him, "A phone, a laptop, and yes, a car." The car had not been part of our initial deal.

I studied hard at Triple D. I took many crash courses to learn what I had to in this very technical business. But I had grown up taking my toys apart, figuring out how they worked, and putting them back together. I was a gifted mechanic. I took a mechanical aptitude test and missed only two questions on it. I started to believe I wasn't as dumb as I had thought I was and had untapped talents.

Justin sent me to the Northeast for a month at the training center for Chesterfield, our number-one supplier. I met with engineers and salespeople from all over the world. Being around excited and passionate people in this business was a great experience though at times I felt like a deer caught in headlights. I was failing most of the tests and started second-guessing my ability. I had always known I wasn't the sharpest tool in the shed, but I was determined to hang in there. I was comforted by the idea God had this.

Each week at the hotel, I found a special ribbon in my Bible. Sheree, who cleaned my room, was leaving them for me. She encouraged me in godly ways, and we became friends—nothing more; I was not ready for a relationship. I had ended up breaking the heart of every girl I had dated. I was an insecure jerk, an unrefined warrior. I reminded myself that I had to stay single and tied to God.

I was assigned a sales territory; I had a customer base. I'd been well trained and equipped thanks to Justin. It was at that point up to me. I looked at a map and found a particular town in the heart of my territory. I went there, and God led me to an 800-square-foot bungalow with affordable rent in a good neighborhood. Triple D arranged to deliver my belongings there.

Praise Jesus, I finally got settled in. I had no one to worry about, no one trying to hurt me, a promising career, and a God who treated me like a son. And a beautiful Baptist church was right across the road. They still played the organ there, but I didn't care—it was home. I went to my first service that Sunday and was met by some very nice people. I was on my way to healing.

I got involved in children's ministry and eventually joined the praise and worship group when we started a second service. The second service became our contemporary service, and it really took off. I enjoyed playing my guitar and singing for God. I was meeting many nice people. I started dropping my guard for longer periods and became more trusting of others.

The kids and others from church started coming over to my place to play volleyball and horseshoes in my backyard. I was starting to feel human, see in color, and deal with life from a different perspective, vision, and plan. God continued to heal me and give me more wisdom. He was "Alter"ing the "Pain" of each event in my life by teaching me the meaning of life. Part of life means being a servant, and that's a tough job. He was teaching me to disarm chaos by recognizing the opportunity in it. I started realizing that Jesus was enriching the soil where I had been planted and was pruning my branches as I grew so I could bear fruit for those I wanted to serve. I realized I was nothing without my caretaker. I was a servant warrior strong enough to serve others.

My career was taking shape. I became more comfortable and confident with life, but I was lonely. I thought I'd try dating again. I dated two girls one after the other and realized I wasn't ready. I was still healing and had too much baggage. I worked harder on my relationship with God. I prayed and read the Bible. Things were going well at Triple D, but sales can be stressful.

I started exercising again, and that was a good way to relieve stress. I had to deal with my tobacco issue; I was chewing as well as smoking, and I loved it. I chewed when I fished, hunted, watched a movie, after every meal, riding horses, on and on. I fell asleep with a dip in my mouth more times than I care to admit. I could have easily become addicted to drugs and alcohol, but thanks to the short leash God had me on, I stayed away from drugs though I had been around them when I was growing up.

On January 1, 2000, I quit cold turkey. My body makeup at that time had to be 5 percent muscle and water, 5 percent fat, and 90 percent nicotine. But with God as my accountability partner, I never used tobacco again other than an occasional cigar, and I even gave that up too as well as caffeine. Sheesh! What's left in life, right? I took a week off work when I was quitting, and it was the rottenest vacation I ever had. One night, I screamed at God with tears in my eyes, *Why are you taking tobacco from me?*

Just then, I heard a knock at the door. It was our church praise and worship pastor. I had to answer because I was sure he had heard my yelling. I was embarrassed when I answered the door. He asked me if I was okay. I explained I was withdrawing from tobacco and had been having a discussion with God about that. I told him it wasn't the first angry discussion I'd had with Him and probably wouldn't be the last. I could tell he was very concerned about me. Once again, God had sent one of His own to rescue me; He was giving me support whenever I needed it. He never made it easy for me; He just made it doable

After one week of being clean from nicotine, I went back to work and began exercising and running. I started going to the YMCA. I knew God needed me to be healthy. I was learning to treat my body as a temple of the Holy Spirit. I no longer belonged to myself. (1 Corinthians 6:19-20) "Don't you realize that your body is a temple of the Holy Spirit, who lives in you and was given to you by God? You do not belong to yourself for God bought you with a high price. So you must honor God with your body."

I started eating better as well, and I felt spiritually stronger every month. Life was calming down. I was meeting people who were less likely to come and go in my life. I'd made more friends than I ever had before. I was following God's ways, not my own. I began to trust more, and that led to being open to more people. God had given me a new start. I don't want to sell my mother short; she had raised me with some good morals and values and had taught me a lot about survival, but I had grown up without a good father figure and was still socially awkward. My ways lacked knowledge, experience, and wisdom.

My first experience with snow in the Midwest happened on a Saturday not long after I had moved in. It was awesome! It came down in huge flakes. Southwestern boys don't know what to do with snow. I went to the mostly empty church parking lot and started doing donuts. The pastor, who was working late, came out. When he realized it was me, he shook his head and walked away chuckling. I whooped around the parking lot like a madman. I was a drifter drifting in the snow.

A police officer pulled into the lot and asked all the typical questions. I was so giddy that I said, "I was hired to do snow removal. No, really, officer, I received the pastor's permission to do this, but just for you, I'll stop." He watched me drive away and pull into my home across the street. The event made it into the pastor's sermon the next morning. Turns out the police officer went to that church also. I had a reputation for being a problem child. How was it that they all loved me so?

I wanted to party some more in the snow, so I pulled out my new lawnmower and started mowing it. I carved the words *I love you, Mom* in the snow just before the lawnmower seized up. I got up on the roof and took a picture of it to send my mom. I began to slide down the steep-pitched roof. *Oh goodness, this could hurt.* The new camera that I needed for work was going to be ruined. I had only four inches of snow to buffer my fall. I hit the ground hard on my butt.

My sweet neighbor had witnessed the whole thing. She came over to make sure I didn't need CPR because I'd had the air knocked out of me. I caught my breath and explained what I had tried to do. She told me she had never heard of anyone mowing snow. "Go take a warm bath, young man." "Yes ma'am!" I said.

Thirty minutes later, she came over. I was so sore I almost couldn't make it to the door. But there she was with some homemade stew. On Monday, I took my lawn mower back to Sears. "How did this happen?" I was asked.

I was bent over in pain. "Well, I was mowing yesterday and it just stopped."

"Um, sir," he said, "it snowed all day yesterday. Most people have winterized their mowers by now."

"I mowed the snow. I wrote 'I love you, Mom' in the snow for my mother, who lives in the desert."

He was so touched by my story that he warrantied it with no further questions. Honesty really does pay off.

Back at home, I lit seven candles, turned off the lights, and began reading the Bible. I was going into prayer-warrior mode. The most amazing thing happened. You can call me a quack—no offense taken— but I felt the most incredible joy coming over me. I had just spent two of the last 12,045 days of my life alone, having fun, feeling no hurt, seeing in color, playing like a boy, and bigger than all that, I wanted to send an I love you to my mom. I'd always told her I loved her, but I had never felt it that strongly before. I believed I was well underway to completely forgiving my mother and also forgetting.

I also started feeling her pain. For the first time in my life, I was completely and emotionally "altered" of "pain" for long enough that I felt compassion for someone other than myself. I felt genuine love in my heart for her. I felt like the Grinch who stole Christmas when his heart began to grow and gain love and wisdom. I saw that all the candle flames were bent at about a 45-degree angle and were pointing at me. I had lit seven candles, not realizing the importance of that number. The flames weren't flickering; it was as if time had stopped. I was in a trance. I looked at my Bible. My portable heater fan was blowing pages over even though the flames on the candles were completely still. I set my hand on my Bible to stop the pages from flipping and saw that my hand was resting on a verse. Here's what I read in my NIV version. (Luke 17:4) "Jesus commanded, "Even if they sin against you seven times in a day and seven times come back to you saying 'repent,' you must forgive them." The pages of the thin paper had blown over, which took me from my intentional reading that evening and made it God's intention, but the candles were as still as ice. I thought about it and concluded that light is as solid and as revealing as are the promises in God's Word if you believed. I had lit seven candles for no particular reason. I was in the midst of a final and true forgiveness of my mom when God delivered Luke 17:4 to me by His breath.

God knew why I had lit seven candles; He wanted to teach me to forgive my mother, and my heart ached at the thought. That night, I forgave my mother not seven times but seven times seven times. I forgave her and fell in love with her again. I cried myself to sleep on the table where I had my study and prayer. I woke up to the smell of burning hair from one of my candles. I had snot running down my nose. I was a healing wreck for sure. I put on a Fernando Ortega CD and listened to Jesus, "King of Angels, Heaven's light" as a spiritual nightcap.

The next morning, I awoke with one thing on my mind. I asked God to grant me the right words to say to my mom. I called her. "Hello?" I sensed she was pleased that I had called. "Hey Mom, I have to tell you what I did last night. I fell off the roof just for you."

"You what?"

"I fell off of the roof because of you. I mean because of me. No, strike that. Because I love you. I mowed the snow and ruined my mower, climbed the roof, took a picture, then fell off. All to tell you I love you."

She laughed. "Son, you could have just called to tell me that rather than hurt yourself and ruin a mower. Are you okay?"

As goofy of a start to a conversation as that was, it had worked. Phew! *God, you're good.*

"I'm fine. I have a picture of my 'I love you, Mom.' I'll send it to you."

It was a great, lighthearted way to start what could have been a very awkward conversation. We talked for a long time. I shared with her many of the transformations in my life over the last year. She was a good listener, a good student, and a good mother in this discussion.

"Mom, I've been plagued with flashbacks," There was no reason to go into specifics; she remembered those days as well as I did. I could only imagine the pain, suffering, and guilt she went through as she relived the memories. God reminded me that Mom hadn't known better and neither had I until I had become a man of God through Christ Jesus. God was teaching me so much more than forgiveness.

Mom didn't know how to repent and unlock her prison doors. Someone had to begin this process. It isn't until we have a foundation—the stronger the better—that we find the strength to act outside our comfort zones more and more. We're like construction cranes with strong outriggers. I had to forgive, and my foundation allowed me to do that and find the freedom it can bring.

She needed to talk too. How was she to have known Daemon had been a beast considering how well I had hidden that? We both needed to forgive to lose our baggage and set ourselves free. That call I made to her was the beginning of something special. God, you are good and merciful always! Thank you for investing in us when no one else would. Now, no one can convince me God isn't real or can't be felt or seen. He had fathered me. He'd been there all the time for me. He was more than patient with me when I stumbled, and I always ended up further ahead each time. I lose some battles, but I'm winning the war. (Galatians 2:20) "My old self has been crucified with Christ. It is no longer I who live, but Christ lives in me. So I live in this earthly body by trusting in the Son of God, who loved me and gave himself for me."

Mother and I began to talk regularly. One day, she told me she had a confession to make and a celebration to share. She said Pamela and I had set an example of what she wanted and needed. She invited Jesus into her heart. I wept for joy. My life was getting better all the time as were those of my loved ones. I was feeling joy, love, and peace. I had my mother back, and she had Jesus.

I got beside myself long enough to learn that my mother had a story too. She had been abused. She had been married to an alcoholic. She had attended a Catholic boarding school. She had stories just as I did. How self-centered I had acted all these years. Mother, I forgive you, and I love you. Please forgive me too. Welcome to the love of God.

Mom was to be baptized a couple months later. I flew out and surprised her. I was in awe of God when I saw the joy on her face after she was submersed. When the baptism bash was over, several relatives and friends of mom's celebrated with us at her and John's home. I think he thought the whole thing was weird. I knew at one time he'd known Jesus Christ, but he had lost his way. I was worried by his mannerisms and the emptiness in his eyes. I had had that same look for many years. He had lost his spirit, and he had lost his son, Leon. He would never be the same again. I felt bad for John. I worked hard to smile and tell him I loved him out of respect.

John read the card I had given Mom on her baptism and blurted out, "Oh for crying out loud!" I was embarrassed. He was a cowboy type straight off the ranch. He had also lived a hard life. Some days, he was a perfect gentleman, but other days, he was a lost soul who drank too much alcohol and smoked weed. His pride never let him admit he was empty. He had chased off his kids. My sisters supported him and claim to have had a decent relationship with him, but I struggled with that. I needed more from a father than he could offer.

None of that derailed my new relationship with Mom. I was so proud of her and how far she had come. I wanted badly to tell her the deepest, darkest secrets of Daemon, but we never went into details about it. I could tell she didn't want to go there. Well, neither did I. Our pasts won't fix themselves as my Christian beliefs teach me, but her baptism was a time to celebrate.

I went home sure that my mom had a new life ahead of her. I couldn't wait to see what our lives had in store for one another. I gave my burdens to God. I had a different kind of healing to do. The scars will always be there, but they're only scars. I wasn't afraid of Mom or my past any longer. Did you know that scars are tougher than undamaged healthy skin?

I made it home safely and fell asleep to Fernando Ortega's "Jesus King of Angels."

Jesus, King of angels, Heaven's light
Shine Your face upon this house tonight
Let no evil come into my dreams
Light of Heaven keep me in Your peace

Remind me how You made dark spirits flee
And spoke Your power to the raging sea.

I could feel Jesus holding me; I knew He was in favor of the pleasant changes happening in my life. I was a changed man who is still changing. I heard God's whisper and smelled His sweet breath. I could feel Him touching my soul, head, and heart. *Am I a Jesus freak? If this is how it feels, I'm a Jesus freak for life.* Most men in my position would have committed suicide, become addicted to drugs, succumbed to alcohol, or ended up in prison. By the grace of God, I'm not an ordinary freak—I'm a special freak. (Psalms 73:28) "But as for me, how good is it to be near God! I have made the sovereign Lord my shelter; and I will tell everyone about the wonderful things You do." I am a God-fearing freak. (Romans 15:4) "Such things were written in the scriptures long ago to teach us. And the scriptures give us hope and encouragement as we wait patiently for God's promises to be revealed."

He has kept all His promises to me. I read the Bible out of fear for God. I believe He means what He says.

Jesus sees me as something precious to Him. I think (Colossians 2:6–15) says it well. Here's my paraphrase.

"And now, just as I accepted Christ Jesus as my Lord, I must continue to follow Him. Let my roots grow down into to Him, and let my life be built on Him. Then my faith will grow strong in the truth I was taught and I will overgrow with thankfulness. Don't let anyone capture me with empty philosophies and high-sounding nonsense that comes from human thinking and from the spiritual powers of this world, rather than from Christ. For in Christ lives all the fullness of God in a human body. So I am also complete through my union with Christ, who is head over every ruler and authority. When I came to Christ, I was "circumcised," but not by a physical procedure. Christ performed a spiritual circumcision—the cutting away of my sinful nature. For I was buried with Christ when I was baptized. And with Him I was raised to new life because I trusted the mighty power of God who raised Christ from the dead. I was dead because of my sins and because of my sinful nature, I was not yet cut away. Then God made me alive with Christ, for He forgave all of my sins. He cancelled the record of all of the charges against me and took it away by nailing it to the cross. In this way, He disarmed the spiritual rulers and authorities. He shamed them publicly by His victory over them on the cross. So now I am not of the law but I am from every word that God speaks to me and I will follow his ways every day that I am alive because He is alive, alive, alive forever amen! Praise God in the highest."

That's a good explanation of my transformation.

I had spent a couple of years growing my career, my territory, my customer base, my love for God and friends, healing, and being alone with God. I was convinced I wasn't equipped to handle an intimate relationship. But as my baggage was being lifted off my shoulders, I realized I was a different person. People weren't trying to hurt me as they had in the past. I had purpose and direction. I was maturing spiritually and emotionally. My sins had been forgiven, and I had a Father who was teaching me life. My foundation was getting stronger; it was no longer the one I had built on mud and sand when I was a child. (Luke 6:47-49) "I will show you what it's like when someone comes to me, listens to my teaching, and then follows it. It is like a person building a house who digs deep and lays the foundation on solid rock. When the floodwaters rise and break against that house, it stands firm because it is well built."

I continued to grow and enjoy church and my church family. I felt God smiled when I sang and played guitar at services. I led a men's ministry in the church, an incredible experience. We had a good showing of men, and we went deep together. Shortly after our men's ministry started, we learned our pastor had cancer. We all endured a very painful death within our church. But God is good, and we endured the grieving process.

On Easter Eve in 2000, we were rehearsing for the next day. I was all set to sing "Easter Song" the following morning. I had a good feeling running through my bones and my soul about celebrating Jesus's resurrection the next day. (Matthew 28:1-6) "Early on Sunday morning, as the new day was dawning, Mary Magdalene and the other Mary went out to visit the tomb. Suddenly there was a great earthquake! For an angel of the Lord came down from heaven, rolled aside the stone, and sat on it. His face shone like lightening, and His clothing was as white as snow. The guards shook with fear when they saw Him, and they fell into a dead faint. Then the angel spoke to the woman. "Don't be afraid!" he said. "I know you are looking for the Jesus, who was crucified. He isn't here! He is risen from the dead just as He said would happen."

Back home, I lit some candles and prayed Jesus would touch me, be with me, and listen to our church sing to Him on Sunday morning. I asked Jesus to shine His face upon me and our team as we glorified Him with our worship.

Chapter 18

❦

The Resurrected Spirit: April 23, 2000

I remembered the dream I had had that had prompted me to call Justin and move to the Midwest. When I awoke, I was trembling with excitement for my future. I had been praying like crazy for wisdom and to become God's warrior. I would often joke and tell Jesus in my prayers that I wanted to be the one to throw Satan in the fiery lake of hell in the end times. Of course, we all know that will be Jesus's job, but wouldn't it be an honor to do it? I prayed to God that I might be a warrior who headed up one of heaven's armies. I prayed myself to sleep and had a dream.

I was in a dark, evil room that reeked of a dead man's breath. I could feel the presence of the beast. I asked Jesus to stand by me. His presence trumped my fear. I stared at the floor for fear of making contact with the eyes of Satan, but I finally lifted my head. I saw two faint blue lights. I stepped toward them. The floor was cold. The air chilled me to my bones. I realized the lights were actually eyes a wonderful, powerful shade of blue. I thought I was staring into Jesus's eyes. His face kept getting closer until He was just inches from me. The spiritual feeling was strong. Jesus was protecting me by showing me His presence.

Then I saw the scale on his face and smelled his putrid breath. His eyes turned from that blue to a fiery red. He lifted me off the ground with his powerful hand that could have encircled my waist and squeezed. My guts were taking the path of least resistance. I grabbed his head, looked into his piercing eyes, and tried to squeeze out the name Jesus with what little air I had. He dropped me. But I had been badly injured. I could feel death coming upon me. The beast's eyes became so bright that in their light I saw silhouettes of spirits everywhere flailing about as if trying to find something. They were in frantic pursuit of nothingness. "God! I ask you in the name of Jesus to give me the power to fight this beast. I'm ready!"

Satan transformed himself into Daemon. He had the eyes of the beast that would look at me when I was being violated. I became weak-kneed. I began to sing, "Our God is an awesome God. He reigns from heaven above with wisdom, power, and love. Our God is an awesome God."

I regained my composure and strength. I stood. I thought that if I sang that song again, I might become even stronger and braver. "Our God is an awesome God. He reigns from heaven above with wisdom, power, and love. Our God is an awesome God."

I felt even stronger. I sang again. Each time I did, the Beast seemed to become weaker and I stronger. I heard a voice singing with me, and one of the lost souls, a spirit, was turning into a human being before my eyes. She was a beautiful girl with an angelic voice who had just been freed from her own bondage by the power of God. I loudly commanded her to sing out loud and strong. She had tears in her eyes. She began to glow. We were having church. The Beast was flailing about; he knew what was happening. I heard another voice. An elderly man was transforming. Each spirit that transformed gave off a light that grew brighter and brighter.

Finally, all the spirits had transformed, and the Beast was blinded by the light. I jumped onto his naked body and twisted his head but couldn't get him to fall. I saw a sword hanging on the wall. I snatched it and read on it, "This is my Word, your sword." I yelled, "Satan, in the name of Jesus begone!" I swung the sword at him it seemed in slow motion. Satan fell to the floor. The room went dark, but the feeling of evil had gone. It was a peaceful darkness.

The ground left me. The walls moved away. I was floating. I heard voices all around me. One voice called me an uncleave and said I was not like the rest. The voice that I recognized as the powerful voice in my dreams before was asking one question after another to a panel of people as if we were in a courtroom. "Is he ready?" one voice asked. "No, he is not," said the voice I had recognized.

Since that dream, I ask God every night, "Am I ready yet?" Every night, I hear crickets. Someday, I'll be ready. I just need to stay true to the Almighty. Dear God, allow me to be present when you capture the Beast, amen. (Revelations 19:19-21) 1says this... "Then I saw the beast and the kings of the world and their armies gathered together to fight against the one sitting on the horse and his army. And the beast was captured, and with him the false prophet who did mighty miracles on behalf of the beast- miracles that deceived all who had accepted the mark of the beast and who worshipped his statue. Their entire army was killed by the sharp sword that came from the mouth of the one riding the white horse. And the vultures all gorged themselves on the dead bodies."

On Easter Sunday, I woke and relived the dream I had had. I wrote it down. I was excited to get to church. For the first time, I really felt a calling to a ministry. God was working in my heart. My love for Him was growing exponentially.

I took a shower and did the backstroke like the guy in the old Zest soap commercial: "You aren't fully clean until you're zestfully clean." My energy level was off the charts. I put on my Sunday clothes and ran to church.

I was singing the Easter Song, a tough one for me to sing. When my song was up, I sang, "Hear the bells ringing. They're singing that you might be born again. Hear the bells ringing. They're singing that Christ is risen from the dead." I cried as I finished singing. I went behind the curtain and dropped to my knees.

While I was singing, I remembered that God had given me a son on Christmas Day. I had a spiritual birthday that day, Easter Sunday, two thousand years after Christ's resurrection. I was thirty-three turning thirty-four in another two hours at ten minutes till one o clock PM, Jesus's age when He was resurrected. My birthday won't fall on Easter again in my lifetime; that day was very special to me; it was a reminder God was with me always. I truly had my spirit back! It was resurrected along with Jesus on that very important day. It was a gift from God. I was alive, praise Jesus! I don't feel set apart from anyone else, but God surely showed His face to me that day. Two significant dates in my life that represented the birth, death, and resurrection of Christ. How cool was that?

Chapter 19

❦

The Gift

One day when I was running in the park, I noticed a beautiful girl running. She reenergized some of my male testosterone to my embarrassment. I looked down when I ran past her to keep me accountable and safe. I hadn't had that feeling in a long time. I was having the same feelings that had gotten me into trouble before. I didn't want to wreck anyone else's life. I no longer think that, praise God, but back then, I worried about that. I even stopped running in the park to avoid her.

But she carried herself differently than other women did. She seemed more intelligent, confident, and mature than me. I was quickly forgetting I had been wonderfully made by God and was selling myself short. In (1 Corinthians 6:11) we read, "I was once like that (a marriage wrecker). But I was cleansed (I was forgiven and taught ... new and improved); I was made Holy; I was made right with God by calling on the name of the Lord. Jesus Christ and by the spirit of our God."

It was time for me to really believe that God had transformed me. (Job 33:4) "For the spirit of God has made me, and the breath of the Almighty gives me life." (Psalms 139:13+14) says "You made all the delicate, inner parts in my body and knit me together in my mother's womb. Thank you for making me so wonderfully complex! Your workmanship is marvelous- how well I know it." I also believe that what we think about we bring about. I wiped my conscience clear and asked God's forgiveness for having wrong thoughts about the woman. I asked for a change of heart and for my humanness to be overlaid with God's promises to me. I had seen many lovely women in my life, so why was I so attracted to her? I'd never spoken to her. It was a perfect example of the inner struggle I was still having with myself and proof I wasn't ready to take on a relationship.

She drew me back to running in the park like a magnet. Boom. She was running with an older guy. I thought, *That's it. She's married. Problem solved.* I was a little bummed though. But when I saw her other times running with her black Lab, I started thinking she was single. *Here we go again. God, are you telling me something?* God was using this to test me and let me approach it differently. I did just that. I knew He would yoke me with a soulmate in His time.

She'd run counterclockwise, so I ran clockwise to increase my chances of seeing her. My engineering brain at work. Jackpot. I'd see her three or four times per run. *Maybe I can throw her a smile and a hello. Maybe her dog will trip me. God? A little help here? My eyes are on you, God, but she's awfully pretty.*

The first time I passed her, I muttered a hi even though I didn't want to. God must have prompted that. She didn't answer. *Maybe that was her answer. Or maybe she hadn't heard me. Will I pass her again? Or was that her last lap for the day? … Here she comes again. Okay, do I say hi again? No, you dork. That would be creepy.* My heart was beating harder. I just knew God was up to something. A squirrel ran across the trail in front of us, and her Lab shot right out in front of me, pulling her my way. Be careful what you ask for. God had clearly heard me think, *Maybe her dog will trip me.* The dog tripped me. Not a flat-on-my-face trip, but I put some theatrics and acrobatics into it anyway. She apologized several times before I said a word. *Okay, so she's talking to you. Come on, bozo! No pickup lines. Be natural.* I prayed God would put some words in my mouth. If they were His, they'd be just fine.

We spoke about five minutes. My heart was beating out of my chest. I felt nervous. *Come on, Alter boy, think of something to say like, "What's your name?"* "What's your name?" "Jan." *Wow! She answered me.* So question number two. "Do you run here often?" *Okay, really stupid question. We've been seeing each other for like months on this track.* She chuckled. "Yes I do, and I know you do too." *Duh.* I was embarrassed, but her comment was cute.

After some more small talk, that was it. But I went home pumped up. I made a big pot of Hamburger Helper to celebrate and ate the whole thing to replace the calories I'd burned running nearly five miles longer than normal to see her as many times as I could.

I prayed particularly intensely that night to God to keep me within the parameters He wanted for me. "Jesus, King of angels, heaven's light, shine your face upon this house tonight. Let no evil come into my dreams. Light of Heaven keep me in your peace."

I awoke the next morning with pep in my step. Yes, I had my spirit back with a passion. My soul was as plump as the Pillsbury Doughboy. I couldn't take my mind off Jan though. I was nervous, excited, and scared. *God, did I speak your words when I was asking Jan questions? They were questions a fifth grader would ask. I'd have thought you were more eloquent than that, God. What am I doing? I don't need any chaos. I need more peace and healing, right? God? You there?*

But I remembered that when Jan and I spoke, I felt something in the air that gave me courage and the conviction it was okay. *I'd never felt that way before, God. I have to assume you set this up. Very funny about the dog-tripping thing, by the way.*

I had looked forward to my run after work that day. The time couldn't come fast enough. I ran for a few miles before I saw her and her dog. I was excited. *So be a stud, not a dud.* We waved. We stopped. We said hello. I thought I saw a spark in her eye. She seemed pleased to see me. We spoke for several minutes. I was more comfortable than I'd been the day before.

We kept this ritual up for several more runs on the following days. One time, we walked together for a while just talking about general things. I learned that she had three kids. I asked her, "May I share my phone number with you in case you'd want to run with me?" "Yes." *Oh boy. What's your phone number again, genius?* I went to my car and wrote it down for her, gave it to her, and drove off. *Oh no! I think I just gave her the wrong number. Alter!* I turned around and nearly caused an accident. I swung back into the parking lot as she was approaching her van. I could tell by the way she was looking at me that she was wondering what I was up to. "Jan, I gave you the wrong phone number." I was so glad she laughed. She thought it was funny. I gave her the right number.

I wanted her to call me that night, but I had an inkling she wouldn't.

She didn't. She didn't call the next night either. I ran ten miles the next time out hoping to see her. I figured at least I'd end up in the best shape ever. *God, let her be here today and settle my nerves.* Sure enough, there she was pulling into the parking lot. I met up with her at her van, and we started walking the trail. I asked her if she would run the Turkey Trot with me the next day, Thanksgiving, a 5.2-mile run. She obliged, and so we did. It was a wonderful time. We talked so much that we lost track of our gait and time; regardless, we both won in our age group. I am pretty sure that we were the only ones in our age group. I won a can of yams and she won a can of cranberry sauce. I wasn't sure if she considered that a date or not. I asked her out to breakfast afterward. She accepted. We had a great talk. I was pretty sure that was a date.

We parted ways. I was still waiting for my first phone call from her when the phone rang. Aww, shoot. It was Kristen. I loved my sister, but she wasn't Jan. And then my call waiting beeped. "Bye Kristen call you later." I punched the button. "Hello?"

"Hey Alter!"

Oh yeah! We spoke for an hour. It was a very comfortable discussion. Kristen tried calling me back. *Sorry, sissy. That's not happening tonight. And God? You're so good.*

That night, I had flashbacks to my marriages. *God, I can't do this again. I'm too excited. I'm afraid I've taken back control of my life. This might not be what you want for me.* I actually made up my mind to not court Jan any longer. I felt guilty for wanting this woman in my life. I apologized to God during my prayers that night. In my dream that night, I received a clear message indicating that Jan and I would be married. It came in that voice I had heard several times before. I awoke. *Dear God, was that you?* The last time I had heard that voice, I had taken a leap of faith and moved. *God, should I be excited?* The last time I listened to that voice, my life took a turn for the definite better. Yes, this was real. I'd get married!

The next day, I went to the park and walked over to her. "Jan, I had a dream last night." She asked me to share it. Any normal human being wouldn't have, but listen to why I did. I was sure the voice that had sent me to the Midwest had brought Jan and me together. "Jan, God told me you and I would be married." You could have heard a pin drop even by the noisy road next to us.

Jan thought for a moment. Then she spoke. "Alter, *I* didn't have that same dream." But we took our walk anyway. Our discussion became quite humorous. That allowed me to open up a bit and tell her why I was so confident about us. Jan recognized my faith, but she was still freaked out by my mention of marriage. We barely knew each other. And I was a big, socially awkward dork. But I now realize my desire to share my dream with her was proof of my faith in God. Especially when He spoke.

Jan and I continued to date. She sized me up. In time, we felt it was time to meet her kids. *Oh boy!* I wasn't a good husband much less a good father. *Am I capable of this?* I was trembling but more out of excitement than doubt. *God, if you can pull this one off, you're the bomb.*

I pulled up in Jan's driveway in December 2001. Her home was new. The yard was well kept. I was impressed that a single mother was able to work, maintain a house, and ride herd on three kids. I was nervous when I knocked. The door opened. A well-mannered young man with glasses and an attractive smirk greeted me with these exact words: "Hello, sir, and welcome to my home. Please come in." Steven was a handsome, well-spoken seven-year-old going on thirty.

Jan was in the kitchen. Steven and I sat at the counter. In walked another handsome young man, Kevin, who turned out to be fifteen. He was shy and hesitant to meet me. I could see and feel his pain and confusion. I'd learned to read facial and body language at an early age just to survive. And then Kara came in because Jan had coerced her. She clearly didn't want to meet me, but she was still curious. She said hi and left. Jan apologized quietly.

I was fine with all that. I knew I could connect with people of all ages. "So Steven, tell me about yourself."

"I'm seven years old, and I go to school. I like bugs and snakes and dinosaurs."

"A young man after my heart." I told him about rattlesnakes back home. He was intrigued.

"I would like to draw you a picture, Mr. Alter. It's okay if you want to watch." He drew a rattlesnake. He printed my name on it. He had asked me how to spell Pain. I began spelling my last name and added letter after letter until he picked up on my funning around. He laughed.

My visit purposefully was rather short this night, as it should have been, but I started spending more and more nights with Jan and her kids. I was slowly learning their insecurities and fears. I soaked up information like a sponge. Our relationship was growing but in a healthy way. We decided one night to brace ourselves and let our skeletons out of the closet. I was afraid that once she heard mine, she'd escort me out and tell me I was a stick of dynamite as the last woman I had dated had said. *God, how honest am I supposed to be? Some flashcards please?*

The fact I had told her at the park that we'd be married because my voice had told me that was as honest as anyone could have been. God had been honest with me, so I wanted to be honest with Jan. It made no difference that she hadn't had my dream. I'd be the leader in our relationship God had designed for us. I would set an example of honesty and integrity. She would follow me because of those things. God worked into my thoughts some crucial wisdom for our difficult discussion. I worried, however, that once I told her about my past, she'd immediately worry about the safety and emotional well-being of her kids.

Steven greeted me when I arrived that night. I joined Jan and Steven for his nightly prayer. His childlike innocence was healing for me. He was quickly growing in my heart. Steven still wouldn't make eye contact with me though. He was going to be tough to get to know. I needed patience and wisdom. Kevin was in bed. Kara was next. I stayed away from her as she was still very emotional. She wouldn't go to bed and leave her mother alone with me. She regularly came out of her room to check on us. I learned that Jan and her kids were all saved; we were evenly yoked from that perspective, but I was faced with getting spiritually unclothed in front of Jan. At least I had an inflated spirit to work with at that point. How sweet was that?

After all the kids were asleep, I said, "Jan, give me an update on your kids. How are they doing?" Jan told me of a little meltdown Kevin had had. He was sure his mother was in a relationship with a man who would become a monster. I asked her why she thought he would say that. She explained it to me. I understood. I tucked away what I learned about the kids so I could pray about them. Kara was not ready for another man in her life. I assumed she was holding her allegiance to her father. I hoped that was the case. She had a high level of fear, angst, and trepidation as most eleven-year-olds would have if their parents were divorcing. I cried myself to sleep many times feeling the pain these kids were feeling. It isn't so much one or the other parent's fault as much as is the divorce itself. The separation of kids' parents feels so unnatural, plain wrong. I had something in common with them. I thought I could build on that.

I gave Jan the short, less-graphic version of my story, but it had enough details to test her spiritual and emotional integrity. She was rock solid. *Is she in shock? Maybe she thinks my story can't be true? Maybe she has an emotional and spiritual maturity I didn't know existed?*

She had been raised in a Christian home by two amazing parents who are still married almost sixty years later. She had been loved, supported, and led by strong leaders with servants' hearts. She was emotionally mature and had a knowledge of grace. She was an educated and smart woman with a lot of horsepower upstairs. She has walked with God all her life and had no idea what it must have been like for me. Yet she believed Jesus had shed His blood on the cross for our sakes. She also convinced me that she wasn't surprised I had a story and that she could put it all in God's hands. She demonstrated her faith wonderfully that night. I had learned so much about her integrity, faith, and love for Christ that night that I went home knowing we'd be together forever.

Jan wanted to share her story with me though I was sure mine had worn her out. Growing up in Christian homes doesn't mean we don't have stories. I was very proud of her for sharing with me. She was brave, transparent, and humble; she was the real deal. With her, what you see is what you get, no filters. I realized I'd never have to doubt her.

I went home praying Jan would see value in my life and consider me someone who had gained experience and wisdom from his trials. I prayed she would rest well after having spilled her heart out to a man she was still getting to know. *Dear God, I'm so comfortable with how things went tonight that even if Jan decided to put a roadblock up between us, I'd gladly be her friend for life. It's an honor just to know this very special woman. Please refill Jan's heart with your overflowing grace and love with everything she spilled out tonight. Your cup overflows, amen.*

Being authentic brings integrity, realness, and readiness. We didn't judge each other that night. We expressed compassion and a desire to learn more about each other and to support each other. We drew closer. Without God's love and grace, intimate communication can turn to fear, judgment, and false notions and kill a relationship before it even starts.

Our liking for one another was growing. We worried about each other's story; we had to work through them, but we had a better understanding of them. I worked on my relationships with the kids. Kara finally stopped crying when I came over, but she continued being protective of her mother. I liked that about her. I spent time with the kids but didn't overdo it. Once, I asked Steven to get ice cream with me. Kevin overheard us and wanted to go. I watched Kara, who had also overheard me, get weaker and weaker. She caved in and said she wanted to go. I saw a transformation in her demeanor. It was nice to spend time with them together. Kara was so insecure and frustrated, but I knew that if I was patient, that would change.

Jan, the three kids, and I headed out for ice cream. Steven said, "Mr. Alter? Stop the car." I stopped. "Yes, Steven?" "I just want you to know it's totally okay with me if you want to marry my mom." The other two kids went off on Steven. I had as much fun watching Kevin and Kara react to Steven's comment as I had hearing his comment.

Kevin and Kara weren't ready for that bomb, and Jan was about in tears she was laughing so hard at his sincerity. I caught my breath and said, "Buddy, I'll keep that in mind. It would be an honor to be a part of this family. Who knows? Maybe someday ..." all the while knowing God had predestined Jan's and my marriage. Once, I had been hopeless, spiritless, and incapable of being a responsible husband much less a father. At that time, I realized I was being groomed for both.

Steven said, "Yeah, no rush, but I just wanted you to know." I was falling in love with that boy.

I wanted to respect their father and be a neutral party who would bring father and children together. I wanted to help mentor and raise them, not replace their father. It was always about the kids for me. I had to often mentor Jan about their best interests. Parents can frequently use their kids to manipulate each other; that's all too common, but it's bad for the kids, who can end up thinking a divorce is their fault. That ice cream trip was a good bonding moment.

Jan started introducing me to her friends and family. And we were running at the park almost nightly. One time, two cute girls came running by. They stared at me and said, "Hiiiiiiiiii!" Yes, it was a prolonged hi. "Jan, that was weird. What was that all about? Do you know them?" "No," she said. So I dropped the matter.

Until we passed them again. I busted them. I caught them staring back at Jan and me. "What's going on?"

"Alter," Jan said, "I have to tell you something. That was my sister and her best friend having to get a little snapshot of you." We laughed. It hadn't gone the way she had wanted it to, but it was cute and comical. After our run, we all met in the parking lot and talked. It was fun to meet them. I liked both of them—two peas in a pod.

I met her parents at a get-together at her sister and brother-in-law's home. I spoke with them for quite a while, and I met others in her family. Jan's younger sister, one of her four sisters, was married to a very nice fellow. Their three children were confused about Jan and me, having known her ex, whom they called uncle. Her family sized me up. They were worried about Jan, who was healing from a bad divorce, but they didn't ask too many questions, and I walked away unharmed.

Jan and I fell in love. I took her to the southwest to meet my family, and we received their approval. I proposed to her when we were visiting the Grand Canyon right at sunset at my favorite spot. She cried and said yes. I may sound a little cocky, but I knew God had this. He plans perfectly when we let Him.

Is it possible to heal, grow, and be ready for such a change in five years? Yes, if you give your life to God.

Chapter 20

❧ ❧

Marriage Number Three: Given by God

On July 20, 2002, I became the stepfather of three precious kids. I counted on God to teach me how to do that. Kara didn't want the wedding to happen. She wasn't interested in the pictures part. I was, however, impressed with her demeanor considering all her angst. Kevin was a gentleman. He didn't want to accept it, but he acted in a mature manner. I was proud of him. Steven was bouncing off the walls with excitement. He was my blessed assurance.

Douglas, my soon-to-be father-in-law, said, "Alter, you do know you're taking on the whole package, right?"

"Yes, sir, I'm all in. God has this." We embraced and we shed tears together. He expressed a father's love for his daughter and her husband.

I'd learned that getting married wasn't nearly as difficult as being married. I moved into their home to keep the kids rooted. I joined Jan's church for the same reason and even joined her Bible study and Sunday school group. It was a bit awkward; I felt resistance from a few people in the class. I thought it was because I'd stepped in where Jan's ex had stepped out. I began to feel as though Jan and I were the black eyes of the church.

Three weeks after we started attending Sunday school class, Jan and I received a letter asking us to leave the class. It was too painful for some of the friends of Jan's ex. We struggled, cried, and prayed over that. No one knew Jan's side of the story, just his. She and I decided to let God handle our future. I talked to the pastor, who told me in essence to worry less about being excommunicated and worry more about making a difference.

Christians have to bear pain for one another and accept those who fall and not condemn them but lift them up in prayer. Rather than making a big stink, we started our own Sunday school class in the church we called Real Encounters. The name served us well. We were real; transparent; eager to learn, please, and love one another well; accept one another; and tell our stories—no condemnation or judging. It was a safe place to go every week. I was the leader of the class, and I taught what I had learned about surviving life's difficulties. Our class grew. Things improved in church for us.

All churches are full of sinners; how quickly some of us can forget that. At Real Encounters, I learned the power of being transparent as a body, and I learned the tough job of leading. That takes heightened senses, but I had those due to my past.

Chapter 21

❧ ☙

The Reunion

Jan, the kids, and I made it through some difficult times. They were all trying to accept me into their lives, but that was all I could ask for. During that time, God decided to close another ugly chapter in my life.

While leading our Real Encounters class at church, I had shared about having a son whom I had lost track of. Our group stopped and prayed over me. I felt the warmth of this prayer go through my bones. I was so at peace and settled. The power of prayer is amazing.

Three days later, I received a phone call from child protective services back home saying they had a child by the name of Jason with them. They asked if I was his father. I said I was. "How did you get my number?" I asked.

"From a directory, sir."

I was livid. "If you could find me so easily, why did I spend every last dollar I earned for the last fifteen years trying to find him? Where is he? Is he okay? What happened?"

"Sir, I'll explain everything. But you'll have to come here in person to prove your identity."

"I'll be there in two days!"

Jan and I hopped a flight the next day. I couldn't wait to see my boy. *Dear God, you answered my prayers and the prayers of my fellow prayer warriors just two nights ago. Thank you, Father, but what now?* The voiced in my head said, *Calm down. Your prayers have been answered. Trust your Daddy.*

Jan was in a whirlwind of emotions. *God, you teamed me up well with*

Jan. She and I can take this on. Our marriage is an amazing story only you could tell best.

We went to child protective services right when they opened. I saw Bobbie my first ex wife in the parking lot walking on her hands. She was wasted. We walked in, and I was escorted to admissions. I talked to the woman who had called me. She told me Jason was in child protective services because his mother had tried to kill herself. She had been let out of the hospital just recently. "Which hospital?" I asked. "Drug or mental rehab? My wife and I just met her in the parking lot, where she was walking on her hands. I'm not sure she's stopped abusing drugs."

The woman filed for a mandatory drug test on her. She told me the system was so messed up. At least she admitted it. She said she'd be fired if her superiors caught wind of her negative comments. I filled out a bunch of paperwork. I met my fifteen-year-old son, a handsome lad. He had thicker bones than I did, but our builds were similar, and same color hair, identical ears, same olive skin tone, and same brown eyes.

He and I spent two hours getting acquainted without Bobbie being there. So many emotions were running through my overwhelmed brain. I'd made a deal with God for him that had changed my life. But he was madder than a hornet. "Why didn't you try harder to find me? Who do I believe, you or Mom? Why don't you go home?" I answered him as best I could, not wanting to tell him everything. I had no idea what he had been through, and I didn't want to trash his mother in front of him. He said he remembered seeing me at the school yard one day and my telling him I was his real father at the park.

Bobbie was eventually allowed back into the room. "Jason, has Alter been lying to you again?"

"I think so, but I don't know for sure."

"Jason, don't believe anything Alter says. He's here only to get you out of this place. He'll hand you over to me and will head home, right, Alter?"

I knew better than to answer because if Jason heard me say anything conflicting, he would have freaked out. I knew at some point I'd see the judge and learn the whole story. I had my recorder with me and recorded all our conversations. I had serious concerns about her agenda. I wanted to take my son home with me, and I was pretty sure that would happen based on what I was hearing from the staff. I wondered what would happen to Jason's little half brother. How do you separate brothers? I'd lost Leon and could testify how difficult that was.

Jan and I went to lunch and spoke at length about all the what ifs. What was in the best interest of Jason and his little brother? How would our family handle the addition of one or two angry children?

After lunch, Jan and I went back to child protective services. I was angry about how easy it had been for them to find me while I had spent years trying to find Jason. I about had the woman in tears. I apologized. It was an emotional day. I had years of pent-up anger, pain, and sadness. But I shut my mouth long enough to hear the woman out.

"Alter and Jan," said Jason's administrator, "Bobbie has hit rock bottom. She took all the pills she had but was resuscitated. She'd been living in a truck with a camper shell. The boys lived with her. They didn't attend school. They were traumatized by their mother's attempted suicide and taken into child protective services."

Apparently, Bobbie and her husband had divorced some time back. *The mother of my child has nearly died, and he and his half brother were living in the back of a pickup?* If Bobbie had included me in Jason's life, I would have never allowed them to get that badly off.

The administrative representative gave me some court papers. I'd finally get my chance in court. "What should I expect in court tomorrow?" I asked the administrator.

"Just show up and answer all questions honestly."

I'd waited fifteen years for this opportunity—fifteen Christmases and fifteen birthdays.

As I was walking into court the next day, Bobbie pulled me aside. I reached into my suit jacket and clicked on the record button. "Alter, you shouldn't agree to accept the judge's position that you should have sole custody of Jason. He won't do well without me. Don't try to get even with me."

"You agreed to joint custody which you violated for fifteen years and now you're asking me to be mature? You broke the law by hiding Jason and changing his last name. The court is finally siding with me. You expect me to roll over?" Bobbie was visually rocked; she knew she was in deep trouble. "I'm going into court," I said. "You coming?"

"Yes," she replied. "I'll pray for both of us." She told me to keep my prayers to myself.

The judge arrived, and the case was read. The judge was familiar with Bobbie's attempted suicide. The judge asked Bobbie, "Do you have any further comments or additions to the case?"

"No ma'am," Bobbie replied in disgust.

"Alter Pain, you're the father of Jason?"

"Yes, your honor, since the day he was born."

"I asked a simple yes or no question, Mr. Pain."

"I apologize, your honor, yes." I nearly snapped back at her, but I spoke calmly. This judge was demanding my respect yet didn't have any to offer me. *God, keep my tongue in my mouth. Don't let me blow this with sarcasm because of my pent-up emotions.*

"Mr. Pain, please state your name and spell it for the record."

"Alter Pain. A-L-T-E-R P-A-I-N."

"Your occupation for the record?"

I responded as asked.

"Please state your case, Mr. Pain."

I spent fifteen minutes explaining the long and tedious efforts I had made to find Jason, whose last name had been changed to that of her current husband. I could tell the judge was visibly taken aback by my story and had a difficult time hiding her emotions. She moved her dagger-like eyes over to Bobbie after she had already tried interrupting her several times. "Miss Bobbie, what is your agenda here today? What would you like to see happen?"

"I would like to see the father of Jason, Alter Pain, get custody of Jason Pain."

"Thank you. I couldn't agree with you more, young lady. You just made my job much easier. Mr. Pain, what would you like to see happen?"

"Your honor, I would like sole custody of Jason. I would like for her to responsibly earn her right back to shared custody. I would like to know she's clean from drugs and making sound choices before she's awarded any kind of custody."

Bobbie blew up, and the judge gave Bobbie a verbal smack on the hand. "Young lady, what's all the angst for? Did you not just agree to this?"

"No ma'am, I'm being railroaded."

"Your honor?" I interjected. "I have a tape recorded version of her real agenda, which is not at all matching up with her rant." Bobbie turned pale. I ask the judge if I could submit it as evidence.

"That won't be necessary, Mr. Pain. I have all the evidence a judge could ask for."

I did, however share with the judge verbally what Bobbie had said. I felt I had been finally heard after all these years.

It was time for her ruling. I prayed quietly and with passion. "I hereby grant you, Alter Pain, sole custody of Jason Daniel. You must spend two weeks building a relationship with Jason before he will be allowed to travel with you to his new life. We will reconvene in two weeks for an update and make a final decision." Bang. The gavel spoke.

Bobbie and I were in tears for different reasons. Bobbie thought she would get Jason back from me after I was awarded custody. Her tactics had failed. I went to Jan to explain the situation; I tried to get the words out. I felt a twinge of sorrow for Bobbie until she walked by and called me some bad things. I could feel Bobbie's evil presence.

Jan and I spoke to our case specialist; she had the paperwork drawn up and ready for me to sign. The sweet administrator closed the door to her office and gave me a big hug. She said, "God bless you." I knew she was a Christian, and I felt the Holy Spirit in the room. I was allowed to visit Jason ten hours per day.

Jan knew our lives were about to change. Jason would be a handful when he found out he was coming back with us. It was time to put our hope and faith in Christ. God carried me so many times in my life because I kept my eyes on Him.

Jan flew home to make arrangements for Jason's arrival. There was much to do. The kids were wondering what was going on. I missed Jan terribly. But Jason and I would get through the next two weeks with God by our side.

Things went very well the first week. I didn't tell him I'd be taking him home with me, nor did Bobbie. We were afraid of rocking his world. I learned that Jason and his brother were very insecure. Jason kept asking me, "Why didn't you try harder to find me?" The fact that my story didn't match his mother's confused him. I wasn't going to convince him overnight. I praise God for instilling in me the wisdom and patience I needed to be rock solid with four kids.

I wanted Bobbie out of the picture so I could be alone with him. The second week was a tense time. Jason knew something was up. I took the counselor's suggestion and told him we were leaving; that would give him a few days to process the move and prepare to say good-bye to his brother. I said, "Jason, your mother and I went to court. The judge ruled that I'm now your legal guardian. I promise that your mother will be active in your life, and as long as she continues to improve, she'll have the right to visit you and for you to visit her. You're coming to live with me."

I told him about my stepchildren. He seemed a little excited. He had thought this was what would happen. But the next few days were difficult; Jason became withdrawn.

The judge wanted to see us the next day. Bobbie asked me to meet her at a park. I took my tape recorder. She had finally come to realize she'd lost her boy. In a last-ditch effort to find pity, she invited me to the home where she was staying with a police officer. Bobbie was on drugs and shacked up with a cop. I quickly realized he had taken her in out of convenience.

She plucked at my heartstrings, but I couldn't get past the years that she kept me from Jason out of spite and selfishness. She needed help starting her truck. She claimed the battery was dead. She also couldn't find her key. I saw where Jason and his little brother were living. My heart bled. I thought of all the times I was nearly homeless but God had protected me. *God, why didn't you protect these boys and their mother?* So much I didn't understand still. I was careful to tape our discussions. I was afraid she was trying to set me up somehow. Getting Jason out of there was the right thing.

In court, the judge asked me how things had gone with Jason. "Very well, thank you," I replied. They had proof of my interactions with Jason and proof Bobbie had been a nuisance. The judge commended me for my actions and apologized for the legal system. I muttered one word audibly with tears in my eyes: "God." I cried because I had been legally awarded Jason and someone in the legal system had apologized for what I had been through. *God, you're so good.*

Bobbie came into the courtroom. She was very high. I was asked to leave. I could hear the judge lighting into her. I prayed for her, Jason, Jason's little brother, and her whole family. I was taking Jason seventeen hundred miles from his home and family. That sad reality trumped the excitement I wanted to feel.

Just a few weeks after my being prayed over that I would be reunited with my son, I was taking him home with me. He said his good-byes. It was painful for him to watch his mother and half brother fade in the rearview mirror. His little brother was in pain, and Bobbie looked like she was crying and cursing me.

Jason asked, "Why aren't you crying?"

"I'm out of tears," I said.

"You're not the one having your family ripped apart!"

"Jason, this isn't easy on any of us. I feel your pain, buddy."

I consoled him all the way home. What a journey the last three weeks had been. Jan had done a remarkable job preparing the kids and the home to accept one more child. We didn't have enough room; Jason joined Kevin and Steven in their room. I was proud of the way the boys handled Jason's arrival especially after they had had to accept me into their lives. They did as well as could be expected and welcomed him. Jason was very quiet and scared.

Jason didn't have many clothes, and those he had were tattered. We got him a new wardrobe, shoes, and toiletries. We enrolled him in the eighth grade with Kara. Before the end of our first day back, Bobbie had called Jason four times. Jason would go private and disappear while talking to his mother. I knew we were going to have to put a cap on the phone calls particularly if it became a behavioral problem with Jason.

After just one week of living with us, Jason began hiding at people's houses; he claimed that we were beating him and that his living conditions were horrific. The police were called; they assessed the situation and completely understood his behavior as we did. We had a structure to our family, and that was something Jason had never had before.

Bobbie's phone calls to Jason increased in number and became manipulative, so we trimmed back the number to three or four a week rather than three or four a night. Jason had thrown Jan's phone into the toilet and laughed in her face. He said it had been an accident. Jason stole from my change jar to call his mother from pay phones. We found out from a neighbor that Bobbie and Jason were plotting an escape.

I could feel Bobbie's evil when she would call Jason. She told me she knew how to talk to spirits, predict people's futures, and cast spells. She told me I would die of throat and jaw cancer; I told her that God would decide when and how I died. Her youngest boy, who was about ten, often called and threatened our lives. Our kids were starting to get nervous and even afraid of Jason, his little brother, and Bobbie.

I called Jason's stepfather. "Payton, it's Alter Pain. We have a lot to talk about, like the years you hid my son from me. But let's talk about more important things first, like how you and I can team up to make this transition easier on the boys."

He and I had several good discussions over the coming days. We coached each other as to the best way to handle the situation. Payton felt it would be best if Jason lived with him since that was where his brother lived. It made sense; Payton and his half brother were all Jason knew. But I was worried. "Payton, why would I want to give my son up again so you can disappear with him a second time?"

Payton apologized and admitted he had been under the spell of Bobbie's lies. Bobbie had convinced Payton I was a very bad man. I believe she did have Payton under an evil spell. In the best interests of Jason, he had taken him in as his own and protected him from me while not knowing any better. I wanted him to explain to Jason that I wasn't the bad man Bobbie had made me out to be. Payton did as I asked, and that helped.

Bobbie was frantically searching for a way to get her boys back. Payton's suggestion of taking Jason in made sense in the short term. I felt his best long-term chances were with me and my new family considering the love and support we could provide him. I was determined to make this work for Jason's sake. Things were getting better over the weeks, but I believed Bobbie wouldn't have stopped at anything; I was worried for my family.

Some days later, the same police officer who had come the first time came again. The officer conducted an assessment in and around our home and checked Jason out. He warned Jason not to cry wolf again. The police officer warned him he could end up in juvenile detention.

One week later, the same officer came in again to assess the situation. Ironically, I was on the phone with Bobbie at that moment. He asked to speak to Jason's mom and was heavy handed with her for ten minutes. He shook his head and admitted that we had our hands full with that woman. He told Jason he would put him over his lap and spank him if he pulled that again.

It was embarrassing to have the police come to our house; they had come three times in less than two months. We had many friends and police officers who lived in our neighborhood. *Oh Jesus, am I sinking backward again?* God kept telling me I was equipped to handle the situation, but I wondered if the rest of my family could. Thankfully, that was the last time the police were called to our home.

Two months later, Jason was getting more depressed. He was worried his mother would kill herself. He and I finally started having a better connection at a deeper level. He was still testing me and pushing my buttons, but I caught glimpses of his coming around. Nonetheless, Bobbie's caustic phone calls continued and were affecting the whole family. When Jason finished talking with his mother on one scheduled call, he had tears in his eyes. "Everything okay?" I asked.

"Please mind your own business," he answered.

I gave him time to process whatever he needed to process. Jason was always dramatic, but that time was different; he was genuinely hurting. I entered his room and sat with him. He left for my room. I followed him and blocked him in the doorway. I asked him what was going on. He blurted out, "Mom said you aren't my father!"

I was blown away that Bobbie would say that even it were true. Drugs had affected her judgment. She wanted him back at any cost. I didn't want him to go, and legally, I couldn't let him go. Jason was at first rocked at the news, but then he started realizing his mother was trying to gain some leverage over me to get him back. I couldn't believe Bobbie would tell Jason that she had had an affair. First, he thought Payton was his father. Then he thought I was. At that point, he didn't know who his father was. He was scared she might attempt suicide again.

She had told him his father was Jamie, the guy who was supposedly that prince she had met while she was on vacation with her family. Jason was all over the place with his emotions. It wasn't fair that she had burdened Jason, and I was hurt to hear it as well. I had to control my emotions in front of him, and it wasn't easy.

Jason and I talked about it some more, and it didn't take long for him to say he wanted to go home to his brother. He promised to make our lives miserable until we let him go. He was worried about his mother's behavior and was sure she would try to take her life again. He went off to bed without another word. Our kids were very uneasy. Things were bad in our home. Our family couldn't take much more of this. Our marriage was new, and Jason was newer. *God, is this too much for my new wife and kids to digest?*

I called Bobbie "Bobbie, how could you have done this to our son? What purpose will it serve for you or him?"

"It's to get you out of our lives. Oh and by the way, I'm positive Jason isn't your boy."

"Does this make you proud? Will you stop at nothing? You're becoming harder for me to pray for each day." She came unglued when I made that comment. She told me and my God some bad things. She crossed the line. *God will take care of this. I'm staying away from this one.* I hung up after she told me I would die in disgrace. *How did she get so angry? How has she become so evil? What happened in the last fifteen years?* I was sure she has quite a story.

The next day after school, Jason told me he wanted to know for sure who his father was. He wanted me to take a blood test. I knew he wouldn't rest until he knew who his father was. I figured I had a fifty-fifty chance of being his father. I prayed about it and called my lawyer. He recommended that Jason learn the truth. It would serve me well if I ever had to go back to court. The matter would be settled one way or the other. I told Jason I'd take the blood test.

We had our blood drawn at the same time. On our way home, we talked about what would happen either way. He didn't hesitate to say that if I wasn't his father, he'd search for Jamie. This boy had learned his mother had grossly lied to him three times in two months.

Chapter 22

❧ ❧

The Son

I couldn't sleep. I was waiting for the results of the blood test. I wanted so badly to care for him as my son no matter what. I was so done with not knowing. I would deal with the results no matter what they were.

I took several days off work to prepare for this moment. I assumed I'd be fine with God at my side. One day, Jason came home expecting the results to have arrived in the mail. They hadn't. *This must be a cruel joke.* He and I were nervous, anxious, and confused.

But that night was the best night we'd had together yet. He actually played cards with me. Though I was dead tired, I couldn't sleep. I got up and watched TV. I fell asleep on the couch. I was reminded of my younger days when I slept in my closet.

Finally, I heard the screeching and clacking of the mail slot. The mailman's jeep left. I ran out to the box and grabbed a handful of mail. The letter Jason and I had been waiting for was tucked in there. Tears were streaming down my face. I dropped the envelope, and when I reached down to pick it up, I had a major dizzy spell. I went in so my neighbors wouldn't see me faint. I dropped the mail on the counter and went to the living room to pray. I realized that maybe I didn't want to open it, that maybe I never wanted to know.

No. God wanted Jason and me to face this together; that was His plan. *Should I open it now or wait for Jason?* I decided to wait for Jan. At that point, I didn't want to open it. I was all over the place. *God, I need answers and your wisdom.* When Jan finally got home, I went into the bedroom with the results so she wouldn't have to see me hurting if Jason wasn't mine. *God, I beg you to strengthen me so my reactions will be pleasing to you and my family regardless of what the results are.*

I opened the envelope in private. I studied the results. I began to sob and wail. I was glad the kids weren't home. Jason Daniel was not my son. *Why, God, would you let him be born on Christmas Day and lead me on for so long? I searched for years for this boy. This hurts terribly, Father.*

Jan came in and held me for a long time. The love I felt from her embrace was like God's arms around me. After a lot of tears and once I had regained my composure, I told Jan about my feelings. The longer I spoke, the better I felt. The pain was lessening at least for the time being. We thought he'd be excited to know the truth and would start planning on escaping the Pain residence and search for his biological father. I had a lot of soul searching and praying to do. I needed a verse from God's Word. This is what I found. (Psalms 23:1-4) "The lord is my shepherd; I have all that I need. He lets me rest in green meadows; he leads me beside peaceful streams. He renews my strength. He guides me along right paths, bringing honor to his name. Even when I walk through the darkest valley, I will not be afraid, for you are close beside me. Your rod and your staff protect and comfort me."

Jan and I agreed that the best way to break this to Jason was straight up. That's what I did. I was alone with him after school that day. He was emotionless at first. He had a lot going through his head. He finally broke a smile. He had tears in his eyes. "May I please go and find my real father?" I had a long talk with him before answering that. I made it clear to him I'd be there for him regardless of the outcome. I asked him if he would consider allowing me to father him. I gave him a nickel tour of my life testimony to let him know what my life had been like without an earthly father and God. I told him I was capable, worthy, and willing to be his father and provide him security.

He pretty much blocked me out, but I hoped something I said would germinate. I told him that if he stayed, I'd set up a college fund for him. He shut me down.

"Alter, I want out of here. I want to go back to Mom and find my dad."

I was torn. *Does he stay with me? What's in his best interest?* His ex-step father had offered to care for him and promised not to give him back to his mother. Jason and I didn't know each other. Payton had technically been more his father than I had. He would also be reunited with his little brother if he went home. Payton was capable of caring for the two boys, while Jason was capable of making our lives miserable. *Do I put our family through chaos because of my selfishness, because I can't let go of something I fought so hard for? Then there's the legal system. What to do? God, please give me the words and the wisdom to say and do what's right.* I told Jason, "I want what's best for you. I'd be acting selfishly if I didn't think about your request. I'll pray about it."

Jason was giddy at the thought of being reunited with his brother and stepfather. This poor kid needed to be closer to his mother and brother; I knew he wouldn't stop until he was reunited with her. We all went to bed this evening with much to think about.

Something strange started to come over me as I lay in bed staring at the ceiling in the dark. Jan and I had talked for quite a while. I didn't feel the same weight on my shoulders that I'd been feeling for fifteen years. I felt free of my mental imprisonment. *Am I happy I'm not his father? Should I feel guilty for that?* After a night of heavy thinking and praying, I had some of my answers.

God, you brought me through this for many reasons. I promised to read your Word and listen to you if you would give me a healthy baby boy, and you did. Jason is a reminder of your power and strength and your Son, Jesus Christ. Father, you yearned for me to come to you, and you used the crazy deal I came up with to get me to seek you. It worked. Thank you for fighting for me as you promised you would. But why did I have to suffer for so many years?

Every Christmas, I was reminded of Jesus's and Jason's birthdays. Jesus was sent to earth to be among sinners and feel their pain and suffer with them. Jesus's death on the cross was an immense sacrifice. His resurrection proved Jesus was who He said He was and sealed all God's promises. I was free of guilt and sin, and I could move on as a sinner with a healthy conscience. I could share His story and it to be His. God proved to the world and me intimately that because I too had suffered and kept my word mostly, I could be free of the bondage I felt every day of my life wondering where my son was. I was guilt free for entertaining the idea of letting Jason go. It was God's plan that I let Jason go.

The day Jason was born was the day I had given myself to God. I had grieved for my son and the relationship I'd never had the chance to enjoy with him. I wanted to know my son on his birthday and every day. I was also reminded of Jesus, who had been born for me and had become my Father. Though Christmas Day was always painful for me because it was Jason's birthday, God wanted to turn my attention to Jesus, the Son who would change my life, not the son who caused me so much pain year after year. I remembered that Easter Sunday, April 23, 2000, my birthday, was the day I got my spirit back. Those events had my attention and would have it until I gained everlasting life.

God has kept His promise to me, and I have tried hard to keep my promise to Him. He raised me and taught me at times with a heavy hand to see the truth, the light, and the love of a real father. He taught me courage, wisdom, morals, and values, and he granted me love, peace, and joy. Jason was never my son by blood or relationship. God had planned that. God planned for me to close this chapter in my life. I know that God gave me His Son, not my son. I prayed Jason would get the same loving kindness and attention from the Father that I have. (John 3:16) "For this is how God loved the world: He gave his one and only Son, so that everyone who believes in Him, will not perish but have eternal life."

I woke the next morning with a new heart and a new understanding of God's power. None of this changed my mind about wanting to raise Jason, but I would be okay with it if he chose to find his stepfather. The lies Bobbie had told him, and Payton about me had been exposed. Jason had a much better chance of sorting things out and moving on.

I told my lawyer about all that had happened. I said that it was in Jason's best interest to live with his stepfather and little brother; I was at peace with that. My lawyer told me that he would seek a legal release and separation of all responsibility and legal guardianship. After I consulted with my pastor, I told my lawyer to mail the letter. Seventy-two hours later, I received a letter of approval. It was done. Jason was packing his bag eager to see his brother. He actually hugged me good-bye. The last thing I told him was, "I will always love you, I will always be there for you unconditionally. I'll accept you back if things don't work out."

Payton once again became Jason's legal parent, and I was able to move on and love, nurture, and raise my beautiful stepkids, whom God reassured me would become my world and give me everything I was sorely missing in life—accountability, joy, love, and much more. I'd raise them the way I should have been raised, the way God raised me. I made enough mistakes raising my stepkids to fill the ocean, but I could feel God coaching me and rooting me on. I have tried to make God proud. I love Kevin, Kara, and Steven with all my heart. They're such beautiful people, and they make me proud. I look forward to spending my life and eternity with them.

I've prayed endlessly that Jason would become a fine man. He will always be my boy. I hope one day we can meet again and share our stories. God will bring us together again in His time if it is His will. I love you, Jason. I'm so thankful for your birth; it changed me forever. I hope you'll know the significant role you played in my life one day and others' lives in a way that glorifies God and sets you free.

Chapter 23

❦

The Healing

God wasn't done with me yet. I don't suppose He ever will be. I joke that I was born in uncharted waters and haven't found dry land yet. But my life was improving every day. I still hit speed bumps, but God was leading me. I'm so secure and confident in myself that I hardly recognize myself when I look in a mirror. I still had baggage—the molestation I endured. How God would deal with that remained to be seen, but I was sure God has something up His sleeve as He always does.

Life went on as normal; I continued to heal and build good relationships with the kids. My spiritual drive was to become the best stepdad I could be. Jan and I were active in church and were very consistent followers of Jesus Christ.

We continued to lead Real Encounters; I liked sharing with my brothers and sisters in Sunday school how God had unpacked one of the most difficult chapters in my and my family's lives. Things were going as well as could be expected. I believe in miracles because I am one. Someone pinch me.

Our Real Encounters Sunday school class was growing; we had moved to a bigger room, and that was becoming too small for us. God was at work. After a year or longer of leading the Sunday school class, I was asked by the church to sign a document, a contract all leaders were to sign. The spiritual indemnification clause was too much for me to grasp. It required me to be pretty awesome and holy in order to lead. I was a sinner with a big past; I didn't think I could live up to the terms of the document, so I stepped down from my leadership position without being told I had too. Again, I didn't make a stink, but I was baffled. My Christian walk apparently had a meaning that was different from those others in the church had. I had a different perspective on what it meant to nurture others particularly those who had endured much pain. Those who have been Christians all their lives can have a much different perspective on Christianity than those who have come to Christ with burdens and out of chaos have. We share the same joy but have different perspectives.

Some Christians actually believe they're worthy and capable of signing these documents, but not me, not the way it was written. I didn't feel I could live sin free. I thought that was the whole purpose of our class. "Thank you, Jesus, for dying for my sins" were my last words as I gave up my leadership responsibility. I wasn't being sarcastic; I just couldn't understand the document and felt I didn't need to. The fact that Christ died for me so I could serve others as a sinner was what I thought it was all about. I couldn't become holy, so I couldn't sign that document. Our class did life together with God as our focal point— nothing more complicated than that.

One day, I stopped off at the bleachers of a baseball diamond to watch a friend's daughter play softball. I was walking my Akita, Dakota; he was a puppy cuter than cute. A young man came up; he wanted to meet Dakota. He knew me from church. That was the first time we had really talked, and we did so for an hour. I could tell he had a story. I can usually look into another person's eyes and tell a lot due to my heightened senses my past brought on in me. But I couldn't with him. He was a burn victim; some would consider him hard to look at because of his facial disfigurement, but I had no problem recognizing his humanness and normalness. It's just that I couldn't read his facial expressions due to his scars.

I liked Gilbert. He seemed open to talk with me and comfortable in our discussions. He and I were about the same height and weight, and he was in his early twenties. He attended the same university my stepkids later attended. Our discussion at the ballpark was the beginning of a lifelong friendship.

One Saturday morning in Anderson, Indiana, in 2003, Jan and I read in the papers that Gilbert had been arrested. I felt called to visit

Gilbert in jail, so I did. I've learned to respond to God's callings out of my healthy fear and respect for Him. He had no idea I was coming. As I waited for him, I heard cell doors crashing closed and smelled floor cleaner. I heard faint cries for freedom, the obnoxious voices of lawbreakers, and the sounds of drug addicts in withdrawal—cries of hopeless agony. I was getting a weird feeling. I'd heard those sounds in my youth.

Gilbert showed up. I picked up the phone on my side of the glass, and he picked up on his side. I could tell by his voice he didn't want to see me. "Why did you come here?"

"Because God spoke to me. I don't want to be here either, Gilbert." He was taken aback by that. "That's right, Gilbert. I don't know why you're here or why God called me to visit you. Gilbert, why are you here? Normally, they put that in the newspaper."

"I've been charged with molesting a very young girl. Alter, it's really bad. I'm guilty."

He told me as much as he could, and I absorbed as much as I could until I shut down. He had no idea of the molestation I had suffered and how hard it was for me to hear what he had done. I tried to hide my emotions. *God, why did you put me face to face with a child molester? Come on!*

Our visit was short. I couldn't handle any more that day. I told Gilbert that God had already forgiven him and that he had to move on by repenting and accepting His grace. I told him I had to process this. I was a little hard on him, but I kept my composure.

Outside, I threw up my breakfast. I emotionally lost it. *God, why do you continue to drag me into chaos? Why do you abuse me like this? Wasn't it enough that I went through this once already?* I got in my car and pounded the steering wheel like a madman. A woman knocked on my window. She wanted to know if I was okay. I bit her head off. She walked away shaking her head. As I drove past her, I apologized. I went home and was quiet for several hours. I shared as much as I could with Jan. I went to bed.

I read in the papers the next morning that Gilbert had been befriended and trusted by the young victim's family. I knew of the family, which made it even harder for me to accept that I had been called into Gilbert's life. I got sicker the more I thought about it. After I was done feeling sorry for myself and quit ranting to God about poor me and why, why, why, God tugged again at my heart to visit Gilbert. *Father, I'm not ready for this right now!* But God knew I'd never be ready. The Holy Spirit called me to forgive Gilbert and let him know he had already been forgiven.

When I visited him the next time, I was still freaked out, but I hid my emotions well. I wanted tell him how I felt about child molesters, but then I asked myself, *Why are you here?* I settled in and asked Gilbert, "Gilbert why, man? Why aren't you crying? Don't you have any remorse?" Gilbert told me his tear ducts had been burned beyond usability. I started to get the picture a little. "But why, Gilbert?"

"Alter, I need to talk about this with someone, but I can't open up to you right away."

"Let's take baby steps."

I prayed about this and listened to God. Subsequent visits were easier for me to handle. Each day, he told me a little more of his story. He gave me permission to share it. Brace yourself.

Gilbert had been verbally, spiritually, physically, mentally, and sexually abused. He had a little sister whom he loved and protected. They were very young when the molestations started, and perverted customers paid to watch their sexual molestation. As the kids reached the age of reasoning and were capable of crying out about the molestation, their parents decided to quiet the evidence of their crimes.

One day while drunk and high on drugs, Gilbert's father set fire to their trailer home. The kids were in it. Gilbert frantically looked for his sister. The fire department arrived. He was rescued by a brave firefighter. Gilbert was trying to tell them his sister was still in the trailer. He broke free and ran as fast he could back to the trailer. He went through the flames to find his sister. She was dead. Gilbert was rescued again, but he had been burned from head to toe.

After several more visits, I learned why Gilbert had molested the girl. He had lived all his adult life alone. Most people shunned him because of his facial injuries. He had few true friends. He'd never had a girlfriend. He had written off his chances of ever having an intimate relationship with any woman. He figured he would never be married, and he suffered from PTSD and depression.

On the day that Gilbert crossed the line, he was looking for a way to fulfill his needs, wants, and dreams and did so with a defenseless child. As sick as that was and as sick as he was, I believe it was less an act of perversion and more an act of extreme need.

Because I was actively pursuing Gilbert's story, people asked me, "Why are you befriending him?" I'd say, "Gilbert and I are brothers in Christ. I'll let God work this out. It isn't for me or anyone else to question. As long as he's a Christian, even though he has sinned, I'll remain his brother." Some didn't understand; they thought I condoned what Gilbert had done. The family of the victim was upset with me as well., but they didn't know my story. Gilbert wasn't a monster. He was human being who had made a huge mistake he would and should pay dearly for.

After each visit, I came home with a clearer understanding of why God had made me face up to Gilbert. He had let so many people down, but I decided not to be like that. I certainly didn't condone his crime, but I felt the need to forgive him and mentor him.

God called on me to get into the mind of a child molester so I could heal and be a servant at the same time. Only God could pull that off. I hadn't faced my fears until then. I was able to forgive Daemon, though I never learned his story. These molesters were products of their upbringing, events, stresses, lies they had been told, and lies they told themselves. They had found children weaker than them who were seeking attention as the molesters were searching for love in their twisted ways.

I healed tremendously, made a new friend, learned how to forgive as I'd never experienced forgiveness before, and served a person who had committed a horrible crime. Talk about being humbled. I was ridiculed for serving a child molester who looked like a monster. But he was someone with a great heart who loved God and sought forgiveness. God gave him grace.

I encourage you to remember all your sins tonight. Have you ever cheated on your spouse? Have you lied? Stolen anything? Cursed your parents? Do you look at porn? Don't look in the mirror if you don't want to see the truth. We're all sinners. Without God, we have no hope of redemption. I'm not preaching. I'm telling you exactly how it is.

Condemn your neighbor only if you're worthy enough. If you're not but you act as if you are, you're a hypocrite. This is the worst thing a Christian who preaches the gospel can be. Get right with yourself before presenting yourself as a Christian.

God gave me a new friend in Gilbert, freed me from mental imprisonment, and taught me how to truly forgive and extend grace even though I might desire revenge. God taught me how to love anything or anybody; He is turning me into a warrior. He has begun to close the most painful chapter in my life. I am free because I did what He expected of me. I'm not saying I'm good; I'm saying He is good and makes me feel good.

Gilbert was going to court. I told his attorney I'd stand not in his defense but in his support. I didn't want a lighter sentence for him; I wanted to make sure he received some help while in prison. I was willing to tell my story as a victim. I was willing to discuss the similarities and differences between Gilbert and Daemon. Gilbert and his attorney accepted my offer. That meant I'd be sitting in the courtroom full of some really upset people, family members, and even friends who may not be friendly to me for much longer. I stood to lose a lot. I was concerned but not deterred. I knew God was good all the time. I could count on that.

I hadn't woken up one morning and decided to go to court on behalf of a child molester. I didn't want to smear my reputation, but I knew I had to do what my heart had been commanded to do. I'd heard the victim's family had forgiven Gilbert as hard as that would be to do. I knew God had been a huge part of that; the family was surely well grounded in Christ. I wished they all knew my heart and why I was there, but it wouldn't have been right to them. I hope that someday this family will know my true story. Perhaps this book might answer a lot of questions for a lot of people as to why I supported Gilbert.

This is another great example of why it's important for all of us to tell our stories. God's plan can't work perfectly if we detour around His will and plan for us. God doesn't call any of us to shine the light on ourselves for our own benefit; He will use us to be a part of His total plan. It won't be easy for us. It will be a sacrifice. But it will always be about the total picture. We will benefit in unimaginable ways. His rewards will be greater than our pain and sacrifice. This is hard to explain to anyone who's hurting. It almost seems like magic, but it's not. It's raw God power. The incredible relational value we experience by being used by God is as close as we'll get to touching God in the flesh. We have to experience it.

I was on the stand looking at the family that was hurting horribly. I could see they were frustrated with Gilbert, who was showing no emotion. They didn't know he couldn't cry or contort his face in a way that would show others the emotions he was experiencing. His blank look hurt his case. The judge clearly thought Gilbert wasn't human; I'm sure others judged him the same way because of his facial disfigurement. He was a human being whose pressure valve had popped.

The prosecution turned whatever I said around. He made it sound as though I were condoning Gilbert's crime. I shared a bit of my story to show that Gilbert's and my story were similar in some ways. The prosecuting attorney was quick to point out that after all my heartache, I had turned out okay as if he were a psychologist. How little he actually knew about Gilbert or me. I hadn't turned out okay; I had turned out a very broken and insecure individual who trusted few if any. My past would have ruined me had it not been for the grace of God. The only difference between Gilbert and me was one decision. I'd had many opportunities to pull the trigger and kill Daemon. I had wanted to at times and had thought about it. I just happened to not break while Gilbert did break. He had made a bad choice. I had faith that he had learned from it and wouldn't make the same mistake twice.

I got off the stand and was trying to recover from this unnerving experience. I could tell Gilbert would get the maximum penalty, but that wouldn't stop his love for God. I wanted him to get into a program that would help him deal with his past, his appearance, and his pain. The judge gave him the maximum—fifty years. I'm sure if Gilbert had been able to show his emotions as most others could, his sentence could have been lighter. He needed help. I prayed to see his problem fixed, not compounded.

Gilbert is where he deserves to be. He knows my feelings about this.

He also knows I'm his brother in Christ who will never forsake him. I'll always love him and be there for him. If he hadn't shared his story so transparently with me, I'd still be in my mental prison concerning my molestation at the hands of a child predator. God knows this and now so do I. Thank you, Gilbert, for your friendship and for what you brought to my life. Thank you, God, for putting this sex offender in my path. It was your divine spiritual power; it couldn't be anything else.

Chapter 24

The Letter

Dear Daemon,

Prior to this letter and prior to a man named Gilbert who came into my life as a sex offender like yourself, I thought you were a beast, Satan in the flesh. You crushed me, Daemon. I depended on you to be a father to me. I trusted you would keep me safe from harm and teach me about life. I thought that with you, I'd have a chance to experience what life was like with a father.

I experienced that for a short time with you. Then something went terribly wrong. Your eyes turned yellow. Your breath became putrid with the smell of death. When I looked into your eyes, you were no longer there. You were empty. There was no soul. There was nothing. You scared me. You threatened my life and even tried to take it from me. You took my heart, soul, and spirit and devoured them like a ravaged beast. But that wasn't enough; you tried to take my flesh too; you failed, though. Satan had found his way into your heart, and you were possessed.

You lost, Daemon, you lost bad. Your kind will never be found in heaven. You will never know what it's like to have a relationship with Christ. You're burning in hell. Dark demons are eating you from the inside out and have gouged out your eyes. There is no happiness where you are at, no joy, nothing to look forward to. You'll be in a dark world for eternity. You're in the bottom of the lake of fire, Daemon, and I can't help you.

God has laid on my heart that I should write this letter. I can only imagine now that Satan's hand will be forced by God to deliver it to you. This letter will burn Satan's hand before he's finished reading it, and it will forever be a reminder of another defeat for the two of you. That's right, Daemon. You lost, and Satan has been defeated by God once again. Praise Jesus! I am free from you, Daemon, and my imprisonment. All that remains are my scars. They no longer mean anything that represents the dark, only the light. They are a reminder to me who my God is, not who you are. They remind me of the day we triumphed over you and your buddy Satan. Did you know my God is your God too? The only difference between you and me is that you'll never be with Him. (Mark 9:42) "But if you cause one of these little ones who trusts in me to fall into sin, it would be better for you to be thrown into the sea with a large mill stone hung around your neck." Daemon the mill stone is still around your neck. You are now at the bottom of the sea of fire.

Satan will read this letter to you, Daemon, because you've been burned and can no longer hold anything in your hands or read anything. Satan's mouth and tongue will burn as if he had sipped acid. God will watch Satan read this letter to you, and it will be the hardest thing ever for Satan to say or for you to hear. Hear these final ending words because I mean them with all my heart. You will never hear from me again because this chapter is officially closed. Thank you, Jesus.

I forgive you, Daemon. I will always love you. I wish we could try life over again and right our wrongs. I pray God will break His own rules and take you back to be His own so you no longer have to experience hell. I'm moving on. I hope by some miracle that we will embrace in heaven. I have prayed and prayed many times that someday I would end up a general in God's army. I pray I can convince God to pardon the souls in hell. It's a stretch, but I love you this much. I know longer ask why. I just rejoice in my freedom from you. I thank you for the strength you have given to me through the trials of my childhood; they made me a warrior who ultimately conquered you and your kind. Praise be to God.

With unconditional love,
Alter

Chapter 25

❦

It is Done

It's a new day. I'm on our deck. The dust is settling around me. There's an abundance of peace and joy in the air. The birds are singing, the flowers are blooming, and I hear kids playing in the streets. God's sweet breath is a cool breeze on my face. I wonder if I'm dreaming. Where is all this peace coming from? Am I in heaven? What's different? Why am I feeling so free? Someone pinch me.

I have just completed a review of my life as if taking inventory of everything that had happened to me before God had called me to the Midwest. It has taken six years for God to close every painful chapter in my life and bring me to today. I'll experience pain in the future, I'm sure, but every bad decision I'd ever made prior to my calling to follow Him has been forgiven, every rock in my bag has been removed, and every issue I have faced has been resolved. God has shone His face on me and kept every promise He ever made. Today, I breathe a new breath. I think a new way. I am free. I now have a future with a strong foundation of faith. I have a clean slate. I have a beautiful family. God has blessed me with a great career. I have an incredible relationship with Christ I didn't think was possible.

My career began to blossom. After ten or so years with Triple D, I wanted to test the mechanical aptitude God had granted me. I had no degree, just the talent the Lord has blessed me with and the people He sent to mentor me. I got a job with System Alliance Groups dealing with much larger pumps and systems in the power industry and nuclear world. I was like a kid in a candy store. I was honored and humbled to become a profit center for this wonderful company. The owners became my mentors; they gave me a chance of a lifetime. I learned the business, and God blessed me with great customers and coworkers. What a pleasure it was to work there.

One of the owners taught me the business. He'd travel with me to my customers, and I learned something new each day. This challenge in career paths is exactly what I needed to see how far I could go with my career. My idea of success is to create opportunity from chaos, to work hard, and find myself free, worthy, and useful as a servant to others. I wanted to teach others how to create success for themselves. God delights in opportunities from weakness. What a good example for me also.

Jan and I could afford to purchase our dream home; that was a benchmark for me in my hard life. It was a handsome home (though that never really mattered to me). It was a safe home, a great place to raise kids, and God was the center of it.

I had always wanted to sail. I told Jan I wanted a sailboat and began selling her on the reason. I felt it would take me even closer to God—I would feel His whispers in my ear—and she and I would be the crew. It would relax me from the stresses of life. I'd never sailed, but I prayed about it, and God wanted me to relax and continue healing. He even provided the means for us to buy a forty-foot sailboat that turned out to be a real hoot. I became known as the crazy man on the docks, the guy who had bought a sailboat without even knowing how to sail. Well, I hired a captain until I was sure-footed enough to solo with it.

Our family had many good times aboard. It was a time that I could be the captain of my marriage. The only time I barked orders at my wife was on the boat. Ha! It provided us with the relaxation that we yearned for after what we had gone through as a family.

The family slowly but steadily drew closer; the kids were more accepting of me. Every family discussion, every pain or hurt, every new trial or tribulation was turned into an opportunity for growth just as God had taught me. I wasn't capable of being a good father on my own, but I was capable of following God's ways rather than my own.

We still had moments of frustration as all families do, but we were transparent with each other about our weaknesses and strengths alike. People can't help you if they don't know you need help, so showing your weaknesses is a benefit more than it is an embarrassment. Kevin, Kara, and Steven have given me everything I needed to be able to experience what it feels like to be a father. Their father shared his kids with me, and I was blessed.

My career blossomed, and the Lord blessed me and my family financially. I was traveling a lot more, which was a regret, but I watched my kids grow and go to college. Their father and Jan and I paid half the cost for their cars; they had to work for their halves.

Every year I fall deeper in love with Jan. Our journey has been incredible. We've always gotten over and past the difficult times. What a special gift God gave me in Jan. I love you so much, Jan. Over my career, I've enjoyed holding seminars and teaching. I've recorded more than 300 seminars, some technical and others motivational. At one point, I had my school approved by the Nuclear Regulatory Commission Center. I began to teach nuclear engineers about pumps and systems. I did a short solo at a nuclear symposium and have taught at several universities including the University of Arizona, Cleveland State, and Indiana University by invitation.

After more than ten successful years with System Alliances Groups (SAG), I decided I really wanted to serve others with what I had learned, so I started thinking of ways I could do that. I was challenged at SAG, but I wanted more. Headhunters were after me, but I thought I'd like my own company. I knew many employees at a company I became interested in purchasing. At SAG, I was a technical specialist for eight Midwest states. I had approached Pumps and Systems Solutions (PSS) while employed at SAG to see if they'd be interested in a strategic alliance with us. We formed a relationship and eventually shared a great volume of business together. I worked with some very talented employees at PSS. I grew to love and respect the owner, Mitch, a friend and mentor who became my partner.

Mitch and I realized we had something to offer each other. He appreciated the time I spent with his sales staff and my technical strengths I shared with them. We began to discuss a succession plan so he could ultimately retire.

I left SAG, a great company, after ten years there. It was a leader in the repair of boiler feed pumps, reactor feeds, and cooling systems for the nuclear industry. I left for nothing more than a chance to become a servant leader. I had learned way too much about life and didn't want to waste my knowledge. I felt strongly that I had more to offer employees than a just a paycheck.

PSS was a small, $12 million company when I started there in April 2013 as the sales and business development manager. That worked out well, so Mitch promoted me to chief operating officer. We continued to grow, and I became president. Today, I'm also part owner and the CEO of this amazing company with amazing people.

Mitch is still the chairman of the board and primary owner. I've recently hired a vice president who is revered by thousands of our customers in more than fifty countries. He had mentored hundreds of successful specialist in this business, including me when I started in the business. He became one of my best friends and confidants. Today, he's my business partner and right hand man. Somebody pinch me please. Is God not good?

Having a nice home, a good career, and nice things is not a sin in itself, but if you don't glorify God with them by sharing them and thus making them holy, they're a big waste. I want to offer my heart, my possessions, my whole life to others. I want to serve them.

I love each of you. God bless you! I pray you will invite Jesus into your heart. God will find favor in each of your struggles. I pray that God will bring you peace and joy. Never give up. God created you to be a warrior and a part of His plan, so He made you wonderfully. If you've strayed from God, come back home where you belong! "Turn us again to yourself, O Lord God of Heavens Armies. Make your face shine down upon us. Only then will we be saved." (Psalms 80:19)

Chapter 26

❧ ✦

Divine Intervention

Do you believe in divine intervention? I do. I've shared with you some of my dreams and visions that I couldn't have made up. I believe God talks to us in many ways. We have all been gifted with a uniqueness no one else possesses. We are each uniquely identified by Christ. He may communicate differently with us. Would it not be a shame if we missed the opportunity to hear or see God? We must all heighten our senses and use more of our brains.

There's tremendous power in our brains, God's creation, so let's utilize it and sharpen all our senses. Look at everything and realize it's all there because of God. Nothing happens by chance. Nothing. There's a plan behind everything. I've highlighted some events, words, and interventions that sometimes would be ignored or not thought of as God's way of communicating with us. He's always working in our lives

March 20, 2016

Another significant day in my life. I was at church with Jan. It was a beautiful moment when three lost souls would come to Christ; it had been an emotional day for me already. When church was over, Jan and met up with some friends who had just returned from Israel. A young man who had strayed from Christ for a few years told me he noticed tension in Israel between Christians and Muslims. He could clearly see signs that Israel was a ticking bomb as had been foretold in Revelation; fascinating stuff.

Jan and I ate at our favorite breakfast place. One of the waitresses we'd grown to love boldly asked us if we would go to the convenience store and buy the girls some malt shakes. After breakfast, Jan and I did. We had the chance to be servants in the moment—the very thing we're called to do.

The day before, we'd bought a ca. 1830s desk. I loaded it with some of my books, one of which was the Bible Ron, my brother-in-law, had given me years earlier. He had helped me come to Christ, if you remember. I hadn't opened that particular Bible in more than twenty years. I dusted it off and opened it. I'd forgotten Ron had written in it, "Alter Pain came to Christ Tuesday, March 20, 1990" inside. The inside cover illustrated that I was clearly not the first owner of that Bible. It had been published in 1966, the year I was born. Hmmm … I can't make this up.

Well, the day was March 20, 2016, exactly twenty-six years later. I became a bit sentimental about that. He had died by then, so I searched for his obit. I wanted to put it in that Bible. I found it and did some calculating. Ron had passed away on March 21, 2014, twenty-four years and a day after he had helped me come to Christ. The next day was the anniversary of Ron's going to heaven. I was reminded how precious it was to witness three lost souls come to Christ that day, and I was reminded by God that I too had an anniversary when I came to Christ.

In addition, while I was looking for Ron's obituary, a coin the size of a dime fell from a shelf. I picked it up to put it in my change bucket. But then I saw it was an Israeli coin of all things. Someone else must have mistaken it for a dime and put it in circulation. This happened just after I'd been warned about the clock ticking in Israel. God was telling me Jesus was coming. And it kept getting better …

On top of all this, after having received all these communications from God, I started feeling guilty about not writing more of this book. I'd been dragging my heels on that. So I started to write. Just then, Bill Lyons, a friend, gave me an accountability phone call. Bill was Tim LaHaye's best friend since high school or college; Tim had written the *Left Behind* series with Barry Jenkins. Jan and I had visited Tim and Beverly LaHaye and Bill and Barry Lyons for a week just a few months prior. I realized God wanted my hand in writing my testimony.

All the events of that day! Friends, none of it had happened by chance. Elevate your senses and be aware that God is moving in you all the time and is speaking to you all the time. You've had days like mine—through a sequence of events, people, circumstances, and sometimes power from the Holy Spirit, God was saying something to you. If your senses were heightened, you realized God was inviting you into a dialogue with Him.

Consider every event in your life part of God's promises to you. He has you positioned where you need to be for His purposes. He's with you everywhere and waiting for you to react to His signs He wants you to recognize. He communicates with you through dreams, visions, and events and even through your conscience, gut, and heart. It takes practice to hear His whispers, notice His power, and experience a relationship with Him on a deeper level. He is waiting for you to say, "I do," "I will," and "I am yours, God," so answer Him!

I'm honored that God chose me to be one of His warriors and experience suffering so I would really get it. I feel I don't deserve to be His warrior, but I would go through all my challenges again to become one. My pain could never match the pain Jesus went through on the cross to redeem us all. God promises us all a room in His kingdom, which none of us deserves, but that's His amazing promise to us! Our sins have been forgiven through Christ's sacrifice, and we are free from sin's bondage.

Life is hard. God knows that. He has no intention of making it easy because He wants to prepare us for His kingdom. Is it just me, or are others realizing many are grappling with ADD, ADHD, OCD, PTSD, and other disorders more? I don't know the percentages, but I see plenty of people all around struggling with their issues at work, home, and in daily life. It's tougher for many to find a balance in life. I've seen more people coming from rough backgrounds and as a result not investing in each other in real time—maintaining relationships seems to be getting tougher if not more painful and risky, and we all need relationships.

We no longer have to work at maintaining our relationships because Facebook reminds us of birthdays and anniversaries. We can take pills for hangovers rather than intentionally cut down on our drinking. And the government is handing out pharmaceuticals to protect us from overdosing on illegal drugs. Dating sites relieve us of the effort we would otherwise put into engaging in courtship as we are wired to do. None of this can ever replace the human touch, the human eye, the human voice telling us, "I love you." We have learned to seek the paths of least resistance.

We have to wake up, show up, and act responsibly. We need each other even though we fear being hurt, of having someone leave our lives without an apology for doing so. We have to be accountable to others as well as ourselves. We have to invest in others for the sake of our mental health. We can tend to pet our pets more than our spouses and text others more than we call them. We have to make a concerted effort to show others we care about them, want to hear their voices, and want to love them more.

Let's stop allowing Facebook to put Hallmark out of business. Let's not let virtual reality trump reality. Let's invest our time in others one on one. If we become humble, we'll find it easier to invest in our friends truthfully and avoid using alternatives to that. If we're hurting, depressed, or anxious, we should love on others with real hugs, not smiley faces on the computer.

Everyone experiences chaos—some of it due to uncontrollable circumstances and some of it created personally—but chaos represents opportunity, so embrace chaos and find the opportunity it contains. Our attitude is critical here; if you can't find a solution to your chaos, invent one.

I want to allow my relationships to fuel my passion to move forward and help me find peace and success and help others find the same; we'll be on the same team. Relationships are the key to success. I'm talking about relationships with God, spouses, families, and friends. This includes fellow employees, customers, and so on. We can't fly solo; that leads to isolation and loneliness. (Psalms 16:9) says that "we can make our plans but the Lord determines our steps." It takes an investment of determination, dedication, perseverance, humility, and a servant's heart to establish and maintain healthy relationships, and that's not an easy job. Marriages require work, but so do careers. I have 1300 relationships with my customers on top of my personal ones. Someone tell me that's not work. But God can help us find a balance; He gives us more than we can handle and I believe this to be true; He grants us armor for our protection against Satan, who loves to weasel his way into our hearts when we are weak. God's armor includes His Word, promises, light, love, truth, Jesus Christ, prayer, and our faith. We're well protected when we are overwhelmed. It's even better when we also accept and protect each other in the name of Jesus. (Romans 15:7) says "Therefore accept each other the same as Christ has accepted you so that God will be given glory."

Relationships are so complicated that we can't nurture them on our own. We need God just as much as He needs us. We have to be dynamic and open to change. We must remain loyal to God and always be ready for battle. (Ephesians 6:11) asks us to "Put on all of Gods armor so that we will be able to stand firm against all tragedies of the devil." This armor is many things. The Word, (read it), Gods promises (always kept), our faith (level of faith) and to trust in the Lord with all of our heart is armor. Additionally, love, truth, light, Jesus Christ, and prayer are all ingredients of this gift of Armor. You are well protected with your eyes on Jesus. We must learn how to survive outside our comfort zones. We have to respect everyone and see to their needs; we have to let God take care of our needs. This is the beginning of success, joy, and something very special.

I will train more to be in heaven's army. I will remain loyal to my Christian brothers and sisters and help God bring as many lost sheep to Christ as possible. I will fight off demons. Alone, I am weak, but "with God's help we will do mighty things, for he will trample down our foes" (Psalm 108:13). Read the book of Exodus for a great example of God's power and willingness to go before us and fight.

Chapter 27

❧❧

Experience and Wisdom

Experience and wisdom are gained by going through the difficulties of life. Wisdom can be a gift from God, but when you ask Him for that, be sure that your faith is in Him alone. (James 1:5-6) "If you need wisdom, ask our generous God, and he will give it to you. He will not rebuke you for asking. But when you ask Him, be sure that your faith is in God alone." Be careful of what you ask for, and be ready. Go one step further—use your story and wisdom for God's glory. (Job 12:13) says that "True wisdom and power are found in God; council and understanding are His." What use would we be if we didn't use our wisdom to serve those in need to glorify God? Wisdom comes with age (Job 32:7) "I thought, those who are older should speak, for wisdom comes with age."

Life has certainly taught me a lot. I have also gained much wisdom. I have learned some very important steps to living life safely while keeping down the chaos. I didn't find this wisdom in a book or learn life from a psychologist. In fact, I had never been to a psychologist at least related to my own issues. I have found peace and joy from Jesus Christ. God has been my mighty counselor. (Isaiah 9:6) "For a child is born to us, a son is given to us. The government will rest on His shoulders. And He will be called: Wonderful Counselor, Mighty God, Everlasting Father, Prince of Peace."

I often reflect on the trials and tribulations I have faced before and after I accepted Jesus into my heart. I have learned that the trials and tribulations never stop; how I handle them now is night-and-day different from how I used to handle them. My attitude, my hope, my passion, and desire to stay free are some major differences. This is all wisdom. Remember that wisdom is nothing without one's desire to share it, teach it, or counsel others with it.

You can teach forgiveness by your actions. You can forgive all walks of life and actually love them well. I forgave Daemon, my molester, and Gilbert, the burn victim with a child molestation story. I came to face my demons by becoming his friend. I forgave my mother. She too was a product of her upbringing and has a story. How can I condemn her? I love her. I have no ill will toward anyone in my life.

I acquired this ability to forgive by first asking for forgiveness. There is no credit to be given or received for what I have learned and what wisdom I have gained. But there is the promise of freedom, everlasting life, and joy. I have learned that when you fall, you can get up and try again until you get it right. I have learned that life is much like a river; there's lots of life going on around me. It doesn't start or stop for me, nor can I start or stop it unless I build a dam. It isn't always smart to build a dam because life then starts backing up. So I may as well learn how to go with the current.

I have learned that no one will make a difference for me but that I can make all the difference by letting God counsel me and then take action. I have learned that God will not do everything for me and that by letting Him guide me does not mean I can coast. Working for God does take work, sacrifice, and humility. God taught me to keep my eye on the prize in spite of those who will try to hurt me, destroy me, and try to cause me to stumble and sin. His Word taught me that I am loved and special to Him and that nothing will change that. I learned the true meaning of love when Jesus died on the cross for me; that said it all. I am no longer afraid to die for Christ.

I have learned that each time I tell my story, I learn a little more about the complexity of myself, this world, and its people. It has freed me from my own imprisonment and at times helped others become free as well. I have learned that following God and professing my faith is much less awkward than being in jail, having no joy, or being depressed and socially awkward. I have learned that by turning my cheek only for the other to be struck stings only for a moment but that the message sent to the afflicter stings for an eternity.

I have learned through Christ's example of true leadership that servanthood makes a powerful statement and has a profound, positive effect on all people and things. After enough abuse by enough people, I have learned that there is only one true God who knows me, one true Father who is blameless and who has never lied to me. I learned that I had never lost my spirit but had guarded it rather than letting God in to fill it.

I learned that when God talks to me, He means business. When He calls me, I go to Him at a run. Fearing God means being in awe of Him and responding to Him. I learned that nothing in life—no possession, no position—is bigger than God, who reigns over all. As I have matured, I have come to know that my life isn't mine anymore. I have learned that my story isn't my story anymore, it's God's story for His glory. The more I gave my story to God, the easier it was to tell. He really does take all the worrying and angst away.

I have learned not to judge others until I learn their stories. If I take time to invest in others' lives, I'll learn their stories and no longer judge but participate in their best interests. I have learned that tithing is not an act of emotions but a responsibility; it's a show of spiritual rather than financial wealth. It's a show of obedience, character, and a servant heart. It reminds me that none of this is mine, that it is God's. I have learned that money can be a root of evil but that it's fine if you're a responsible servant with it rather than coveting it. It's okay to have nice things to share, not to hoard. I learned that hard work is an example for others as well as yourself; the biggest reward is your accomplishment when it affects others positively. All other good things will come naturally from my efforts. And finally, I have learned that I am but a speck on this planet but am as big as the moon in God's eyes. And so are you. God loves you unconditionally. I write this on behalf of the more than 7.4 billion people on earth. I proudly write before each of you that my story is no fluke. It's real, it's God's and it's yours. Now let's go fill heaven up, shall we?

Chapter 28

❧ ❧

The Characters

This story is a story of God, not Alter Pain. If you look at the bigger picture, you will see that life goes on all around us. We are nothing more than a part of the web of life that God weaves. This story certainly doesn't show how great I am. I am a jacked-up and derailed train wreck with all the scars to prove it. I am not proud of this story. I am, however, in awe of what God was able to accomplish through a sinner like me. God must first work in you before He can work through you. Let Him in, and let Him work you over. I can't explain it as well as He can demonstrate it.

One of the most difficult things I have ever done in my life was write this book. I didn't write it to prove anything. I wrote it because I was led to write it. It should have been written long ago. I hemmed and hawed for years before finally having the courage to write it.

I will now bring all the major characters forward as of this day, June 9, 2016.

Alphonse

Dad was miserable up to the day he died. He had a small-man complex; he never got over losing mother in their divorce. He smoked and drank heavily. He wasn't healthy for much of his life. He was very insecure. He was extremely abusive to mother but less abusive to us kids.

Regardless of all the bad memories of him, I have some good ones. He was a man of his word. He always kissed me goodnight. Once, he gave me a Christmas present of some army trucks and characters that needed assembly. Dad helped me, and I remember looking up to him thinking he was so cool and smart and could do anything. I can remember building a tin shed in our backyard. I learned to build something with him. I hung onto these memories because I don't have many more. We did fish a couple of times alone together. We did go to an amusement park alone together when I lived with him in in the Northeast for a brief period.

He died several months before Jan and I married. I went to visit him twice before he died. The first visit was to share with him that I was a Christian and how that had changed my life. We spent several hours talking about the fact that it wasn't too late for him to invite Jesus into his heart. He admitted he was still wishy-washy about his beliefs on Christianity. He went around the barn with his feelings. He had a hard time talking, so he would write his feelings on paper. I wish I had saved the notes. I suppose I thought I'd never need them because I'd remember them. I'll never forget our discussions and how much they meant to me.

We talked about the past. He regretted hurting Mom. He regretted being an alcoholic and a smoker. He still very much disliked Grandmother Amelia. We would cry and take a break because he was out of breath. I unpacked a little more of my life story. He cried when I got to the molestation part. We watched the news about Bin Laden being in hiding. Dad was passionate about catching him. He was a true patriot who loved his country.

I toured the home where he was staying. The employees were so kind; some asked me if I needed counseling; I was told my dad didn't have long to live. They didn't know the power God had given me to deal with such closures. I was at peace and made very clear to Dad's doctor of my belief in Christ.

Dad wanted to give me closure. He apologized for hurting mother, for laying a hand on us kids, for throwing that statue that hit me—he apologized for an hour straight. He wouldn't apologize about the fights he had with Grandmother Amelia or her husband, Pepe. He was bitter and felt they were a big part of ruining his and Mom's lives. I suspect he was right. Nonetheless, we were clearing the air. I was so proud in the moment of being his son even it lasted only a few short days.

God had given me the courage to clear the air with dad. I wasn't bitter or angry. I was regretful that we hadn't done this sooner. I told him that if he wanted to die hating Meme, I would not force him to reverse his feelings. He needed something to hang onto that gave him a sense of control over his dignity and beliefs. I was more concerned about his belief in Jesus Christ. He explained that he believed in the Bible but that giving himself to a God that remained absent from his life was too much for him to process. I know, though, that my story resonated with him.

We talked about the wonderful things God had done for me in Dad's absence. The fact that I held no grudge, judgement, condemnation, or anxiety convinced him of that. God didn't stop life from happening, but he molded me into a man in Dad's absence. I asked him to thank God for that. He did. He sobbed. We were getting right with each other.

We did a lot of writing and sign language. It was getting late. I was wearing Dad out. I knew he would die, but I did not want to be the death of him. We parted ways. I asked him, "Dad, would you please consider inviting Jesus into your heart?" He gave me a thumbs-up. I quickly walked back to his bed. "Dad, I'll say a prayer. Say it with me in your heart." I prayed, "Jesus, I believe you are the Son of God, that you died on the cross, then rose from the dead to save me and give me eternal life. Thank you, Father, for this sacrifice. I don't want to die without knowing you. Please make yourself available to me. I want you in my heart, amen."

I asked him if I could check on him in the morning. He gave me a thumbs-up. I acted as though I were leaving. I hid in a recliner near his bed.

Dad suddenly started breathing erratically. I jumped up. Tears began streaming down my face and I stroked his thinning, grey hair. He looked so much older than fifty-seven. I was sure he would die any minute. I prayed that he had said the prayer with me. *God, give me a sign that Dad will be in heaven with you. I need this more than anything.* I stayed as long as I could. I needed sleep and food.

I ate in the cafeteria and went to my aunt's, where I was staying. I slept well and was so thankful for my aunt. The next day, I visited Dad again. His breathing was even more shallow than the previous day. He managed to eat a small breakfast but clearly was worn out from our discussion the day before. It had taken a lot out of us. I explained I had to get back to work. He understood.

We spent several hours saying good-bye. I was sure it would be the last time I'd see him. Why was I so emotionally in love with a man I hardly knew? It was because God made me right with him by His mercy and grace and His Son, Jesus Christ. Thank you, Jesus. "Dad, I need to know I'll see you again and that this isn't good-bye. Did you say the prayer and accept Jesus into your heart?" Dad held both thumbs up. Praise God! I could rest knowing I'd see my father in heaven. Saying good-bye was so difficult. I loved my Dad. I cried all the way home. Eleven hours of shedding tears.

On February 22, 2002, an outwardly simple but very complex man went to be with Jesus. Pamela and I went to his funeral. I was blessed to have had the opportunity to speak on behalf of the mourners. Praise God! I let Dad go. This chapter closed gracefully.

The Boy Who Shot Daemon

My friend Stan, who had introduced me to Daemon, told me years later that the boy who had killed Daemon got a lesser sentence than expected and later became a pastor. I don't know the whole story so I can't elaborate. If you recall, I went to bat for him after the murder. God is good and closed this worrisome chapter in my life.

Stan

May you rest in peace, Stan. You are a brother in Christ. Stan was in shock when I shared my story of Daemon. He renewed his vows to Christ with me in our last discussion. He died a few months later.

Peter

Bobbie's brother, who had stolen my identity, ended up in prison, and God served him up a little wisdom of His own. I don't know what happened to him after prison, but I have forgiven him. I have prayed many a prayer for Peter. At one time, I wanted revenge, but now, I pray he's found peace through Christ Jesus. This chapter was closed gracefully.

Leslie

Bobbie's mother and Telly, her boyfriend at the time, were never caught for skipping out with the rent money they had collected. She lived a hard life and didn't need any get evens from me; her wrongs have haunted her in many ways. I have continued to pray for her. I am not sure if she is alive, but I've forgiven her. This chapter was closed gracefully.

Jason

Rumor had it that his mother ran off with him. I pray for Jason and miss him. He was born on a special day and was an answer to my biggest prayer ever. I found God because of the deal that God allowed me to make with Him and then I later found Christ. Thank you, God and Jason. God closed this chapter of my life.

John

Mom assured me he went to church with her the weekend before his death. He had invited Jesus into his heart. I can now rest knowing we are brothers in Christ. He was never my father; being his brother is as good as it can get, praise Jesus. I look forward to seeing him in heaven. God closed this chapter in my life.

Daemon

He is no longer the Beast; I have forgiven him. He lost his earthly life and was condemned to hell. That breaks my heart, but I'm no longer broken because of him, praise Jesus! God closed this chapter.

Bobbie

I hope she's alive and well. I pray the Lord has found her and will keep her. I have truly forgiven her. God closed this chapter.

Payton

I have no idea where Bobbie's ex is either. I believe he regrets having aided Bobbie by keeping Jason hidden from me. He believed all her lies but soon learned the truth. I forgive him. God closed that chapter.

Jan

God gave me Jesus, who gave me hope. He also gave me Jan, who was so instrumental in giving me the desire to become who I am. She has driven me to naturally want success. My drive to be successful isn't driven by bad things. My motives come from many sources including God, Jan, her kids, and people in need. Having such a good wife makes me want to be a better man. It's a closed circuit; it creates positive energy. Keep God at the center of your circuit and you'll have eternal spiritual energy.

Jan is my earthly rock, the love of my life, the gift of a lifetime, my soulmate, my best friend. She continues to be a rock in our family. I love you forever, Jan. This chapter of my life will be dynamic until death do us part.

Kara

My stepdaughter is now a fine young woman with a huge heart and a great deal of wisdom. She served as a specialist in the government system and is now a teacher for special-needs kids. She loves on families and kids who have had it rough. I'm proud of her. She and her husband are followers of Christ. I love her and my son in law.

Kevin

Kevin has exceeded my expectations, which were pretty high. He is married to a beautiful young woman. I'm proud of the strength, love, and support they show one another. Kevin and his wife are followers of Christ, two lovebirds who bring joy to their friends and family. I love these two.

Steven

He was the little man who invited me into his home, into his mother's life, and into his life. He has filled my heart above its capacity over the last fifteen years. He's twenty-two and is finding himself. We have an amazing relationship. His tender heart and servanthood attitude will bring him a bright future with people. I love you, kiddo!

Meme, Grandma Amelia

Several months before she died, Meme met Jan and fell in love with her. In her last years, she gave herself to Jesus. She was clearly a changed woman. She became the grandmother I had always dreamed of. I experienced her love, smile, happiness, and joy; that was all I needed. I fell in love with Meme and was in awe of the woman she became in two short years. Meme's testimony alone is worth writing about. She died peacefully. God closed this chapter of my life.

Ron

My brother-in-law died of colon cancer and will be missed. He led me to Christ. I know I'll see him in heaven. Ron helped close a very painful chapter in my life.

Leon

My stepbrother, best friend, and confidant is with God. He loved Jesus and me. It took many years for me to heal from his loss. The deeper my love and faith for God, the more I celebrate Leon's absence. It brings joy to my heart to know where he is. I'm jealous he got there first. I love you, brother. He came to me in a dream, and from that moment forward, I was able to move on without him knowing that I would see him again.

Gilbert

My friend and brother in Christ has been in prison for fourteen years. We've written many letters and spoken many times on the phone. I've forgiven him and I know God has as well. He is a special friend, and I'll be there for him when he gets out of prison. Who knows? Gilbert and I may speak out together some day, God willing. Love you, bub. Keep your head up, your nose pointed due north, and your eyes on Jesus. Remember God loves you. You've been given a new chance. Let's do this right, Brother! Gilbert was instrumental in helping me to forgive at a whole new level.

Bill and Barry Lyons

Bill and Barry are special friends with Pastor Tim and Beverly LaHaye. When I felt called to write a book based on my life story, I needed some mentorship. As God would have it, I found Bill and Barry Lyons in the San Diego area; they were neighbors and best friends with Tim and Beverly LaHaye. Barry is one of Tim's editors. I called Bill; he listened to me and was willing to meet with me. Jan and I flew out and spent several days together. They listened to my story and offered me their wisdom. God was the reason I met this wonderful couple who offered to share their time and love with Jan and me. They have an amazing life story to share; what a privilege and honor it was to have them share it with Jan and me. God, you are good. I began writing this book right after we got home from that visit. Jan and I love you very much and thank you. God is still working in their lives as they approach their midnineties.

Tim and Beverly LaHaye

I had read the entire *Left Behind* series Tim LaHaye and Barry Jenkins wrote. I had read most of Tim's books. To be sitting with him at the table laughing, loving, living, and sharing God's testimonies was a tremendous experience. Thank you, Tim and Beverly, for sharing your wisdom and experience in life and writing. Jan and I love you both. Tim has recently passed. I'll see him in heaven.

Kristen

My older sister is the most precious woman I know. She'd give her last penny to someone in need and not think twice about it. She has lately found a new interest in Christ Jesus. She has always believed, but I've always said that if and when Kristen went deep into a relationship with Christ, she would become a saint. Thank you, Kristen, for always loving me, supporting me, and believing in me. You're the best big sister ever. You had seen my worst and picked me up off the ground many times even when you too were weak. I love you so much!

Pamela

My younger sister, affectionately known as peanut, is a saint, a follower of Christ, an amazing sister and child of God, a widow, a tough woman, and a tender woman. She is all things good. Pamela was my mentor and godly example growing up. I always wanted what she had. I didn't know how to get it, and I thought that her belief in Jesus was a bit weird. Pamela, thank you for setting the example I needed. I love you, peanut.

Barbe

My mother! Some of what I wrote in this book could have been viewed as destructive to our relationship. Please remember that I was reenacting my life and that I started with the anger, hurt, and bitterness I felt then. I was committed to being real and transparent, no sugar coating. I was too immature at that age to know that many of the problems I had were caused by me. Though I was young, I believe in the age of self-capable reasoning, and that age is different with each person. I began to understand this mostly as I grew older and closer to God. But as a boy, I had all the ingredients that I needed to make a story God would use for all that is good.

What I failed to understand for many years when I was submersed in self-pity and darkness was that Mom was a beautiful person who had also endured difficult times as a child with her mother. She clearly was abused for twelve or thirteen years by Dad. Everyone reacts differently under stress. I am sure that I don't know the half of her life story, and I'll make a point to learn it. But I do know she has a story. God knows all our stories and is waiting to use them for His glory.

I need her, I love her, and I forgive her. I've asked her for forgiveness as well, and yes, our relationship is as good as it could ever be. Mom has watched her kids grow into their relationships with Christ. She also wanted what we had, and she has found it. She was saved and baptized and now attends church regularly. She is a lovely, kind, gentle woman of whom I couldn't be prouder. Mother, I love you, and I look forward to the remainder of our lives together. God bless you! One huge chapter in my life closed by God.

Chapter 29

ᕙ᎑ ᎑ᕗ

Survival

The following taps into my follow-up life guide. I did zero research on how to survive the trials and tribulations of life. In fact, I've no stats, bibliographies, cowriters, or specialists involved. I wanted to share with you from my own heart, experience, and wisdom about how I survived, what I learned, and how I compartmentalize my ADD brain. Because life is complicated, I'm not suggesting that the way I survived works for everyone. It's possible to live a good life without God, but you will never experience true freedom. What one thinks freedom is may not at all be as great as freedom could be. I challenge each of my readers to test it for themselves.

Okay, we have all been dealt rough hands at one time or another and we have to survive, rise above, or we will fall below. We have to conquer. This chapter will focus briefly on surviving life and staying spiritually and mentally healthy. Much of this is in much greater detail in *The Heartest Story Finally Told—Life Guide*, HSFT for short, which is a supporting book that comes across as a quick guide to life. It's for your personal life story through mine.

Ask yourself these questions and do your best to answer them honestly. This is the very beginning of your new, authentic journey.

1. What does your story mean to you?
2. What do you think that your story means to God?
3. What do you think that your story means to others?

Surviving:

This is your story. The following is very typical of what people's stories mean to themselves. It can hurt, it's tough, and you feel like dying at times, but you survive. You pretend things are okay when they're not. Most people think being in survival mode all the time makes them stronger. Buzzard noise! That makes you weaker because you are in a constant reactive maintenance mode; all your energy is used up fighting to be loved, eat, get attention, be heard, be employed, be happy, make more money, and in extreme cases, fighting for your life, for health care coverage, for sympathy, on and on. You never get ahead; you're too busy surviving and are wiped out every second. Other people see your weaknesses and use you as a doormat. I get it; no one is alone here.

The good news is that if you're still breathing, you've survived and have a chance and a choice. Let's figure out ways of getting out of your mess alive, happy, healthy, and joyfully.

Rising Above:

This is where you let your story be God's story by asking Jesus into your heart. This is where you are in a spiritual preventative maintenance program. You step beside yourself and rise up. You finally realize you can't fight the fight on your own. You're tired and at the bottom, sucked away from reality, and as far as you can get from relationships. You have become a recluse. You would gravitate if you haven't already to quick fixes such as drugs, pornography, or affairs. You can't go any lower. You're afraid to poke your head up because you're sure someone is lurking behind you and ready to take it off.

You're helpless and will die, kill yourself, or fight for your life. Which one will you choose? The right choice—life. Rise above your situation and live again. Smell the flowers and see in color; think with clarity, and take preventative measures so you won't fall or be pushed into the hole again.

You finally admit you can't do it alone. There is no earthly secret to living life with joy because joy comes from God. You try yoga, meditation, exercise, diets, even anxiety and depression medicine, and though those things help and are sometimes prescribed and encouraged, there is still something missing. You become desperate.

Friends, readers, lost souls, rise above yourself and head to the valley where the air is clean and the soil is fertile. Stay there and let your heart and soul heal. The Holy Spirit is waiting to do good things and will take you to new heights you didn't know existed. Once you've healed, have a relationship with Jesus, and become stronger—and that will happen as weird as it sounds—you will become a warrior who makes dark spirits flee. You can't conquer them if you're a weak soul. God will strengthen you, fill you with overflowing life and joy, and equip you with the tools you'll need to fight, including a sword and shield.

Conquering:

This is the point that your story touches others' lives. You enter a predictive maintenance mode. You'll know when you're straying from the pathway God is creating for you. As a warrior, you focus God and the task at hand. All things work in and through Him. No matter how bad it is, your life story is becoming meaningless to you but becoming everything to God. You see you have a place in God's kingdom He prepared for you and you know where you're going. You become confident and bold enough to announce your new home. (John 14:2) Jesus said "There is more than enough room in my Father's home, If this were not so, would I have told you that I am going to prepare a place for you?"

Your task is to stay focused on God. Life soon becomes less about you and more about God and how He uses you to make life better for others. It isn't a mind game or a trick. It's not explainable. What is love really? We all agree love is real. The Bible says that "Love is patient and kind. Love is not jealous or boastful or proud or rude. It does not demand its own way. It is not irritable, and it keeps no record of being wronged." (1 Corinthians 13) So let's look at love again as patient. Were you patient in your time of need? Were you kind? Were you ever jealous of those who had money and fame and had it all together? Did you ever brag or put down another person to make yourself look better or feel better about yourself? Did you ever treat people badly on your best day, which was most people's worst? How would you feel if you could apologize to someone and make wrongs right again? Would you be more attractive? How would you feel if you could forgive and set yourself free from mental anguish and imprisonment?

Yeah, man, love is so much bigger than us. It is so powerful that when we act alone with it, it doesn't make sense. We can't define it or understand it. We don't know how to engage with it properly. Its takes someone or something bigger than ourselves to help us to understand love much less how to become it. Because we have such a difficult time understanding love, we still struggle getting it right. Because of this, God has given us grace upon grace. He has forgiven our sins. Without the crucial gifts of love, grace, and forgiveness, our world would be spiritless. God gave us grace because He loved us so. He gave us His Son so we could be forgiven of our sins and get new starts in life. We would die out of ourselves and into His love.

I'm not a psychologist, a pastor, or a counselor. I'm man who became a warrior for God. Seriously, how could I not? God has done some incredible work in my life. The time and investment He has in me and the child I'm becoming as He designed me to are remarkable. This story is much bigger than me. No games, no polls, no percentages no counseling—just life, experience, and wisdom. Don't miss your opportunity to dig yourself out of a hole with the right kind of help. God is ready when you are.

Chapter 30

❦ ❧

Take Action- Own It

I've prepared a follow-up Life Book to *The Heartest Story Finally Told: Jesus's Glory Divinely Bold*. It will include ten sessions, chapters, or stepping stones—call them whatever you wish. God took me through these steps His gift to me, so I'm sure they're trustworthy and biblically sound. This Life Book, which I wrote based on my experience and wisdom, will be your study guide for all ten steps. It can be used by individuals, in group therapy, small life groups, Sunday school classes, and church sermons. You can do this. God can help you.

I'm honored to be a part of your life on this journey. It doesn't matter if you have never been in a relationship with Christ, have become lost and want to come home, or have been a Christian all your life, this is a clean, clear, decisive, and simple guide to living with God. If you walk away not knowing Christ after reading this autobiography, if nothing else, the seed will have been planted and will grow. When you finally get it, no matter how bad your troubles are, God will clean up your life one chapter at a time. This is something none of us can do alone.

Here's more detail on what each session will look like if you move forward with the HSFT Life Guide.

1. **Jesus Christ Must Become Your Lord and Savior; There Is No Other Way**

The next steps moving forward will be considered Christianity, the beginning of something very special. It's new, refreshing, and exciting.

From the moment we enter into a relationship with Jesus Christ, we must keep it simple. One of the biggest problems I have witnessed in new believers is that their faith starts off simple and then turns complex. The biggest step, which some call the leap of faith, requires you to give up your life. That sounds weird, but you aren't giving up your life as in physical death; you're giving up controlling your life. You go from survival mode or run-to-failure maintenance, which we all know hasn't worked.

You move toward finding your spirit, reducing chaos, getting out of mental prison, and finding peace and joy. At that point, you're living in predictive maintenance in which your destiny is God's and you fight for Him, a loving God, not a hateful life. Predictive maintenance means that you don't necessarily predict what happens next but know you're in good hands; He's already designed your future. You know through faith that everything will be okay because of His promises to you through His Word. God keeps up your maintenance program from this point forward.

Jesus Christ must be your Lord and Savior. None of this exciting stuff can happen unless you know and believe the following.

Christ's mother didn't have sex with a human being to get pregnant; she was impregnated by the Holy Spirit. God sent Jesus to be our Savior. God struggled with the fact that humanity couldn't become sin free by itself; humanity also couldn't obey the Ten Commandments. God wanted Jesus to feel all that we felt—pain, temptation, battle, death, sickness, mental anguish, and so on.

Christ walked the earth and did some crazy cool things. He was named Jesus, King of the Jews. Jesus grew up like any child, but He was also drawn to God's Word and studied it like no other.

On the day He was baptized, the heavens opened up. He began His ministry on earth. He walked with many, but twelve men in particular became his posse. They spread the word of what God has done, was doing, and would do. Jesus became a phenomenon. He healed the sick, made the blind see, and even brought dead people back to life. Jesus's rise in popularity caused great unrest among the high-level priests and religious people. They felt threatened; they thought He was pursuing power to take control of the land and its people. Jesus didn't care about fame, power and fortune; He cared about all Gods people. He was a King all right, the King of love, servanthood, peace, and joy. He is the way, the truth, and the light.

The religious leaders didn't understand and felt the need to remove this threat, so they did. The Romans arrested Him, beat Him up badly, spit on him, disrobed him, mocked him, whipped him, and crucified Him. When He died, the temple curtain was torn in half, and other strange events occurred. This stuff happened; it isn't talked about just in the Bible, it's also in history books. Scientists and atheists can't explain it away. The history of this God destroys the big bang theory. Poof! Oh look! An explosion made life. That wouldn't go over well even in a good science fiction movie. If God weren't real, there would be nothing to argue over. The fact that Jesus is alive and well after more than 2,000 years says it all. I don't think you or I will be remembered and worshipped in 2,000 years, do you?

Jesus rose from the dead after having predicted His death and resurrection more than once. He rose, the heavens opened up, and our sins were forever forgiven. We now have a way to heaven through Christ Jesus. We will live eternally. No other God gives us this promise. Jesus shed His blood so you and I could get through the messiness of our lives and remain sane, have something to hold onto, enjoy the security of everlasting life, and best of all, join His kingdom and experience heaven.

I now have faith, promise, hope, and joy. I can't explain it from a spiritual standpoint. I don't understand God's power, but I know it's real.

Read the book of Matthew in the New Testament. In case you don't have a Bible handy, I have included all of Matthew in the following pages. I encourage you to read this word for word and write down your questions. Matthew was one of Jesus's apostles who lived with and knew Jesus well.

Matthew 1
The Ancestors of Jesus the Messiah

1*This is a record of the ancestors of Jesus the Messiah, a descendant of David and of Abraham:*

2*Abraham was the father of Isaac.*

Isaac was the father of Jacob.

Jacob was the father of Judah and his brothers.

3*Judah was the father of Perez and Zerah (whose mother was Tamar).*

Perez was the father of Hezron.

Hezron was the father of Ram.

4*Ram was the father of Amminadab.*

Amminadab was the father of Nahshon.

Nahshon was the father of Salmon.

5*Salmon was the father of Boaz (whose mother was Rahab).*

Boaz was the father of Obed (whose mother was Ruth).

Obed was the father of Jesse.

6*Jesse was the father of King David.*

David was the father of Solomon (whose mother was Bathsheba, the widow of Uriah).

7*Solomon was the father of Rehoboam.*

Rehoboam was the father of Abijah.

Abijah was the father of Asa.

8*Asa was the father of Jehoshaphat.*

Jehoshaphat was the father of Jehoram.

Jehoram was the father of Uzziah.

9*Uzziah was the father of Jotham.*

Jotham was the father of Ahaz.

Ahaz was the father of Hezekiah.

10*Hezekiah was the father of Manasseh.*

Manasseh was the father of Amon.

Amon was the father of Josiah.

11*Josiah was the father of Jehoiachin and his brothers (born at the time of the exile to Babylon).*

12*After the Babylonian exile:*

Jehoiachin was the father of Shealtiel.

Shealtiel was the father of Zerubbabel.

13*Zerubbabel was the father of Abiud.*

Abiud was the father of Eliakim.

Eliakim was the father of Azor.

14*Azor was the father of Zadok.*

Zadok was the father of Akim.
Akim was the father of Eliud.
15*Eliud was the father of Eleazar.*
Eleazar was the father of Matthan.
Matthan was the father of Jacob.
16*Jacob was the father of Joseph, the husband of Mary.*
Mary gave birth to Jesus, who is called the Messiah.

17*All those listed above include fourteen generations from Abraham to David, fourteen from David to the Babylonian exile, and fourteen from the Babylonian exile to the Messiah.*

The Birth of Jesus the Messiah

18*This is how Jesus the Messiah was born. His mother, Mary, was engaged to be married to Joseph. But before the marriage took place, while she was still a virgin, she became pregnant through the power of the Holy Spirit.* **19***Joseph, her fiancé, was a good man and did not want to disgrace her publicly, so he decided to break the engagement quietly.*

20*As he considered this, an angel of the Lord appeared to him in a dream. "Joseph, son of David," the angel said, "do not be afraid to take Mary as your wife. For the child within her was conceived by the Holy Spirit.* **21***And she will have a son, and you are to name him Jesus, for he will save his people from their sins."*

22*All of this occurred to fulfill the Lord's message through his prophet:*
23*"Look! The virgin will conceive a child!*
She will give birth to a son,
and they will call him Immanuel,
which means 'God is with us.'"

24*When Joseph woke up, he did as the angel of the Lord commanded and took Mary as his wife.* **25***But he did not have sexual relations with her until her son was born. And Joseph named him Jesus.*

Matthew 2
Visitors from the East

1*Jesus was born in Bethlehem in Judea, during the reign of King Herod. About that time some wise men from eastern lands arrived in Jerusalem,* *asking,* **2**"*Where is the newborn king of the Jews? We saw his star as it rose, and we have come to worship him.*"

3*King Herod was deeply disturbed when he heard this, as was everyone in Jerusalem.* **4***He called a meeting of the leading priests and teachers of religious law and asked, "Where is the Messiah supposed to be born?*"

5"*In Bethlehem in Judea," they said, "for this is what the prophet wrote:*

6*And you, O Bethlehem in the land of Judah,*

are not least among the ruling cities of Judah,

for a ruler will come from you

who will be the shepherd for my people Israel.'"

7*Then Herod called for a private meeting with the wise men, and he learned from them the time when the star first appeared.* **8***Then he told them, "Go to Bethlehem and search carefully for the child. And when you find him, come back and tell me so that I can go and worship him, too!*"

9*After this interview the wise men went their way. And the star they had seen in the east guided them to Bethlehem. It went ahead of them and stopped over the place where the child was.* **10***When they saw the star, they were filled with joy!* **11***They entered the house and saw the child with his mother, Mary, and they bowed down and worshiped him. Then they opened their treasure chests and gave him gifts of gold, frankincense, and myrrh.*

12*When it was time to leave, they returned to their own country by another route, for God had warned them in a dream not to return to Herod.*

The Escape to Egypt

13*After the wise men were gone, an angel of the Lord appeared to Joseph in a dream. "Get up! Flee to Egypt with the child and his mother," the angel said. "Stay there until I tell you to return, because Herod is going to search for the child to kill him.*"

14*That night Joseph left for Egypt with the child and Mary, his mother,* **15***and they stayed there until Herod's death. This fulfilled what the Lord had spoken through the prophet: "I called my Son out of Egypt.*"

16*Herod was furious when he realized that the wise men had outwitted him. He sent soldiers to kill all the boys in and around Bethlehem who were two years old and under, based on the wise men's report of the star's first appearance.* **17***Herod's brutal action fulfilled what God had spoken through the prophet Jeremiah:*

18*"A cry was heard in Ramah—*
weeping and great mourning.
Rachel weeps for her children,
refusing to be comforted,
for they are dead."

The Return to Nazareth

19*When Herod died, an angel of the Lord appeared in a dream to Joseph in Egypt.* **20***"Get up!" the angel said. "Take the child and his mother back to the land of Israel, because those who were trying to kill the child are dead."*

21*So Joseph got up and returned to the land of Israel with Jesus and his mother.* **22***But when he learned that the new ruler of Judea was Herod's son Archelaus, he was afraid to go there. Then, after being warned in a dream, he left for the region of Galilee.* **23***So the family went and lived in a town called Nazareth. This fulfilled what the prophets had said: "He will be called a Nazarene."*

Matthew 3
John the Baptist Prepares the Way

1*In those days John the Baptist came to the Judean wilderness and began preaching. His message was,* **2***"Repent of your sins and turn to God, for the Kingdom of Heaven is near."* **3***The prophet Isaiah was speaking about John when he said,*

"He is a voice shouting in the wilderness,
'Prepare the way for the lord's coming!
Clear the road for him!'"

4*John's clothes were woven from coarse camel hair, and he wore a leather belt around his waist. For food he ate locusts and wild honey.* **5***People from Jerusalem and from all of Judea and all over the Jordan Valley went out to see and hear John.* **6***And when they confessed their sins, he baptized them in the Jordan River.*

7*But when he saw many Pharisees and Sadducees coming to watch him baptize, he denounced them. "You brood of snakes!" he exclaimed. "Who warned you to flee God's coming wrath?* **8***Prove by the way you live that you have repented of your sins and turned to God.* **9***Don't just say to each other,*

'We're safe, for we are descendants of Abraham.' That means nothing, for I tell you, God can create children of Abraham from these very stones. **10**Even now the ax of God's judgment is poised, ready to sever the roots of the trees. Yes, every tree that does not produce good fruit will be chopped down and thrown into the fire.

11"I baptize with water those who repent of their sins and turn to God. But someone is coming soon who is greater than I am—so much greater that I'm not worthy even to be his slave and carry his sandals. He will baptize you with the Holy Spirit and with fire. **12**He is ready to separate the chaff from the wheat with his winnowing fork. Then he will clean up the threshing area, gathering the wheat into his barn but burning the chaff with never-ending fire."

The Baptism of Jesus

13Then Jesus went from Galilee to the Jordan River to be baptized by John. **14**But John tried to talk him out of it. "I am the one who needs to be baptized by you," he said, "so why are you coming to me?"

15But Jesus said, "It should be done, for we must carry out all that God requires." So John agreed to baptize him.

16After his baptism, as Jesus came up out of the water, the heavens were opened and he saw the Spirit of God descending like a dove and settling on him. **17**And a voice from heaven said, "This is my dearly loved Son, who brings me great joy."

Matthew 4
The Temptation of Jesus

1Then Jesus was led by the Spirit into the wilderness to be tempted there by the devil. **2**For forty days and forty nights he fasted and became very hungry.

3During that time the devil came and said to him, "If you are the Son of God, tell these stones to become loaves of bread."

4But Jesus told him, "No! The Scriptures say,
'People do not live by bread alone,
but by every word that comes from the mouth of God.'"

5Then the devil took him to the holy city, Jerusalem, to the highest point *of the Temple,* **6***and said, "If you are the Son of God, jump off! For the Scriptures say,*

'He will order his angels to protect you.

And they will hold you up with their hands

so you won't even hurt your foot on a stone.'"

7*Jesus responded, "The Scriptures also say, 'You must not test the lord your God.'"*

8*Next the devil took him to the peak of a very high mountain and showed him all the kingdoms of the world and their glory.* **9***"I will give it all to you,"* *he said, "if you will kneel down and worship me."*

10*"Get out of here, Satan," Jesus told him. "For the Scriptures say,*

'You must worship the lord your God

and serve only him.'"

11*Then the devil went away, and angels came and took care of Jesus.*

The Ministry of Jesus Begins

12*When Jesus heard that John had been arrested, he left Judea and returned to Galilee.* **13***He went first to Nazareth, then left there and moved to Capernaum, beside the Sea of Galilee, in the region of Zebulun and Naphtali.* **14***This fulfilled what God said through the prophet Isaiah:*

15*"In the land of Zebulun and of Naphtali,*

beside the sea, beyond the Jordan River,

in Galilee where so many Gentiles live,

16*the people who sat in darkness*

have seen a great light.

And for those who lived in the land where death casts its shadow,

a light has shined."

17*From then on Jesus began to preach, "Repent of your sins and turn to God, for the Kingdom of Heaven is near."*

The First Disciples

18*One day as Jesus was walking along the shore of the Sea of Galilee, he saw two brothers—Simon, also called Peter, and Andrew—throwing a net into the water, for they fished for a living.* **19***Jesus called out to them, "Come, follow me, and I will show you how to fish for people!"* **20***And they left their nets at once and followed him.*

21*A little farther up the shore he saw two other brothers, James and John, sitting in a boat with their father, Zebedee, repairing their nets. And he called them to come, too.* **22***They immediately followed him, leaving the boat and their father behind.*

Crowds Follow Jesus

23*Jesus traveled throughout the region of Galilee, teaching in the synagogues and announcing the Good News about the Kingdom. And he healed every kind of disease and illness.* **24***News about him spread as far as Syria, and people soon began bringing to him all who were sick. And whatever their sickness or disease, or if they were demon possessed or epileptic or paralyzed—he healed them all.* **25***Large crowds followed him wherever he went—people from Galilee, the Ten Towns, Jerusalem, from all over Judea, and from east of the Jordan River.*

Matthew 5
The Sermon on the Mount

1*One day as he saw the crowds gathering, Jesus went up on the mountainside and sat down. His disciples gathered around him,* **2***and he began to teach them.*

The Beatitudes
3*"God blesses those who are poor and realize their need for him,*
for the Kingdom of Heaven is theirs.
4*God blesses those who mourn,*
for they will be comforted.
5*God blesses those who are humble,*
for they will inherit the whole earth.
6*God blesses those who hunger and thirst for justice,*
for they will be satisfied.
7*God blesses those who are merciful,*
for they will be shown mercy.
8*God blesses those whose hearts are pure,*
for they will see God.
9*God blesses those who work for peace,*

177

for they will be called the children of God.

10*God blesses those who are persecuted for doing right,*
for the Kingdom of Heaven is theirs.

11*"God blesses you when people mock you and persecute you and lie about you and say all sorts of evil things against you because you are my followers.* **12***Be happy about it! Be very glad! For a great reward awaits you in heaven. And remember, the ancient prophets were persecuted in the same way.*

Teaching about Salt and Light

13*"You are the salt of the earth. But what good is salt if it has lost its flavor? Can you make it salty again? It will be thrown out and trampled underfoot as worthless.*

14*"You are the light of the world—like a city on a hilltop that cannot be hidden.* **15***No one lights a lamp and then puts it under a basket. Instead, a lamp is placed on a stand, where it gives light to everyone in the house.* **16***In the same way, let your good deeds shine out for all to see, so that everyone will praise your heavenly Father.*

Teaching about the Law

17*"Don't misunderstand why I have come. I did not come to abolish the law of Moses or the writings of the prophets. No, I came to accomplish their purpose.* **18***I tell you the truth, until heaven and earth disappear, not even the smallest detail of God's law will disappear until its purpose is achieved.* **19***So if you ignore the least commandment and teach others to do the same, you will be called the least in the Kingdom of Heaven. But anyone who obeys God's laws and teaches them will be called great in the Kingdom of Heaven.*

20*"But I warn you—unless your righteousness is better than the righteousness of the teachers of religious law and the Pharisees, you will never enter the Kingdom of Heaven!*

Teaching about Anger

21*"You have heard that our ancestors were told, 'You must not murder. If you commit murder, you are subject to judgment.'* **22***But I say, if you are even angry with someone, you are subject to judgment! If you call someone an idiot, you are in danger of being brought before the court. And if you curse someone, you are in danger of the fires of hell.*

23 *"So if you are presenting a sacrifice at the altar in the Temple and you suddenly remember that someone has something against you,* 24*leave your sacrifice there at the altar. Go and be reconciled to that person. Then come and offer your sacrifice to God.*

25 *"When you are on the way to court with your adversary, settle your differences quickly. Otherwise, your accuser may hand you over to the judge, who will hand you over to an officer, and you will be thrown into prison.* 26*And if that happens, you surely won't be free again until you have paid the last penny.*

Teaching about Adultery

27 *"You have heard the commandment that says, 'You must not commit adultery.'* 28*But I say, anyone who even looks at a woman with lust has already committed adultery with her in his heart.* 29*So if your eye—even your good eye—causes you to lust, gouge it out and throw it away. It is better for you to lose one part of your body than for your whole body to be thrown into hell.* 30*And if your hand—even your stronger hand—causes you to sin, cut it off and throw it away. It is better for you to lose one part of your body than for your whole body to be thrown into hell.*

Teaching about Divorce

31 *"You have heard the law that says, 'A man can divorce his wife by merely giving her a written notice of divorce.'* 32*But I say that a man who divorces his wife, unless she has been unfaithful, causes her to commit adultery. And anyone who marries a divorced woman also commits adultery.*

Teaching about Vows

33 *"You have also heard that our ancestors were told, 'You must not break your vows; you must carry out the vows you make to the lord.'* 34*But I say, do not make any vows! Do not say, 'By heaven!' because heaven is God's throne.* 35*And do not say, 'By the earth!' because the earth is his footstool. And do not say, 'By Jerusalem!' for Jerusalem is the city of the great King.* 36*Do not even say, 'By my head!' for you can't turn one hair white or black.* 37*Just say a simple, 'Yes, I will,' or 'No, I won't.' Anything beyond this is from the evil one.*

Teaching about Revenge

38"*You have heard the law that says the punishment must match the injury: 'An eye for an eye, and a tooth for a tooth.'* **39***But I say, do not resist an evil person! If someone slaps you on the right cheek, offer the other cheek also.* **40***If you are sued in court and your shirt is taken from you, give your coat, too.* **41***If a soldier demands that you carry his gear for a mile, carry it two miles.* **42***Give to those who ask, and don't turn away from those who want to borrow.*

Teaching about Love for Enemies

43"*You have heard the law that says, 'Love your neighbor' and hate your enemy.* **44***But I say, love your enemies! Pray for those who persecute you!* **45***In that way, you will be acting as true children of your Father in heaven. For he gives his sunlight to both the evil and the good, and he sends rain on the just and the unjust alike.* **46***If you love only those who love you, what reward is there for that? Even corrupt tax collectors do that much.* **47***If you are kind only to your friends, how are you different from anyone else? Even pagans do that.* **48***But you are to be perfect, even as your Father in heaven is perfect.*

Matthew 6
Teaching about Giving to the Needy

1"*Watch out! Don't do your good deeds publicly, to be admired by others, for you will lose the reward from your Father in heaven.* **2***When you give to someone in need, don't do as the hypocrites do—blowing trumpets in the synagogues and streets to call attention to their acts of charity! I tell you the truth, they have received all the reward they will ever get.* **3***But when you give to someone in need, don't let your left hand know what your right hand is doing.* **4***Give your gifts in private, and your Father, who sees everything, will reward you.*

Teaching about Prayer and Fasting

5"*When you pray, don't be like the hypocrites who love to pray publicly on street corners and in the synagogues where everyone can see them. I tell you the truth, that is all the reward they will ever get.* **6***But when you pray, go away* *by yourself, shut the door behind you, and pray to your Father in private. Then your Father, who sees everything, will reward you.*

7"*When you pray, don't babble on and on as people of other religions do. They think their prayers are answered merely by repeating their words again and again.* **8***Don't be like them, for your Father knows exactly what you need even before you ask him!* **9***Pray like this:*

Our Father in heaven,
may your name be kept holy.
10*May your Kingdom come soon.*
May your will be done on earth,
as it is in heaven.
11*Give us today the food we need,*
12*and forgive us our sins,*
as we have forgiven those who sin against us.
13*And don't let us yield to temptation,*
but rescue us from the evil one.

14"*If you forgive those who sin against you, your heavenly Father will forgive you.* **15***But if you refuse to forgive others, your Father will not forgive your sins.*

16"*And when you fast, don't make it obvious, as the hypocrites do, for they try to look miserable and disheveled so people will admire them for their fasting. I tell you the truth, that is the only reward they will ever get.* **17***But when you fast, comb your hair and wash your face.* **18***Then no one will notice that you are fasting, except your Father, who knows what you do in private. And your Father, who sees everything, will reward you.*

Teaching about Money and Possessions

19"*Don't store up treasures here on earth, where moths eat them and rust destroys them, and where thieves break in and steal.* **20***Store your treasures in heaven, where moths and rust cannot destroy, and thieves do not break in and steal.* **21***Wherever your treasure is, there the desires of your heart will also be.*

22"*Your eye is a lamp that provides light for your body. When your eye is good, your whole body is filled with light.* **23***But when your eye is bad, your whole body is filled with darkness. And if the light you think you have is actually darkness, how deep that darkness is!*

24"*No one can serve two masters. For you will hate one and love the* *other; you will be devoted to one and despise the other. You cannot serve both God and money.*

25*"That is why I tell you not to worry about everyday life—whether you have enough food and drink, or enough clothes to wear. Isn't life more than food, and your body more than clothing?* 26*Look at the birds. They don't plant or harvest or store food in barns, for your heavenly Father feeds them. And aren't you far more valuable to him than they are?* 27*Can all your worries add a single moment to your life?*

28*"And why worry about your clothing? Look at the lilies of the field and how they grow. They don't work or make their clothing,* 29*yet Solomon in all his glory was not dressed as beautifully as they are.* 30*And if God cares so wonderfully for wildflowers that are here today and thrown into the fire tomorrow, he will certainly care for you. Why do you have so little faith?*

31*"So don't worry about these things, saying, 'What will we eat? What will we drink? What will we wear?'* 32*These things dominate the thoughts of unbelievers, but your heavenly Father already knows all your needs.* 33*Seek the Kingdom of God above all else, and live righteously, and he will give you everything you need.*

34*"So don't worry about tomorrow, for tomorrow will bring its own worries. Today's trouble is enough for today.*

Matthew 7
Do Not Judge Others

1*"Do not judge others, and you will not be judged.* 2*For you will be treated as you treat others. The standard you use in judging is the standard by which you will be judged.*

3*"And why worry about a speck in your friend's eye when you have a log in your own?* 4*How can you think of saying to your friend, 'Let me help you get rid of that speck in your eye,' when you can't see past the log in your own eye?* 5*Hypocrite! First get rid of the log in your own eye; then you will see well enough to deal with the speck in your friend's eye.*

6*"Don't waste what is holy on people who are unholy. Don't throw your pearls to pigs! They will trample the pearls, then turn and attack you.*

Effective Prayer

7 *"Keep on asking, and you will receive what you ask for. Keep on seeking, and you will find. Keep on knocking, and the door will be opened to you.* **8***For everyone who asks, receives. Everyone who seeks, finds. And to everyone who knocks, the door will be opened.*

9 *"You parents—if your children ask for a loaf of bread, do you give them a stone instead?* **10***Or if they ask for a fish, do you give them a snake? Of course not!* **11***So if you sinful people know how to give good gifts to your children, how much more will your heavenly Father give good gifts to those who ask him.*

The Golden Rule

12 *"Do to others whatever you would like them to do to you. This is the essence of all that is taught in the law and the prophets.*

The Narrow Gate

13 *"You can enter God's Kingdom only through the narrow gate. The highway to hell is broad, and its gate is wide for the many who choose that way.* **14***But the gateway to life is very narrow and the road is difficult, and only a few ever find it.*

The Tree and Its Fruit

15 *"Beware of false prophets who come disguised as harmless sheep but are really vicious wolves.* **16***You can identify them by their fruit, that is, by the way they act. Can you pick grapes from thornbushes, or figs from thistles?* **17***A good tree produces good fruit, and a bad tree produces bad fruit.* **18***A good tree can't produce bad fruit, and a bad tree can't produce good fruit.* **19***So every tree that does not produce good fruit is chopped down and thrown into the fire.* **20***Yes, just as you can identify a tree by its fruit, so you can identify people by their actions.*

True Disciples

21 *"Not everyone who calls out to me, 'Lord! Lord!' will enter the Kingdom of Heaven. Only those who actually do the will of my Father in heaven will enter.* **22***On judgment day many will say to me, 'Lord! Lord! We prophesied in your name and cast out demons in your name and performed many miracles* *in your name.' 23But I will reply, 'I never knew you. Get away from me, you who break God's laws.'*

Building on a Solid Foundation

24"Anyone who listens to my teaching and follows it is wise, like a person who builds a house on solid rock. 25Though the rain comes in torrents and the floodwaters rise and the winds beat against that house, it won't collapse because it is built on bedrock. 26But anyone who hears my teaching and doesn't obey it is foolish, like a person who builds a house on sand. 27When the rains and floods come and the winds beat against that house, it will collapse with a mighty crash."

28When Jesus had finished saying these things, the crowds were amazed at his teaching, 29for he taught with real authority—quite unlike their teachers of religious law.

Matthew 8
Jesus Heals a Man with Leprosy

1Large crowds followed Jesus as he came down the mountainside. 2Suddenly, a man with leprosy approached him and knelt before him. "Lord," the man said, "if you are willing, you can heal me and make me clean."

3Jesus reached out and touched him. "I am willing," he said. "Be healed!" And instantly the leprosy disappeared. 4Then Jesus said to him, "Don't tell anyone about this. Instead, go to the priest and let him examine you. Take along the offering required in the law of Moses for those who have been healed of leprosy. This will be a public testimony that you have been cleansed."

The Faith of a Roman Officer

5When Jesus returned to Capernaum, a Roman officer came and pleaded with him, 6"Lord, my young servant lies in bed, paralyzed and in terrible pain."

7Jesus said, "I will come and heal him."

8But the officer said, "Lord, I am not worthy to have you come into my home. Just say the word from where you are, and my servant will be healed. 9I know this because I am under the authority of my superior officers, and I have authority over my soldiers. I only need to say, 'Go,' and they go, or 'Come,' and they come. And if I say to my slaves, 'Do this,' they do it."

10*When Jesus heard this, he was amazed. Turning to those who were following him, he said, "I tell you the truth, I haven't seen faith like this in all Israel!* 11*And I tell you this, that many Gentiles will come from all over the world—from east and west—and sit down with Abraham, Isaac, and Jacob at the feast in the Kingdom of Heaven.* 12*But many Israelites—those for whom the Kingdom was prepared—will be thrown into outer darkness, where there will be weeping and gnashing of teeth."*

13*Then Jesus said to the Roman officer, "Go back home. Because you believed, it has happened." And the young servant was healed that same hour.*

Jesus Heals Many People

14*When Jesus arrived at Peter's house, Peter's mother-in-law was sick in bed with a high fever.* 15*But when Jesus touched her hand, the fever left her. Then she got up and prepared a meal for him.*

16*That evening many demon-possessed people were brought to Jesus. He cast out the evil spirits with a simple command, and he healed all the sick.* 17*This fulfilled the word of the Lord through the prophet Isaiah, who said,*
"He took our sicknesses
and removed our diseases."

The Cost of Following Jesus

18*When Jesus saw the crowd around him, he instructed his disciples to cross to the other side of the lake.*

19*Then one of the teachers of religious law said to him, "Teacher, I will follow you wherever you go."*

20*But Jesus replied, "Foxes have dens to live in, and birds have nests, but the Son of Man has no place even to lay his head."*

21*Another of his disciples said, "Lord, first let me return home and bury my father."*

22*But Jesus told him, "Follow me now. Let the spiritually dead bury their own dead."*

Jesus Calms the Storm

23*Then Jesus got into the boat and started across the lake with his disciples.* 24*Suddenly, a fierce storm struck the lake, with waves breaking into the boat.*

But Jesus was sleeping. **25**The disciples went and woke him up, shouting, "Lord, save us! We're going to drown!"

26Jesus responded, "Why are you afraid? You have so little faith!" Then he got up and rebuked the wind and waves, and suddenly there was a great calm.

27The disciples were amazed. "Who is this man?" they asked. "Even the winds and waves obey him!"

Jesus Heals Two Demon-Possessed Men

28When Jesus arrived on the other side of the lake, in the region of the Gadarenes, two men who were possessed by demons met him. They lived in a cemetery and were so violent that no one could go through that area.

29They began screaming at him, "Why are you interfering with us, Son of God? Have you come here to torture us before God's appointed time?"

30There happened to be a large herd of pigs feeding in the distance. **31**So the demons begged, "If you cast us out, send us into that herd of pigs."

32"All right, go!" Jesus commanded them. So the demons came out of the men and entered the pigs, and the whole herd plunged down the steep hillside into the lake and drowned in the water.

33The herdsmen fled to the nearby town, telling everyone what happened to the demon-possessed men. **34**Then the entire town came out to meet Jesus, but they begged him to go away and leave them alone.

Matthew 9
Jesus Heals a Paralyzed Man

1Jesus climbed into a boat and went back across the lake to his own town. **2**Some people brought to him a paralyzed man on a mat. Seeing their faith, Jesus said to the paralyzed man, "Be encouraged, my child! Your sins are forgiven."

3But some of the teachers of religious law said to themselves, "That's blasphemy! Does he think he's God?"

4Jesus knew what they were thinking, so he asked them, "Why do you have such evil thoughts in your hearts? **5**Is it easier to say 'Your sins are forgiven,' or 'Stand up and walk'? **6**So I will prove to you that the Son of Man has the authority on earth to forgive sins." Then Jesus turned to the paralyzed man and said, "Stand up, pick up your mat, and go home!"

7And the man jumped up and went home! 8Fear swept through the crowd as they saw this happen. And they praised God for sending a man with such great authority.

Jesus Calls Matthew

9As Jesus was walking along, he saw a man named Matthew sitting at his tax collector's booth. "Follow me and be my disciple," Jesus said to him. So Matthew got up and followed him.

10Later, Matthew invited Jesus and his disciples to his home as dinner guests, along with many tax collectors and other disreputable sinners. 11But when the Pharisees saw this, they asked his disciples, "Why does your teacher eat with such scum?"

12When Jesus heard this, he said, "Healthy people don't need a doctor— sick people do." 13Then he added, "Now go and learn the meaning of this Scripture: 'I want you to show mercy, not offer sacrifices.' For I have come to call not those who think they are righteous, but those who know they are sinners."

A Discussion about Fasting

14One day the disciples of John the Baptist came to Jesus and asked him, "Why don't your disciples fast like we do and the Pharisees do?"

15Jesus replied, "Do wedding guests mourn while celebrating with the groom? Of course not. But someday the groom will be taken away from them, and then they will fast.

16"Besides, who would patch old clothing with new cloth? For the new patch would shrink and rip away from the old cloth, leaving an even bigger tear than before.

17"And no one puts new wine into old wineskins. For the old skins would burst from the pressure, spilling the wine and ruining the skins. New wine is stored in new wineskins so that both are preserved."

Jesus Heals in Response to Faith

18As Jesus was saying this, the leader of a synagogue came and knelt before him. "My daughter has just died," he said, "but you can bring her back to life again if you just come and lay your hand on her."

19So Jesus and his disciples got up and went with him. 20Just then a woman who had suffered for twelve years with constant bleeding came up behind him. She touched the fringe of his robe, **21**for she thought, "If I can just touch his robe, I will be healed."

22Jesus turned around, and when he saw her he said, "Daughter, be encouraged! Your faith has made you well." And the woman was healed at that moment.

23When Jesus arrived at the official's home, he saw the noisy crowd and heard the funeral music. **24**"Get out!" he told them. "The girl isn't dead; she's only asleep." But the crowd laughed at him. **25**After the crowd was put outside, however, Jesus went in and took the girl by the hand, and she stood up! **26**The report of this miracle swept through the entire countryside.

Jesus Heals the Blind

27After Jesus left the girl's home, two blind men followed along behind him, shouting, "Son of David, have mercy on us!"

28They went right into the house where he was staying, and Jesus asked them, "Do you believe I can make you see?"

"Yes, Lord," they told him, "we do."

29Then he touched their eyes and said, "Because of your faith, it will happen." **30**Then their eyes were opened, and they could see! Jesus sternly warned them, "Don't tell anyone about this." **31**But instead, they went out and spread his fame all over the region.

32When they left, a demon-possessed man who couldn't speak was brought to Jesus. **33**So Jesus cast out the demon, and then the man began to speak. The crowds were amazed. "Nothing like this has ever happened in Israel!" they exclaimed.

34But the Pharisees said, "He can cast out demons because he is empowered by the prince of demons."

The Need for Workers

35Jesus traveled through all the towns and villages of that area, teaching in the synagogues and announcing the Good News about the Kingdom. And he healed every kind of disease and illness. **36**When he saw the crowds, he had compassion on them because they were confused and helpless, like sheep without a shepherd. **37**He said to his disciples, "The harvest is great, but the *workers are few.* **38***So pray to the Lord who is in charge of the harvest; ask him to send more workers into his fields."*

Matthew 10
Jesus Sends Out the Twelve Apostles

1*Jesus called his twelve disciples together and gave them authority to cast out evil spirits and to heal every kind of disease and illness.* **2***Here are the names of the twelve apostles:*
first, Simon (also called Peter),
then Andrew (Peter's brother),
James (son of Zebedee),
John (James's brother),
3*Philip,*
Bartholomew,
Thomas,
Matthew (the tax collector),
James (son of Alphaeus),
Thaddaeus,
4*Simon (the zealot),*
Judas Iscariot (who later betrayed him).
5*Jesus sent out the twelve apostles with these instructions: "Don't go to the Gentiles or the Samaritans,* **6***but only to the people of Israel—God's lost sheep.* **7***Go and announce to them that the Kingdom of Heaven is near.* **8***Heal the sick, raise the dead, cure those with leprosy, and cast out demons. Give as freely as you have received!*

9*"Don't take any money in your money belts—no gold, silver, or even copper coins.* **10***Don't carry a traveler's bag with a change of clothes and sandals or even a walking stick. Don't hesitate to accept hospitality, because those who work deserve to be fed.*

11*"Whenever you enter a city or village, search for a worthy person and stay in his home until you leave town.* **12***When you enter the home, give it your blessing.* **13***If it turns out to be a worthy home, let your blessing stand; if it is not, take back the blessing.* **14***If any household or town refuses to welcome you or listen to your message, shake its dust from your feet as you leave.* **15***I* *tell you the truth, the wicked cities of Sodom and Gomorrah will be better off than such a town on the judgment day.*

16*"Look, I am sending you out as sheep among wolves. So be as shrewd as snakes and harmless as doves.* **17***But beware! For you will be handed over to the courts and will be flogged with whips in the synagogues.* **18***You will stand trial before governors and kings because you are my followers. But this will be your opportunity to tell the rulers and other unbelievers about me.* **19***When you are arrested, don't worry about how to respond or what to say. God will give you the right words at the right time.* **20***For it is not you who will be speaking—it will be the Spirit of your Father speaking through you.*

21*"A brother will betray his brother to death, a father will betray his own child, and children will rebel against their parents and cause them to be killed.* **22***And all nations will hate you because you are my followers. But everyone who endures to the end will be saved.* **23***When you are persecuted in one town, flee to the next. I tell you the truth, the Son of Man will return before you have reached all the towns of Israel.*

24*"Students are not greater than their teacher, and slaves are not greater than their master.* **25***Students are to be like their teacher, and slaves are to be like their master. And since I, the master of the household, have been called the prince of demons, the members of my household will be called by even worse names!*

26*"But don't be afraid of those who threaten you. For the time is coming when everything that is covered will be revealed, and all that is secret will be made known to all.* **27***What I tell you now in the darkness, shout abroad when daybreak comes. What I whisper in your ear, shout from the housetops for all to hear!*

28*"Don't be afraid of those who want to kill your body; they cannot touch your soul. Fear only God, who can destroy both soul and body in hell.* **29***What is the price of two sparrows—one copper coin? But not a single sparrow can fall to the ground without your Father knowing it.* **30***And the very hairs on your head are all numbered.* **31***So don't be afraid; you are more valuable to God than a whole flock of sparrows.*

32*"Everyone who acknowledges me publicly here on earth, I will also acknowledge before my Father in heaven.* **33***But everyone who denies me here on earth, I will also deny before my Father in heaven.*

34*"Don't imagine that I came to bring peace to the earth! I came not to bring peace, but a sword.*

35*'I have come to set a man against his father,*
a daughter against her mother,
and a daughter-in-law against her mother-in-law.
36*Your enemies will be right in your own household!'*

37*"If you love your father or mother more than you love me, you are not worthy of being mine; or if you love your son or daughter more than me, you are not worthy of being mine.* **38***If you refuse to take up your cross and follow me, you are not worthy of being mine.* **39***If you cling to your life, you will lose it; but if you give up your life for me, you will find it.*

40*"Anyone who receives you receives me, and anyone who receives me receives the Father who sent me.* **41***If you receive a prophet as one who speaks for God, you will be given the same reward as a prophet. And if you receive righteous people because of their righteousness, you will be given a reward like theirs.* **42***And if you give even a cup of cold water to one of the least of my followers, you will surely be rewarded."*

Matthew 11
Jesus and John the Baptist

1*When Jesus had finished giving these instructions to his twelve disciples, he went out to teach and preach in towns throughout the region.*

2*John the Baptist, who was in prison, heard about all the things the Messiah was doing. So he sent his disciples to ask Jesus,* **3***"Are you the Messiah we've been expecting, or should we keep looking for someone else?"*

4*Jesus told them, "Go back to John and tell him what you have heard and seen—***5***the blind see, the lame walk, the lepers are cured, the deaf hear, the dead are raised to life, and the Good News is being preached to the poor.* **6***And tell him, 'God blesses those who do not turn away because of me.'"*

7*As John's disciples were leaving, Jesus began talking about him to the crowds. "What kind of man did you go into the wilderness to see? Was he a weak reed, swayed by every breath of wind?* **8***Or were you expecting to see a man dressed in expensive clothes? No, people with expensive clothes live in palaces.* **9***Were you looking for a prophet? Yes, and he is more than a prophet.* **10***John is the man to whom the Scriptures refer when they say,*

'Look, I am sending my messenger ahead of you,
and he will prepare your way before you.'

11"*I tell you the truth, of all who have ever lived, none is greater than John the Baptist. Yet even the least person in the Kingdom of Heaven is greater than he is!* **12***And from the time John the Baptist began preaching until now, the Kingdom of Heaven has been forcefully advancing, and violent people are attacking it.* **13***For before John came, all the prophets and the law of Moses looked forward to this present time.* **14***And if you are willing to accept what I say, he is Elijah, the one the prophets said would come.* **15***Anyone with ears to hear should listen and understand!*

16"*To what can I compare this generation? It is like children playing a game in the public square. They complain to their friends,*

17*'We played wedding songs,*
and you didn't dance,
so we played funeral songs,
and you didn't mourn.'

18*For John didn't spend his time eating and drinking, and you say, 'He's possessed by a demon.'* **19***The Son of Man, on the other hand, feasts and drinks, and you say, 'He's a glutton and a drunkard, and a friend of tax collectors and other sinners!' But wisdom is shown to be right by its results.*"

Judgment for the Unbelievers

20*Then Jesus began to denounce the towns where he had done so many of his miracles, because they hadn't repented of their sins and turned to God.* **21**"*What sorrow awaits you, Korazin and Bethsaida! For if the miracles I did in you had been done in wicked Tyre and Sidon, their people would have repented of their sins long ago, clothing themselves in burlap and throwing ashes on their heads to show their remorse.* **22***I tell you, Tyre and Sidon will be better off on judgment day than you.*

23"*And you people of Capernaum, will you be honored in heaven? No, you will go down to the place of the dead. For if the miracles I did for you had been done in wicked Sodom, it would still be here today.* **24***I tell you, even Sodom will be better off on judgment day than you.*"

Jesus' Prayer of Thanksgiving

25*At that time Jesus prayed this prayer: "O Father, Lord of heaven and earth, thank you for hiding these things from those who think themselves wise and clever, and for revealing them to the childlike.* **26***Yes, Father, it pleased you to do it this way!*

27*"My Father has entrusted everything to me. No one truly knows the Son except the Father, and no one truly knows the Father except the Son and those to whom the Son chooses to reveal him."*

28*Then Jesus said, "Come to me, all of you who are weary and carry heavy burdens, and I will give you rest.* **29***Take my yoke upon you. Let me teach you, because I am humble and gentle at heart, and you will find rest for your souls.* **30***For my yoke is easy to bear, and the burden I give you is light."*

Matthew 12
A Discussion about the Sabbath

1*At about that time Jesus was walking through some grainfields on the Sabbath. His disciples were hungry, so they began breaking off some heads of grain and eating them.* **2***But some Pharisees saw them do it and protested, "Look, your disciples are breaking the law by harvesting grain on the Sabbath."*

3*Jesus said to them, "Haven't you read in the Scriptures what David did when he and his companions were hungry?* **4***He went into the house of God, and he and his companions broke the law by eating the sacred loaves of bread that only the priests are allowed to eat.* **5***And haven't you read in the law of Moses that the priests on duty in the Temple may work on the Sabbath?* **6***I tell you, there is one here who is even greater than the Temple!* **7***But you would not have condemned my innocent disciples if you knew the meaning of this Scripture: 'I want you to show mercy, not offer sacrifices.'* **8***For the Son of Man is Lord, even over the Sabbath!"*

Jesus Heals on the Sabbath

9*Then Jesus went over to their synagogue,* **10***where he noticed a man with a deformed hand. The Pharisees asked Jesus, "Does the law permit a person to work by healing on the Sabbath?" (They were hoping he would say yes, so they could bring charges against him.)*

11*And he answered, "If you had a sheep that fell into a well on the*

Sabbath, wouldn't you work to pull it out? Of course you would. **12**And how much more valuable is a person than a sheep! Yes, the law permits a person to do good on the Sabbath."

13Then he said to the man, "Hold out your hand." So the man held out his hand, and it was restored, just like the other one! **14**Then the Pharisees called a meeting to plot how to kill Jesus.

Jesus, God's Chosen Servant

15But Jesus knew what they were planning. So he left that area, and many people followed him. He healed all the sick among them, **16**but he warned them not to reveal who he was. **17**This fulfilled the prophecy of Isaiah concerning him:

18"Look at my Servant, whom I have chosen.
He is my Beloved, who pleases me.
I will put my Spirit upon him,
and he will proclaim justice to the nations.
19He will not fight or shout
or raise his voice in public.
20He will not crush the weakest reed
or put out a flickering candle.
Finally he will cause justice to be victorious.
21And his name will be the hope
of all the world."

Jesus and the Prince of Demons

22Then a demon-possessed man, who was blind and couldn't speak, was brought to Jesus. He healed the man so that he could both speak and see. **23**The crowd was amazed and asked, "Could it be that Jesus is the Son of David, the Messiah?"

24But when the Pharisees heard about the miracle, they said, "No wonder he can cast out demons. He gets his power from Satan, the prince of demons."

25Jesus knew their thoughts and replied, "Any kingdom divided by civil war is doomed. A town or family splintered by feuding will fall apart. **26**And if Satan is casting out Satan, he is divided and fighting against himself. His own kingdom will not survive. **27**And if I am empowered by Satan, what about your own exorcists? They cast out demons, too, so they will condemn *you for what you have said.* **28***But if I am casting out demons by the Spirit of God, then the Kingdom of God has arrived among you.* **29***For who is powerful enough to enter the house of a strong man like Satan and plunder his goods? Only someone even stronger—someone who could tie him up and then plunder his house.*

30*"Anyone who isn't with me opposes me, and anyone who isn't working with me is actually working against me.*

31*"So I tell you, every sin and blasphemy can be forgiven—except blasphemy against the Holy Spirit, which will never be forgiven.* **32***Anyone who speaks against the Son of Man can be forgiven, but anyone who speaks against the Holy Spirit will never be forgiven, either in this world or in the world to come.*

33*"A tree is identified by its fruit. If a tree is good, its fruit will be good. If a tree is bad, its fruit will be bad.* **34***You brood of snakes! How could evil men like you speak what is good and right? For whatever is in your heart determines what you say.* **35***A good person produces good things from the treasury of a good heart, and an evil person produces evil things from the treasury of an evil heart.* **36***And I tell you this, you must give an account on judgment day for every idle word you speak.* **37***The words you say will either acquit you or condemn you."*

The Sign of Jonah

38*One day some teachers of religious law and Pharisees came to Jesus and said, "Teacher, we want you to show us a miraculous sign to prove your authority."*

39*But Jesus replied, "Only an evil, adulterous generation would demand a miraculous sign; but the only sign I will give them is the sign of the prophet Jonah.* **40***For as Jonah was in the belly of the great fish for three days and three nights, so will the Son of Man be in the heart of the earth for three days and three nights.*

41*"The people of Nineveh will stand up against this generation on judgment day and condemn it, for they repented of their sins at the preaching of Jonah. Now someone greater than Jonah is here—but you refuse to repent.* **42***The queen of Sheba will also stand up against this generation on judgment day and condemn it, for she came from a distant land to hear the wisdom of Solomon. Now someone greater than Solomon is here—but you refuse to listen.*

43*"When an evil spirit leaves a person, it goes into the desert, seeking rest but finding none.* **44***Then it says, 'I will return to the person I came from.' So it returns and finds its former home empty, swept, and in order.* **45***Then the spirit finds seven other spirits more evil than itself, and they all enter the person and live there. And so that person is worse off than before. That will be the experience of this evil generation."*

The True Family of Jesus

46*As Jesus was speaking to the crowd, his mother and brothers stood outside, asking to speak to him.* **47***Someone told Jesus, "Your mother and your brothers are standing outside, and they want to speak to you."*

48*Jesus asked, "Who is my mother? Who are my brothers?"* **49***Then he pointed to his disciples and said, "Look, these are my mother and brothers.* **50***Anyone who does the will of my Father in heaven is my brother and sister and mother!"*

Matthew 13
Parable of the Farmer Scattering Seed

1*Later that same day Jesus left the house and sat beside the lake.* **2***A large crowd soon gathered around him, so he got into a boat. Then he sat there and taught as the people stood on the shore.* **3***He told many stories in the form of parables, such as this one:*

"Listen! A farmer went out to plant some seeds. **4***As he scattered them across his field, some seeds fell on a footpath, and the birds came and ate them.* **5***Other seeds fell on shallow soil with underlying rock. The seeds sprouted quickly because the soil was shallow.* **6***But the plants soon wilted under the hot sun, and since they didn't have deep roots, they died.* **7***Other seeds fell among thorns that grew up and choked out the tender plants.* **8***Still other seeds fell on fertile soil, and they produced a crop that was thirty, sixty, and even a hundred times as much as had been planted!* **9***Anyone with ears to hear should listen and understand."*

10*His disciples came and asked him, "Why do you use parables when you talk to the people?"*

11*He replied, "You are permitted to understand the secrets of the Kingdom of Heaven, but others are not.* **12***To those who listen to my teaching, more* *understanding will be given, and they will have an abundance of knowledge. But for those who are not listening, even what little understanding they have will be taken away from them.* **13***That is why I use these parables,*

For they look, but they don't really see.
They hear, but they don't really listen or understand.
14*This fulfills the prophecy of Isaiah that says,*
'When you hear what I say,
you will not understand.
When you see what I do,
you will not comprehend.
15*For the hearts of these people are hardened,*
and their ears cannot hear,
and they have closed their eyes—
so their eyes cannot see,
and their ears cannot hear,
and their hearts cannot understand,
and they cannot turn to me
and let me heal them.'

16*"But blessed are your eyes, because they see; and your ears, because they hear.* **17***I tell you the truth, many prophets and righteous people longed to see what you see, but they didn't see it. And they longed to hear what you hear, but they didn't hear it.*

18*"Now listen to the explanation of the parable about the farmer planting seeds:* **19***The seed that fell on the footpath represents those who hear the message about the Kingdom and don't understand it. Then the evil one comes and snatches away the seed that was planted in their hearts.* **20***The seed on the rocky soil represents those who hear the message and immediately receive it with joy.* **21***But since they don't have deep roots, they don't last long. They fall away as soon as they have problems or are persecuted for believing God's word.* **22***The seed that fell among the thorns represents those who hear God's word, but all too quickly the message is crowded out by the worries of this life and the lure of wealth, so no fruit is produced.* **23***The seed that fell on good soil represents those who truly hear and understand God's word and produce a harvest of thirty, sixty, or even a hundred times as much as had been planted!"*

Parable of the Wheat and Weeds

24*Here is another story Jesus told: "The Kingdom of Heaven is like a farmer who planted good seed in his field.* **25***But that night as the workers slept, his enemy came and planted weeds among the wheat, then slipped away.* **26***When the crop began to grow and produce grain, the weeds also grew.*

27*"The farmer's workers went to him and said, 'Sir, the field where you planted that good seed is full of weeds! Where did they come from?'*

28*"'An enemy has done this!' the farmer exclaimed.*

"'Should we pull out the weeds?' they asked.

29*"'No,' he replied, 'you'll uproot the wheat if you do.* **30***Let both grow together until the harvest. Then I will tell the harvesters to sort out the weeds, tie them into bundles, and burn them, and to put the wheat in the barn.'"*

Parable of the Mustard Seed

31*Here is another illustration Jesus used: "The Kingdom of Heaven is like a mustard seed planted in a field.* **32***It is the smallest of all seeds, but it becomes the largest of garden plants; it grows into a tree, and birds come and make nests in its branches."*

Parable of the Yeast

33*Jesus also used this illustration: "The Kingdom of Heaven is like the yeast a woman used in making bread. Even though she put only a little yeast in three measures of flour, it permeated every part of the dough."*

34*Jesus always used stories and illustrations like these when speaking to the crowds. In fact, he never spoke to them without using such parables.* **35***This fulfilled what God had spoken through the prophet:*

"I will speak to you in parables.

I will explain things hidden since the creation of the world."

Parable of the Wheat and Weeds Explained

36*Then, leaving the crowds outside, Jesus went into the house. His disciples said, "Please explain to us the story of the weeds in the field."*

37*Jesus replied, "The Son of Man is the farmer who plants the good seed.* **38***The field is the world, and the good seed represents the people of the Kingdom. The weeds are the people who belong to the evil one.* **39***The enemy*

*who planted the weeds among the wheat is the devil. The harvest is the end
of the world, and the harvesters are the angels.*

40*"Just as the weeds are sorted out and burned in the fire, so it will be at
the end of the world.* **41***The Son of Man will send his angels, and they will
remove from his Kingdom everything that causes sin and all who do evil.*
42*And the angels will throw them into the fiery furnace, where there will
be weeping and gnashing of teeth.* **43***Then the righteous will shine like the
sun in their Father's Kingdom. Anyone with ears to hear should listen and
understand!*

Parables of the Hidden Treasure and the Pearl

44*"The Kingdom of Heaven is like a treasure that a man discovered
hidden in a field. In his excitement, he hid it again and sold everything he
owned to get enough money to buy the field.*

45*"Again, the Kingdom of Heaven is like a merchant on the lookout for
choice pearls.* **46***When he discovered a pearl of great value, he sold everything
he owned and bought it!*

Parable of the Fishing Net

47*"Again, the Kingdom of Heaven is like a fishing net that was thrown
into the water and caught fish of every kind.* **48***When the net was full, they
dragged it up onto the shore, sat down, and sorted the good fish into crates,
but threw the bad ones away.* **49***That is the way it will be at the end of the
world. The angels will come and separate the wicked people from the righteous,*
50*throwing the wicked into the fiery furnace, where there will be weeping
and gnashing of teeth.* **51***Do you understand all these things?"*

"Yes," they said, "we do."

52*Then he added, "Every teacher of religious law who becomes a disciple
in the Kingdom of Heaven is like a homeowner who brings from his storeroom
new gems of truth as well as old."*

Jesus Rejected at Nazareth

53*When Jesus had finished telling these stories and illustrations, he left
that part of the country.* **54***He returned to Nazareth, his hometown. When he
taught there in the synagogue, everyone was amazed and said, "Where does he
get this wisdom and the power to do miracles?"* **55***Then they scoffed, "He's just*

the carpenter's son, and we know Mary, his mother, and his brothers—James, Joseph, Simon, and Judas. **56**All his sisters live right here among us. Where did he learn all these things?" **57**And they were deeply offended and refused to believe in him.

Then Jesus told them, "A prophet is honored everywhere except in his own hometown and among his own family." **58**And so he did only a few miracles there because of their unbelief.

Matthew 14
The Death of John the Baptist

1When Herod Antipas, the ruler of Galilee, heard about Jesus, **2**he said to his advisers, "This must be John the Baptist raised from the dead! That is why he can do such miracles."

3For Herod had arrested and imprisoned John as a favor to his wife Herodias (the former wife of Herod's brother Philip). **4**John had been telling Herod, "It is against God's law for you to marry her." **5**Herod wanted to kill John, but he was afraid of a riot, because all the people believed John was a prophet.

6But at a birthday party for Herod, Herodias's daughter performed a dance that greatly pleased him, **7**so he promised with a vow to give her anything she wanted. **8**At her mother's urging, the girl said, "I want the head of John the Baptist on a tray!" **9**Then the king regretted what he had said; but because of the vow he had made in front of his guests, he issued the necessary orders. **10**So John was beheaded in the prison, **11**and his head was brought on a tray and given to the girl, who took it to her mother. **12**Later, John's disciples came for his body and buried it. Then they went and told Jesus what had happened.

Jesus Feeds Five Thousand

13As soon as Jesus heard the news, he left in a boat to a remote area to be alone. But the crowds heard where he was headed and followed on foot from many towns. **14**Jesus saw the huge crowd as he stepped from the boat, and he had compassion on them and healed their sick.

15That evening the disciples came to him and said, "This is a remote place, and it's already getting late. Send the crowds away so they can go to the villages and buy food for themselves."

16But Jesus said, "That isn't necessary—you feed them."

17"But we have only five loaves of bread and two fish!" they answered.

18"Bring them here," he said. 19Then he told the people to sit down on the grass. Jesus took the five loaves and two fish, looked up toward heaven, and blessed them. Then, breaking the loaves into pieces, he gave the bread to the disciples, who distributed it to the people. 20They all ate as much as they wanted, and afterward, the disciples picked up twelve baskets of leftovers. 21About 5,000 men were fed that day, in addition to all the women and children!

Jesus Walks on Water

22Immediately after this, Jesus insisted that his disciples get back into the boat and cross to the other side of the lake, while he sent the people home. 23After sending them home, he went up into the hills by himself to pray. Night fell while he was there alone.

24Meanwhile, the disciples were in trouble far away from land, for a strong wind had risen, and they were fighting heavy waves. 25About three o'clock in the morning Jesus came toward them, walking on the water. 26When the disciples saw him walking on the water, they were terrified. In their fear, they cried out, "It's a ghost!"

27But Jesus spoke to them at once. "Don't be afraid," he said. "Take courage. I am here!"

28Then Peter called to him, "Lord, if it's really you, tell me to come to you, walking on the water."

29"Yes, come," Jesus said.

So Peter went over the side of the boat and walked on the water toward Jesus. 30But when he saw the strong wind and the waves, he was terrified and began to sink. "Save me, Lord!" he shouted.

31Jesus immediately reached out and grabbed him. "You have so little faith," Jesus said. "Why did you doubt me?"

32When they climbed back into the boat, the wind stopped. 33Then the disciples worshiped him. "You really are the Son of God!" they exclaimed.

34After they had crossed the lake, they landed at Gennesaret. 35When the people recognized Jesus, the news of his arrival spread quickly throughout the *whole area, and soon people were bringing all their sick to be healed.* **36***They begged him to let the sick touch at least the fringe of his robe, and all who touched him were healed.*

Matthew 15
Jesus Teaches about Inner Purity

1*Some Pharisees and teachers of religious law now arrived from Jerusalem to see Jesus. They asked him,* **2***"Why do your disciples disobey our age-old tradition? For they ignore our tradition of ceremonial hand washing before they eat."*

3*Jesus replied, "And why do you, by your traditions, violate the direct commandments of God?* **4***For instance, God says, 'Honor your father and mother,' and 'Anyone who speaks disrespectfully of father or mother must be put to death.'* **5***But you say it is all right for people to say to their parents, 'Sorry, I can't help you. For I have vowed to give to God what I would have given to you.'* **6***In this way, you say they don't need to honor their parents. And so you cancel the word of God for the sake of your own tradition.* **7***You hypocrites! Isaiah was right when he prophesied about you, for he wrote,*

8*'These people honor me with their lips,*
but their hearts are far from me.
9*Their worship is a farce,*
for they teach man-made ideas as commands from God.'"

10*Then Jesus called to the crowd to come and hear. "Listen," he said, "and try to understand.* **11***It's not what goes into your mouth that defiles you; you are defiled by the words that come out of your mouth."*

12*Then the disciples came to him and asked, "Do you realize you offended the Pharisees by what you just said?"*

13*Jesus replied, "Every plant not planted by my heavenly Father will be uprooted,* **14***so ignore them. They are blind guides leading the blind, and if one blind person guides another, they will both fall into a ditch."*

15*Then Peter said to Jesus, "Explain to us the parable that says people aren't defiled by what they eat."*

16*"Don't you understand yet?" Jesus asked.* **17***"Anything you eat passes through the stomach and then goes into the sewer.* **18***But the words you speak come from the heart—that's what defiles you.* **19***For from the heart* *come evil thoughts, murder, adultery, all sexual immorality, theft, lying, and slander.* **20***These are what defile you. Eating with unwashed hands will never defile you."*

The Faith of a Gentile Woman

21*Then Jesus left Galilee and went north to the region of Tyre and Sidon.* **22***A Gentile woman who lived there came to him, pleading, "Have mercy on me, O Lord, Son of David! For my daughter is possessed by a demon that torments her severely."*

23*But Jesus gave her no reply, not even a word. Then his disciples urged him to send her away. "Tell her to go away," they said. "She is bothering us with all her begging."*

24*Then Jesus said to the woman, "I was sent only to help God's lost sheep—the people of Israel."*

25*But she came and worshiped him, pleading again, "Lord, help me!"*

26*Jesus responded, "It isn't right to take food from the children and throw it to the dogs."*

27*She replied, "That's true, Lord, but even dogs are allowed to eat the scraps that fall beneath their masters' table."*

28*"Dear woman," Jesus said to her, "your faith is great. Your request is granted." And her daughter was instantly healed.*

Jesus Heals Many People

29*Jesus returned to the Sea of Galilee and climbed a hill and sat down.* **30***A vast crowd brought to him people who were lame, blind, crippled, those who couldn't speak, and many others. They laid them before Jesus, and he healed them all.* **31***The crowd was amazed! Those who hadn't been able to speak were talking, the crippled were made well, the lame were walking, and the blind could see again! And they praised the God of Israel.*

Jesus Feeds Four Thousand

32*Then Jesus called his disciples and told them, "I feel sorry for these people. They have been here with me for three days, and they have nothing left to eat. I don't want to send them away hungry, or they will faint along the way."*

33The disciples replied, "Where would we get enough food here in the wilderness for such a huge crowd?"

34Jesus asked, "How much bread do you have?"

They replied, "Seven loaves, and a few small fish."

35So Jesus told all the people to sit down on the ground. 36Then he took the seven loaves and the fish, thanked God for them, and broke them into pieces. He gave them to the disciples, who distributed the food to the crowd.

37They all ate as much as they wanted. Afterward, the disciples picked up seven large baskets of leftover food. 38There were 4,000 men who were fed that day, in addition to all the women and children. 39Then Jesus sent the people home, and he got into a boat and crossed over to the region of Magadan.

Matthew 16
Leaders Demand a Miraculous Sign

1One day the Pharisees and Sadducees came to test Jesus, demanding that he show them a miraculous sign from heaven to prove his authority.

2He replied, "You know the saying, 'Red sky at night means fair weather tomorrow; 3red sky in the morning means foul weather all day.' You know how to interpret the weather signs in the sky, but you don't know how to interpret the signs of the times! 4Only an evil, adulterous generation would demand a miraculous sign, but the only sign I will give them is the sign of the prophet Jonah." Then Jesus left them and went away.

Yeast of the Pharisees and Sadducees

5Later, after they crossed to the other side of the lake, the disciples discovered they had forgotten to bring any bread. 6"Watch out!" Jesus warned them. "Beware of the yeast of the Pharisees and Sadducees."

7At this they began to argue with each other because they hadn't brought any bread. 8Jesus knew what they were saying, so he said, "You have so little faith! Why are you arguing with each other about having no bread? 9Don't you understand even yet? Don't you remember the 5,000 I fed with five loaves, and the baskets of leftovers you picked up? 10Or the 4,000 I fed with seven loaves, and the large baskets of leftovers you picked up? 11Why can't you understand that I'm not talking about bread? So again I say, 'Beware of the yeast of the Pharisees and Sadducees.'"

12*Then at last they understood that he wasn't speaking about the yeast in bread, but about the deceptive teaching of the Pharisees and Sadducees.*

Peter's Declaration about Jesus

13*When Jesus came to the region of Caesarea Philippi, he asked his disciples, "Who do people say that the Son of Man is?"*

14*"Well," they replied, "some say John the Baptist, some say Elijah, and others say Jeremiah or one of the other prophets."*

15*Then he asked them, "But who do you say I am?"*

16*Simon Peter answered, "You are the Messiah, the Son of the living God."*

17*Jesus replied, "You are blessed, Simon son of John, because my Father in heaven has revealed this to you. You did not learn this from any human being. 18Now I say to you that you are Peter (which means 'rock'), and upon this rock I will build my church, and all the powers of hell will not conquer it. 19And I will give you the keys of the Kingdom of Heaven. Whatever you forbid on earth will be forbidden in heaven, and whatever you permit on earth will be permitted in heaven."*

20*Then he sternly warned the disciples not to tell anyone that he was the Messiah.*

Jesus Predicts His Death

21*From then on Jesus began to tell his disciples plainly that it was necessary for him to go to Jerusalem, and that he would suffer many terrible things at the hands of the elders, the leading priests, and the teachers of religious law. He would be killed, but on the third day he would be raised from the dead.*

22*But Peter took him aside and began to reprimand him for saying such things. "Heaven forbid, Lord," he said. "This will never happen to you!"*

23*Jesus turned to Peter and said, "Get away from me, Satan! You are a dangerous trap to me. You are seeing things merely from a human point of view, not from God's."*

24*Then Jesus said to his disciples, "If any of you wants to be my follower, you must turn from your selfish ways, take up your cross, and follow me. 25If you try to hang on to your life, you will lose it. But if you give up your life for my sake, you will save it. 26And what do you benefit if you gain the whole world but lose your own soul? Is anything worth more than your soul? 27For the Son of Man will come with his angels in the glory of his Father and will* *judge all people according to their deeds.* **28***And I tell you the truth, some standing here right now will not die before they see the Son of Man coming in his Kingdom.*"

Matthew 17
The Transfiguration

1*Six days later Jesus took Peter and the two brothers, James and John, and led them up a high mountain to be alone.* **2***As the men watched, Jesus' appearance was transformed so that his face shone like the sun, and his clothes became as white as light.* **3***Suddenly, Moses and Elijah appeared and began talking with Jesus.*

4*Peter exclaimed, "Lord, it's wonderful for us to be here! If you want, I'll make three shelters as memorials—one for you, one for Moses, and one for Elijah."*

5*But even as he spoke, a bright cloud overshadowed them, and a voice from the cloud said, "This is my dearly loved Son, who brings me great joy. Listen to him."* **6***The disciples were terrified and fell face down on the ground.*

7*Then Jesus came over and touched them. "Get up," he said. "Don't be afraid."* **8***And when they looked up, Moses and Elijah were gone, and they saw only Jesus.*

9*As they went back down the mountain, Jesus commanded them, "Don't tell anyone what you have seen until the Son of Man has been raised from the dead."*

10*Then his disciples asked him, "Why do the teachers of religious law insist that Elijah must return before the Messiah comes?"*

11*Jesus replied, "Elijah is indeed coming first to get everything ready.* **12***But I tell you, Elijah has already come, but he wasn't recognized, and they chose to abuse him. And in the same way they will also make the Son of Man suffer."* **13***Then the disciples realized he was talking about John the Baptist.*

Jesus Heals a Demon-Possessed Boy

14*At the foot of the mountain, a large crowd was waiting for them. A man came and knelt before Jesus and said,* **15***"Lord, have mercy on my son. He has seizures and suffers terribly. He often falls into the fire or into the water.* **16***So I brought him to your disciples, but they couldn't heal him."*

17*Jesus said, "You faithless and corrupt people! How long must I be with you? How long must I put up with you? Bring the boy here to me."* 18*Then Jesus rebuked the demon in the boy, and it left him. From that moment the boy was well.*

19*Afterward the disciples asked Jesus privately, "Why couldn't we cast out that demon?"*

20*"You don't have enough faith," Jesus told them. "I tell you the truth, if you had faith even as small as a mustard seed, you could say to this mountain, 'Move from here to there,' and it would move. Nothing would be impossible."*

Jesus Again Predicts His Death

22*After they gathered again in Galilee, Jesus told them, "The Son of Man is going to be betrayed into the hands of his enemies.* 23*He will be killed, but on the third day he will be raised from the dead." And the disciples were filled with grief.*

Payment of the Temple Tax

24*On their arrival in Capernaum, the collectors of the Temple tax came to Peter and asked him, "Doesn't your teacher pay the Temple tax?"*

25*"Yes, he does," Peter replied. Then he went into the house.*

But before he had a chance to speak, Jesus asked him, "What do you think, Peter? Do kings tax their own people or the people they have conquered?"

26*"They tax the people they have conquered," Peter replied.*

"Well, then," Jesus said, "the citizens are free! 27*However, we don't want to offend them, so go down to the lake and throw in a line. Open the mouth of the first fish you catch, and you will find a large silver coin. Take it and pay the tax for both of us."*

Matthew 18
The Greatest in the Kingdom

1*About that time the disciples came to Jesus and asked, "Who is greatest in the Kingdom of Heaven?"*

2*Jesus called a little child to him and put the child among them.* 3*Then he said, "I tell you the truth, unless you turn from your sins and become like little children, you will never get into the Kingdom of Heaven.* 4*So anyone who becomes as humble as this little child is the greatest in the Kingdom of Heaven.*

5*"And anyone who welcomes a little child like this on my behalf is welcoming me.* 6*But if you cause one of these little ones who trusts in me to fall into sin, it would be better for you to have a large millstone tied around your neck and be drowned in the depths of the sea.*

7*"What sorrow awaits the world, because it tempts people to sin. Temptations are inevitable, but what sorrow awaits the person who does the tempting.* 8*So if your hand or foot causes you to sin, cut it off and throw it away. It's better to enter eternal life with only one hand or one foot than to be thrown into eternal fire with both of your hands and feet.* 9*And if your eye causes you to sin, gouge it out and throw it away. It's better to enter eternal life with only one eye than to have two eyes and be thrown into the fire of hell.*

10*"Beware that you don't look down on any of these little ones. For I tell you that in heaven their angels are always in the presence of my heavenly Father.*

Parable of the Lost Sheep

12*"If a man has a hundred sheep and one of them wanders away, what will he do? Won't he leave the ninety-nine others on the hills and go out to search for the one that is lost?* 13*And if he finds it, I tell you the truth, he will rejoice over it more than over the ninety-nine that didn't wander away!* 14*In the same way, it is not my heavenly Father's will that even one of these little ones should perish.*

Correcting Another Believer

15*"If another believer sins against you, go privately and point out the offense. If the other person listens and confesses it, you have won that person back.* 16*But if you are unsuccessful, take one or two others with you and go back again, so that everything you say may be confirmed by two or three witnesses.* 17*If the person still refuses to listen, take your case to the church. Then if he or she won't accept the church's decision, treat that person as a pagan or a corrupt tax collector.*

18*"I tell you the truth, whatever you forbid on earth will be forbidden in heaven, and whatever you permit on earth will be permitted in heaven.*

19*"I also tell you this: If two of you agree here on earth concerning anything you ask, my Father in heaven will do it for you.* 20*For where two or three gather together as my followers, I am there among them."*

Parable of the Unforgiving Debtor

21*Then Peter came to him and asked, "Lord, how often should I forgive someone who sins against me? Seven times?"*

22*"No, not seven times," Jesus replied, "but seventy times seven!*

23*"Therefore, the Kingdom of Heaven can be compared to a king who decided to bring his accounts up to date with servants who had borrowed money from him.* **24***In the process, one of his debtors was brought in who owed him millions of dollars.* **25***He couldn't pay, so his master ordered that he be sold—along with his wife, his children, and everything he owned—to pay the debt.*

26*"But the man fell down before his master and begged him, 'Please, be patient with me, and I will pay it all.'* **27***Then his master was filled with pity for him, and he released him and forgave his debt.*

28*"But when the man left the king, he went to a fellow servant who owed him a few thousand dollars. He grabbed him by the throat and demanded instant payment.*

29*"His fellow servant fell down before him and begged for a little more time. 'Be patient with me, and I will pay it,' he pleaded.* **30***But his creditor wouldn't wait. He had the man arrested and put in prison until the debt could be paid in full.*

31*"When some of the other servants saw this, they were very upset. They went to the king and told him everything that had happened.* **32***Then the king called in the man he had forgiven and said, 'You evil servant! I forgave you that tremendous debt because you pleaded with me.* **33***Shouldn't you have mercy on your fellow servant, just as I had mercy on you?'* **34***Then the angry king sent the man to prison to be tortured until he had paid his entire debt.*

35*"That's what my heavenly Father will do to you if you refuse to forgive your brothers and sisters from your heart."*

Matthew 19

Discussion about Divorce and Marriage

1*When Jesus had finished saying these things, he left Galilee and went down to the region of Judea east of the Jordan River.* **2***Large crowds followed him there, and he healed their sick.*

3Some Pharisees came and tried to trap him with this question: "Should a man be allowed to divorce his wife for just any reason?"

4"Haven't you read the Scriptures?" Jesus replied. "They record that from the beginning 'God made them male and female.'" **5**And he said, "This explains why a man leaves his father and mother and is joined to his wife, and the two are united into one.' **6**Since they are no longer two but one, let no one split apart what God has joined together."

7"Then why did Moses say in the law that a man could give his wife a written notice of divorce and send her away?" they asked.

8Jesus replied, "Moses permitted divorce only as a concession to your hard hearts, but it was not what God had originally intended. **9**And I tell you this, whoever divorces his wife and marries someone else commits adultery—unless his wife has been unfaithful."

10Jesus' disciples then said to him, "If this is the case, it is better not to marry!"

11"Not everyone can accept this statement," Jesus said. "Only those whom God helps. **12**Some are born as eunuchs, some have been made eunuchs by others, and some choose not to marry for the sake of the Kingdom of Heaven. Let anyone accept this who can."

Jesus Blesses the Children

13One day some parents brought their children to Jesus so he could lay his hands on them and pray for them. But the disciples scolded the parents for bothering him.

14But Jesus said, "Let the children come to me. Don't stop them! For the Kingdom of Heaven belongs to those who are like these children." **15**And he placed his hands on their heads and blessed them before he left.

The Rich Man

16Someone came to Jesus with this question: "Teacher, what good deed must I do to have eternal life?"

17"Why ask me about what is good?" Jesus replied. "There is only One who is good. But to answer your question—if you want to receive eternal life, keep the commandments."

18"Which ones?" the man asked.

And Jesus replied: "'You must not murder. You must not commit adultery.

You must not steal. You must not testify falsely. **19***Honor your father and mother. Love your neighbor as yourself.'"*

20*"I've obeyed all these commandments," the young man replied. "What else must I do?"*

21*Jesus told him, "If you want to be perfect, go and sell all your possessions and give the money to the poor, and you will have treasure in heaven. Then come, follow me."*

22*But when the young man heard this, he went away sad, for he had many possessions.*

23*Then Jesus said to his disciples, "I tell you the truth, it is very hard for a rich person to enter the Kingdom of Heaven.* **24***I'll say it again—it is easier for a camel to go through the eye of a needle than for a rich person to enter the Kingdom of God!"*

25*The disciples were astounded. "Then who in the world can be saved?" they asked.*

26*Jesus looked at them intently and said, "Humanly speaking, it is impossible. But with God everything is possible."*

27*Then Peter said to him, "We've given up everything to follow you. What will we get?"*

28*Jesus replied, "I assure you that when the world is made new and the Son of Man sits upon his glorious throne, you who have been my followers will also sit on twelve thrones, judging the twelve tribes of Israel.* **29***And everyone who has given up houses or brothers or sisters or father or mother or children or property, for my sake, will receive a hundred times as much in return and will inherit eternal life.* **30***But many who are the greatest now will be least important then, and those who seem least important now will be the greatest then.*

Matthew 20
Parable of the Vineyard Workers

1*"For the Kingdom of Heaven is like the landowner who went out early one morning to hire workers for his vineyard.* **2***He agreed to pay the normal daily wage and sent them out to work.*

3*"At nine o'clock in the morning he was passing through the marketplace and saw some people standing around doing nothing.* **4***So he hired them,*

telling them he would pay them whatever was right at the end of the day.
5*So they went to work in the vineyard. At noon and again at three o'clock he did the same thing.*

6"*At five o'clock that afternoon he was in town again and saw some more people standing around. He asked them, 'Why haven't you been working today?'*

7"*They replied, 'Because no one hired us.'*

"*The landowner told them, 'Then go out and join the others in my vineyard.'*

8"*That evening he told the foreman to call the workers in and pay them, beginning with the last workers first.* **9**When those hired at five o'clock were paid, each received a full day's wage. **10**When those hired first came to get their pay, they assumed they would receive more. But they, too, were paid a day's wage.* **11**When they received their pay, they protested to the owner,* **12**'Those people worked only one hour, and yet you've paid them just as much as you paid us who worked all day in the scorching heat.'*

13"*He answered one of them, 'Friend, I haven't been unfair! Didn't you agree to work all day for the usual wage?* **14**Take your money and go. I wanted to pay this last worker the same as you.* **15**Is it against the law for me to do what I want with my money? Should you be jealous because I am kind to others?'*

16"*So those who are last now will be first then, and those who are first will be last.*"

Jesus Again Predicts His Death

17*As Jesus was going up to Jerusalem, he took the twelve disciples aside privately and told them what was going to happen to him.* **18**"*Listen," he said, "we're going up to Jerusalem, where the Son of Man will be betrayed to the leading priests and the teachers of religious law. They will sentence him to die.* **19**Then they will hand him over to the Romans to be mocked, flogged with a whip, and crucified. But on the third day he will be raised from the dead.*"

Jesus Teaches about Serving Others

20*Then the mother of James and John, the sons of Zebedee, came to Jesus with her sons. She knelt respectfully to ask a favor.* **21**"*What is your request?" he asked.*

She replied, "In your Kingdom, please let my two sons sit in places of honor next to you, one on your right and the other on your left."

22*But Jesus answered by saying to them, "You don't know what you are asking! Are you able to drink from the bitter cup of suffering I am about to drink?"*

"Oh yes," they replied, "we are able!"

23*Jesus told them, "You will indeed drink from my bitter cup. But I have no right to say who will sit on my right or my left. My Father has prepared those places for the ones he has chosen."*

24*When the ten other disciples heard what James and John had asked, they were indignant.* **25***But Jesus called them together and said, "You know that the rulers in this world lord it over their people, and officials flaunt their authority over those under them.* **26***But among you it will be different. Whoever wants to be a leader among you must be your servant,* **27***and whoever wants to be first among you must become your slave.* **28***For even the Son of Man came not to be served but to serve others and to give his life as a ransom for many."*

Jesus Heals Two Blind Men

29*As Jesus and the disciples left the town of Jericho, a large crowd followed behind.* **30***Two blind men were sitting beside the road. When they heard that Jesus was coming that way, they began shouting, "Lord, Son of David, have mercy on us!"*

31*"Be quiet!" the crowd yelled at them.*

But they only shouted louder, "Lord, Son of David, have mercy on us!"

32*When Jesus heard them, he stopped and called, "What do you want me to do for you?"*

33*"Lord," they said, "we want to see!"* **34***Jesus felt sorry for them and touched their eyes. Instantly they could see! Then they followed him.*

Matthew 21
Jesus' Triumphant Entry

1*As Jesus and the disciples approached Jerusalem, they came to the town of Bethphage on the Mount of Olives. Jesus sent two of them on ahead.* **2***"Go into the village over there," he said. "As soon as you enter it, you will see a*

donkey tied there, with its colt beside it. Untie them and bring them to me.
3*If anyone asks what you are doing, just say, 'The Lord needs them,' and he will immediately let you take them."*

4*This took place to fulfill the prophecy that said,*
5*"Tell the people of Jerusalem,*
'Look, your King is coming to you.
He is humble, riding on a donkey—
riding on a donkey's colt.'"

6*The two disciples did as Jesus commanded.* **7***They brought the donkey and the colt to him and threw their garments over the colt, and he sat on it.*

8*Most of the crowd spread their garments on the road ahead of him, and others cut branches from the trees and spread them on the road.* **9***Jesus was in the center of the procession, and the people all around him were shouting,*
"Praise God for the Son of David!
Blessings on the one who comes in the name of the lord!
Praise God in highest heaven!"

10*The entire city of Jerusalem was in an uproar as he entered. "Who is this?" they asked.*

11*And the crowds replied, "It's Jesus, the prophet from Nazareth in Galilee."*

Jesus Clears the Temple

12*Jesus entered the Temple and began to drive out all the people buying and selling animals for sacrifice. He knocked over the tables of the money changers and the chairs of those selling doves.* **13***He said to them, "The Scriptures declare, 'My Temple will be called a house of prayer,' but you have turned it into a den of thieves!"*

14*The blind and the lame came to him in the Temple, and he healed them.* **15***The leading priests and the teachers of religious law saw these wonderful miracles and heard even the children in the Temple shouting, "Praise God for the Son of David."*

But the leaders were indignant. **16***They asked Jesus, "Do you hear what these children are saying?"*

"Yes," Jesus replied. "Haven't you ever read the Scriptures? For they say, 'You have taught children and infants to give you praise.'" **17***Then he returned to Bethany, where he stayed overnight.*

Jesus Curses the Fig Tree

18*In the morning, as Jesus was returning to Jerusalem, he was hungry,* **19***and he noticed a fig tree beside the road. He went over to see if there were any figs, but there were only leaves. Then he said to it, "May you never bear fruit again!" And immediately the fig tree withered up.*

20*The disciples were amazed when they saw this and asked, "How did the fig tree wither so quickly?"*

21*Then Jesus told them, "I tell you the truth, if you have faith and don't doubt, you can do things like this and much more. You can even say to this mountain, 'May you be lifted up and thrown into the sea,' and it will happen.* **22***You can pray for anything, and if you have faith, you will receive it."*

The Authority of Jesus Challenged

23*When Jesus returned to the Temple and began teaching, the leading priests and elders came up to him. They demanded, "By what authority are you doing all these things? Who gave you the right?"*

24*"I'll tell you by what authority I do these things if you answer one question," Jesus replied.* **25***"Did John's authority to baptize come from heaven, or was it merely human?"*

They talked it over among themselves. "If we say it was from heaven, he will ask us why we didn't believe John. **26***But if we say it was merely human, we'll be mobbed because the people believe John was a prophet."* **27***So they finally replied, "We don't know."*

And Jesus responded, "Then I won't tell you by what authority I do these things.

Parable of the Two Sons

28*"But what do you think about this? A man with two sons told the older boy, 'Son, go out and work in the vineyard today.'* **29***The son answered, 'No, I won't go,' but later he changed his mind and went anyway.* **30***Then the father told the other son, 'You go,' and he said, 'Yes, sir, I will.' But he didn't go.*

31*"Which of the two obeyed his father?"*

They replied, "The first."

Then Jesus explained his meaning: "I tell you the truth, corrupt tax collectors and prostitutes will get into the Kingdom of God before you do. **32***For John the Baptist came and showed you the right way to live, but you* *didn't believe him, while tax collectors and prostitutes did. And even when you saw this happening, you refused to believe him and repent of your sins.*

Parable of the Evil Farmers

33*"Now listen to another story. A certain landowner planted a vineyard, built a wall around it, dug a pit for pressing out the grape juice, and built a lookout tower. Then he leased the vineyard to tenant farmers and moved to another country.* **34***At the time of the grape harvest, he sent his servants to collect his share of the crop.* **35***But the farmers grabbed his servants, beat one, killed one, and stoned another.* **36***So the landowner sent a larger group of his servants to collect for him, but the results were the same.*

37*"Finally, the owner sent his son, thinking, 'Surely they will respect my son.'*

38*"But when the tenant farmers saw his son coming, they said to one another, 'Here comes the heir to this estate. Come on, let's kill him and get the estate for ourselves!'* **39***So they grabbed him, dragged him out of the vineyard, and murdered him.*

40*"When the owner of the vineyard returns," Jesus asked, "what do you think he will do to those farmers?"*

41*The religious leaders replied, "He will put the wicked men to a horrible death and lease the vineyard to others who will give him his share of the crop after each harvest."*

42*Then Jesus asked them, "Didn't you ever read this in the Scriptures?*
'The stone that the builders rejected
has now become the cornerstone.
This is the lord's doing,
and it is wonderful to see.'

43*I tell you, the Kingdom of God will be taken away from you and given to a nation that will produce the proper fruit.* **44***Anyone who stumbles over that stone will be broken to pieces, and it will crush anyone it falls on."*

45*When the leading priests and Pharisees heard this parable, they realized he was telling the story against them—they were the wicked farmers.* **46***They wanted to arrest him, but they were afraid of the crowds, who considered Jesus to be a prophet.*

Matthew 22
Parable of the Great Feast

1*Jesus also told them other parables. He said,* **2***"The Kingdom of Heaven can be illustrated by the story of a king who prepared a great wedding feast for his son.* **3***When the banquet was ready, he sent his servants to notify those who were invited. But they all refused to come!*

4*"So he sent other servants to tell them, 'The feast has been prepared. The bulls and fattened cattle have been killed, and everything is ready. Come to the banquet!'* **5***But the guests he had invited ignored them and went their own way, one to his farm, another to his business.* **6***Others seized his messengers and insulted them and killed them.*

7*"The king was furious, and he sent out his army to destroy the murderers and burn their town.* **8***And he said to his servants, 'The wedding feast is ready, and the guests I invited aren't worthy of the honor.* **9***Now go out to the street corners and invite everyone you see.'* **10***So the servants brought in everyone they could find, good and bad alike, and the banquet hall was filled with guests.*

11*"But when the king came in to meet the guests, he noticed a man who wasn't wearing the proper clothes for a wedding.* **12***'Friend,' he asked, 'how is it that you are here without wedding clothes?' But the man had no reply.* **13***Then the king said to his aides, 'Bind his hands and feet and throw him into the outer darkness, where there will be weeping and gnashing of teeth.'*

14*"For many are called, but few are chosen."*

Taxes for Caesar
15*Then the Pharisees met together to plot how to trap Jesus into saying something for which he could be arrested.* **16***They sent some of their disciples, along with the supporters of Herod, to meet with him. "Teacher," they said, "we know how honest you are. You teach the way of God truthfully. You are impartial and don't play favorites.* **17***Now tell us what you think about this: Is it right to pay taxes to Caesar or not?"*

18*But Jesus knew their evil motives. "You hypocrites!" he said. "Why are you trying to trap me?* **19***Here, show me the coin used for the tax." When they handed him a Roman coin,* **20***he asked, "Whose picture and title are stamped on it?"*

21*"Caesar's," they replied.*

"Well, then," he said, "give to Caesar what belongs to Caesar, and give to God what belongs to God."

22*His reply amazed them, and they went away.*

Discussion about Resurrection

23*That same day Jesus was approached by some Sadducees—religious leaders who say there is no resurrection from the dead. They posed this question:* 24*"Teacher, Moses said, 'If a man dies without children, his brother should marry the widow and have a child who will carry on the brother's name.'* 25*Well, suppose there were seven brothers. The oldest one married and then died without children, so his brother married the widow.* 26*But the second brother also died, and the third brother married her. This continued with all seven of them.* 27*Last of all, the woman also died.* 28*So tell us, whose wife will she be in the resurrection? For all seven were married to her."*

29*Jesus replied, "Your mistake is that you don't know the Scriptures, and you don't know the power of God.* 30*For when the dead rise, they will neither marry nor be given in marriage. In this respect they will be like the angels in heaven.*

31*"But now, as to whether there will be a resurrection of the dead—haven't you ever read about this in the Scriptures? Long after Abraham, Isaac, and Jacob had died, God said,* 32*'I am the God of Abraham, the God of Isaac, and the God of Jacob.' So he is the God of the living, not the dead."*

33*When the crowds heard him, they were astounded at his teaching.*

The Most Important Commandment

34*But when the Pharisees heard that he had silenced the Sadducees with his reply, they met together to question him again.* 35*One of them, an expert in religious law, tried to trap him with this question:* 36*"Teacher, which is the most important commandment in the law of Moses?"*

37*Jesus replied, "'You must love the lord your God with all your heart, all your soul, and all your mind.'* 38*This is the first and greatest commandment.* 39*A second is equally important: 'Love your neighbor as yourself.'* 40*The entire law and all the demands of the prophets are based on these two commandments."*

Whose Son Is the Messiah?

41*Then, surrounded by the Pharisees, Jesus asked them a question:* **42***"What do you think about the Messiah? Whose son is he?"*

They replied, "He is the son of David."

43*Jesus responded, "Then why does David, speaking under the inspiration of the Spirit, call the Messiah 'my Lord'? For David said,*

44*'The lord said to my Lord,*

Sit in the place of honor at my right hand

until I humble your enemies beneath your feet.'

45*Since David called the Messiah 'my Lord,' how can the Messiah be his son?"*

46*No one could answer him. And after that, no one dared to ask him any more questions.*

Matthew 23
Jesus Criticizes the Religious Leaders

1*Then Jesus said to the crowds and to his disciples,* **2***"The teachers of religious law and the Pharisees are the official interpreters of the law of Moses.* **3***So practice and obey whatever they tell you, but don't follow their example. For they don't practice what they teach.* **4***They crush people with unbearable religious demands and never lift a finger to ease the burden.*

5*"Everything they do is for show. On their arms they wear extra wide prayer boxes with Scripture verses inside, and they wear robes with extra long tassels.* **6***And they love to sit at the head table at banquets and in the seats of honor in the synagogues.* **7***They love to receive respectful greetings as they walk in the marketplaces, and to be called 'Rabbi.'*

8*"Don't let anyone call you 'Rabbi,' for you have only one teacher, and all of you are equal as brothers and sisters.* **9***And don't address anyone here on earth as 'Father,' for only God in heaven is your spiritual Father.* **10***And don't let anyone call you 'Teacher,' for you have only one teacher, the Messiah.* **11***The greatest among you must be a servant.* **12***But those who exalt themselves will be humbled, and those who humble themselves will be exalted.*

13*"What sorrow awaits you teachers of religious law and you Pharisees. Hypocrites! For you shut the door of the Kingdom of Heaven in people's faces. You won't go in yourselves, and you don't let others enter either.*

15 *"What sorrow awaits you teachers of religious law and you Pharisees. Hypocrites! For you cross land and sea to make one convert, and then you turn that person into twice the child of hell you yourselves are!* **16** *"Blind guides! What sorrow awaits you! For you say that it means nothing to swear 'by God's Temple,' but that it is binding to swear 'by the gold in the Temple.'* **17** *Blind fools! Which is more important—the gold or the Temple that makes the gold sacred?* **18** *And you say that to swear 'by the altar' is not binding, but to swear 'by the gifts on the altar' is binding.* **19** *How blind! For which is more important—the gift on the altar or the altar that makes the gift sacred?* **20** *When you swear 'by the altar,' you are swearing by it and by everything on it.* **21** *And when you swear 'by the Temple,' you are swearing by it and by God, who lives in it.* **22** *And when you swear 'by heaven,' you are swearing by the throne of God and by God, who sits on the throne.*

23 *"What sorrow awaits you teachers of religious law and you Pharisees. Hypocrites! For you are careful to tithe even the tiniest income from your herb gardens, but you ignore the more important aspects of the law—justice, mercy, and faith. You should tithe, yes, but do not neglect the more important things.* **24** *Blind guides! You strain your water so you won't accidentally swallow a gnat, but you swallow a camel!*

25 *"What sorrow awaits you teachers of religious law and you Pharisees. Hypocrites! For you are so careful to clean the outside of the cup and the dish, but inside you are filthy—full of greed and self-indulgence!* **26** *You blind Pharisee! First wash the inside of the cup and the dish, and then the outside will become clean, too.*

27 *"What sorrow awaits you teachers of religious law and you Pharisees. Hypocrites! For you are like whitewashed tombs—beautiful on the outside but filled on the inside with dead people's bones and all sorts of impurity.* **28** *Outwardly you look like righteous people, but inwardly your hearts are filled with hypocrisy and lawlessness.*

29 *"What sorrow awaits you teachers of religious law and you Pharisees. Hypocrites! For you build tombs for the prophets your ancestors killed, and you decorate the monuments of the godly people your ancestors destroyed.* **30** *Then you say, 'If we had lived in the days of our ancestors, we would never have joined them in killing the prophets.'*

31 *"But in saying that, you testify against yourselves that you are indeed the descendants of those who murdered the prophets.* **32** *Go ahead and finish* *what your ancestors started.* **33***Snakes! Sons of vipers! How will you escape the judgment of hell?*

34*"Therefore, I am sending you prophets and wise men and teachers of religious law. But you will kill some by crucifixion, and you will flog others with whips in your synagogues, chasing them from city to city.* **35***As a result, you will be held responsible for the murder of all godly people of all time—from the murder of righteous Abel to the murder of Zechariah son of Berekiah, whom you killed in the Temple between the sanctuary and the altar.* **36***I tell you the truth, this judgment will fall on this very generation.*

Jesus Grieves over Jerusalem

37*"O Jerusalem, Jerusalem, the city that kills the prophets and stones God's messengers! How often I have wanted to gather your children together as a hen protects her chicks beneath her wings, but you wouldn't let me.* **38***And now, look, your house is abandoned and desolate.* **39***For I tell you this, you will never see me again until you say, 'Blessings on the one who comes in the name of the lord!'"*

Matthew 24
Jesus Foretells the Future

1*As Jesus was leaving the Temple grounds, his disciples pointed out to him the various Temple buildings.* **2***But he responded, "Do you see all these buildings? I tell you the truth, they will be completely demolished. Not one stone will be left on top of another!"*

3*Later, Jesus sat on the Mount of Olives. His disciples came to him privately and said, "Tell us, when will all this happen? What sign will signal your return and the end of the world?"*

4*Jesus told them, "Don't let anyone mislead you,* **5***for many will come in my name, claiming, 'I am the Messiah.' They will deceive many.* **6***And you will hear of wars and threats of wars, but don't panic. Yes, these things must take place, but the end won't follow immediately.* **7***Nation will go to war against nation, and kingdom against kingdom. There will be famines and earthquakes in many parts of the world.* **8***But all this is only the first of the birth pains, with more to come.*

9*"Then you will be arrested, persecuted, and killed. You will be hated all* *over the world because you are my followers.* **10***And many will turn away from me and betray and hate each other.* **11***And many false prophets will appear and will deceive many people.* **12***Sin will be rampant everywhere, and the love of many will grow cold.* **13***But the one who endures to the end will be saved.* **14***And the Good News about the Kingdom will be preached throughout the whole world, so that all nations will hear it; and then the end will come.*

15*"The day is coming when you will see what Daniel the prophet spoke about—the sacrilegious object that causes desecration standing in the Holy Place." (Reader, pay attention!)* **16***"Then those in Judea must flee to the hills.* **17***A person out on the deck of a roof must not go down into the house to pack.* **18***A person out in the field must not return even to get a coat.* **19***How terrible it will be for pregnant women and for nursing mothers in those days.* **20***And pray that your flight will not be in winter or on the Sabbath.* **21***For there will be greater anguish than at any time since the world began. And it will never be so great again.* **22***In fact, unless that time of calamity is shortened, not a single person will survive. But it will be shortened for the sake of God's chosen ones.*

23*"Then if anyone tells you, 'Look, here is the Messiah,' or 'There he is,' don't believe it.* **24***For false messiahs and false prophets will rise up and perform great signs and wonders so as to deceive, if possible, even God's chosen ones.* **25***See, I have warned you about this ahead of time.*

26*"So if someone tells you, 'Look, the Messiah is out in the desert,' don't bother to go and look. Or, 'Look, he is hiding here,' don't believe it!* **27***For as the lightning flashes in the east and shines to the west, so it will be when the Son of Man comes.* **28***Just as the gathering of vultures shows there is a carcass nearby, so these signs indicate that the end is near.*

29*"Immediately after the anguish of those days,*
the sun will be darkened,
the moon will give no light,
the stars will fall from the sky,
and the powers in the heavens will be shaken.

30*And then at last, the sign that the Son of Man is coming will appear in the heavens, and there will be deep mourning among all the peoples of the earth. And they will see the Son of Man coming on the clouds of heaven with power and great glory.* **31***And he will send out his angels with the mighty blast of a trumpet, and they will gather his chosen ones from all over the world—from the farthest ends of the earth and heaven.*

32*"Now learn a lesson from the fig tree. When its branches bud and its leaves begin to sprout, you know that summer is near.* **33***In the same way, when you see all these things, you can know his return is very near, right at the door.* **34***I tell you the truth, this generation will not pass from the scene until all these things take place.* **35***Heaven and earth will disappear, but my words will never disappear.*

36*"However, no one knows the day or hour when these things will happen, not even the angels in heaven or the Son himself. Only the Father knows.*

37*"When the Son of Man returns, it will be like it was in Noah's day.* **38***In those days before the flood, the people were enjoying banquets and parties and weddings right up to the time Noah entered his boat.* **39***People didn't realize what was going to happen until the flood came and swept them all away. That is the way it will be when the Son of Man comes.*

40*"Two men will be working together in the field; one will be taken, the other left.* **41***Two women will be grinding flour at the mill; one will be taken, the other left.*

42*"So you, too, must keep watch! For you don't know what day your Lord is coming.* **43***Understand this: If a homeowner knew exactly when a burglar was coming, he would keep watch and not permit his house to be broken into.* **44***You also must be ready all the time, for the Son of Man will come when least expected.*

45*"A faithful, sensible servant is one to whom the master can give the responsibility of managing his other household servants and feeding them.* **46***If the master returns and finds that the servant has done a good job, there will be a reward.* **47***I tell you the truth, the master will put that servant in charge of all he owns.* **48***But what if the servant is evil and thinks, 'My master won't be back for a while,'* **49***and he begins beating the other servants, partying, and getting drunk?* **50***The master will return unannounced and unexpected,* **51***and he will cut the servant to pieces and assign him a place with the hypocrites. In that place there will be weeping and gnashing of teeth.*

Matthew 25
Parable of the Ten Bridesmaids

1*"Then the Kingdom of Heaven will be like ten bridesmaids who took their lamps and went to meet the bridegroom.* **2***Five of them were foolish,* *and five were wise.* **3** *The five who were foolish didn't take enough olive oil for their lamps,* **4** *but the other five were wise enough to take along extra oil.* **5** *When the bridegroom was delayed, they all became drowsy and fell asleep.*

6 *"At midnight they were roused by the shout, 'Look, the bridegroom is coming! Come out and meet him!'*

7 *"All the bridesmaids got up and prepared their lamps.* **8** *Then the five foolish ones asked the others, 'Please give us some of your oil because our lamps are going out.'*

9 *"But the others replied, 'We don't have enough for all of us. Go to a shop and buy some for yourselves.'*

10 *"But while they were gone to buy oil, the bridegroom came. Then those who were ready went in with him to the marriage feast, and the door was locked.* **11** *Later, when the other five bridesmaids returned, they stood outside, calling, 'Lord! Lord! Open the door for us!'*

12 *"But he called back, 'Believe me, I don't know you!'*

13 *"So you, too, must keep watch! For you do not know the day or hour of my return.*

Parable of the Three Servants

14 *"Again, the Kingdom of Heaven can be illustrated by the story of a man going on a long trip. He called together his servants and entrusted his money to them while he was gone.* **15** *He gave five bags of silver to one, two bags of silver to another, and one bag of silver to the last—dividing it in proportion to their abilities. He then left on his trip.*

16 *"The servant who received the five bags of silver began to invest the money and earned five more.* **17** *The servant with two bags of silver also went to work and earned two more.* **18** *But the servant who received the one bag of silver dug a hole in the ground and hid the master's money.*

19 *"After a long time their master returned from his trip and called them to give an account of how they had used his money.* **20** *The servant to whom he had entrusted the five bags of silver came forward with five more and said, 'Master, you gave me five bags of silver to invest, and I have earned five more.'*

21 *"The master was full of praise. 'Well done, my good and faithful servant. You have been faithful in handling this small amount, so now I will give you many more responsibilities. Let's celebrate together!'*

22 *"The servant who had received the two bags of silver came forward and said, 'Master, you gave me two bags of silver to invest, and I have earned two more.'*

23 *"The master said, 'Well done, my good and faithful servant. You have been faithful in handling this small amount, so now I will give you many more responsibilities. Let's celebrate together!'*

24 *"Then the servant with the one bag of silver came and said, 'Master, I knew you were a harsh man, harvesting crops you didn't plant and gathering crops you didn't cultivate.* 25 *I was afraid I would lose your money, so I hid it in the earth. Look, here is your money back.'*

26 *"But the master replied, 'You wicked and lazy servant! If you knew I harvested crops I didn't plant and gathered crops I didn't cultivate,* 27 *why didn't you deposit my money in the bank? At least I could have gotten some interest on it.'*

28 *"Then he ordered, 'Take the money from this servant, and give it to the one with the ten bags of silver.* 29 *To those who use well what they are given, even more will be given, and they will have an abundance. But from those who do nothing, even what little they have will be taken away.* 30 *Now throw this useless servant into outer darkness, where there will be weeping and gnashing of teeth.'*

The Final Judgment

31 *"But when the Son of Man comes in his glory, and all the angels with him, then he will sit upon his glorious throne.* 32 *All the nations will be gathered in his presence, and he will separate the people as a shepherd separates the sheep from the goats.* 33 *He will place the sheep at his right hand and the goats at his left.*

34 *"Then the King will say to those on his right, 'Come, you who are blessed by my Father, inherit the Kingdom prepared for you from the creation of the world.* 35 *For I was hungry, and you fed me. I was thirsty, and you gave me a drink. I was a stranger, and you invited me into your home.* 36 *I was naked, and you gave me clothing. I was sick, and you cared for me. I was in prison, and you visited me.'*

37 *"Then these righteous ones will reply, 'Lord, when did we ever see you hungry and feed you? Or thirsty and give you something to drink?* 38 *Or a*

stranger and show you hospitality? Or naked and give you clothing? **39***When did we ever see you sick or in prison and visit you?'*

40*"And the King will say, 'I tell you the truth, when you did it to one of the least of these my brothers and sisters, you were doing it to me!'*

41*"Then the King will turn to those on the left and say, 'Away with you, you cursed ones, into the eternal fire prepared for the devil and his demons.* **42***For I was hungry, and you didn't feed me. I was thirsty, and you didn't give me a drink.* **43***I was a stranger, and you didn't invite me into your home. I was naked, and you didn't give me clothing. I was sick and in prison, and you didn't visit me.'*

44*"Then they will reply, 'Lord, when did we ever see you hungry or thirsty or a stranger or naked or sick or in prison, and not help you?'*

45*"And he will answer, 'I tell you the truth, when you refused to help the least of these my brothers and sisters, you were refusing to help me.'*

46*"And they will go away into eternal punishment, but the righteous will go into eternal life."*

Matthew 26
The Plot to Kill Jesus

1*When Jesus had finished saying all these things, he said to his disciples,* **2***"As you know, Passover begins in two days, and the Son of Man will be handed over to be crucified."*

3*At that same time the leading priests and elders were meeting at the residence of Caiaphas, the high priest,* **4***plotting how to capture Jesus secretly and kill him.* **5***"But not during the Passover celebration," they agreed, "or the people may riot."*

Jesus Anointed at Bethany

6*Meanwhile, Jesus was in Bethany at the home of Simon, a man who had previously had leprosy.* **7***While he was eating, a woman came in with a beautiful alabaster jar of expensive perfume and poured it over his head.*

8*The disciples were indignant when they saw this. "What a waste!" they said.* **9***"It could have been sold for a high price and the money given to the poor."*

10*But Jesus, aware of this, replied, "Why criticize this woman for doing* *such a good thing to me?* **11***You will always have the poor among you, but you will not always have me.* **12***She has poured this perfume on me to prepare my body for burial.* **13***I tell you the truth, wherever the Good News is preached throughout the world, this woman's deed will be remembered and discussed."*

Judas Agrees to Betray Jesus

14*Then Judas Iscariot, one of the twelve disciples, went to the leading priests* **15***and asked, "How much will you pay me to betray Jesus to you?" And they gave him thirty pieces of silver.* **16***From that time on, Judas began looking for an opportunity to betray Jesus.*

The Last Supper

17*On the first day of the Festival of Unleavened Bread, the disciples came to Jesus and asked, "Where do you want us to prepare the Passover meal for you?"*

18*"As you go into the city," he told them, "you will see a certain man. Tell him, 'The Teacher says: My time has come, and I will eat the Passover meal with my disciples at your house.'"* **19***So the disciples did as Jesus told them and prepared the Passover meal there.*

20*When it was evening, Jesus sat down at the table with the Twelve.* **21***While they were eating, he said, "I tell you the truth, one of you will betray me."*

22*Greatly distressed, each one asked in turn, "Am I the one, Lord?"*

23*He replied, "One of you who has just eaten from this bowl with me will betray me.* **24***For the Son of Man must die, as the Scriptures declared long ago. But how terrible it will be for the one who betrays him. It would be far better for that man if he had never been born!"*

25*Judas, the one who would betray him, also asked, "Rabbi, am I the one?" And Jesus told him, "You have said it."*

26*As they were eating, Jesus took some bread and blessed it. Then he broke it in pieces and gave it to the disciples, saying, "Take this and eat it, for this is my body."*

27*And he took a cup of wine and gave thanks to God for it. He gave it to them and said, "Each of you drink from it,* **28***for this is my blood, which confirms the covenant between God and his people. It is poured out as a* *sacrifice to forgive the sins of many.* **29***Mark my words—I will not drink wine again until the day I drink it new with you in my Father's Kingdom."* **30***Then they sang a hymn and went out to the Mount of Olives.*

Jesus Predicts Peter's Denial

31*On the way, Jesus told them, "Tonight all of you will desert me. For the Scriptures say,*

'God will strike the Shepherd,
and the sheep of the flock will be scattered.'

32*But after I have been raised from the dead, I will go ahead of you to Galilee and meet you there."*

33*Peter declared, "Even if everyone else deserts you, I will never desert you."*

34*Jesus replied, "I tell you the truth, Peter—this very night, before the rooster crows, you will deny three times that you even know me."*

35*"No!" Peter insisted. "Even if I have to die with you, I will never deny you!" And all the other disciples vowed the same.*

Jesus Prays in Gethsemane

36*Then Jesus went with them to the olive grove called Gethsemane, and he said, "Sit here while I go over there to pray." ***37***He took Peter and Zebedee's two sons, James and John, and he became anguished and distressed.* **38***He told them, "My soul is crushed with grief to the point of death. Stay here and keep watch with me."*

39*He went on a little farther and bowed with his face to the ground, praying, "My Father! If it is possible, let this cup of suffering be taken away from me. Yet I want your will to be done, not mine."*

40*Then he returned to the disciples and found them asleep. He said to Peter, "Couldn't you watch with me even one hour?* **41***Keep watch and pray, so that you will not give in to temptation. For the spirit is willing, but the body is weak!"*

42*Then Jesus left them a second time and prayed, "My Father! If this cup cannot be taken away unless I drink it, your will be done." ***43***When he returned to them again, he found them sleeping, for they couldn't keep their eyes open.*

44*So he went to pray a third time, saying the same things again.* **45***Then he came to the disciples and said, "Go ahead and sleep. Have your rest. But* *look—the time has come. The Son of Man is betrayed into the hands of sinners.* **46***Up, let's be going. Look, my betrayer is here!"*

Jesus Is Betrayed and Arrested

47*And even as Jesus said this, Judas, one of the twelve disciples, arrived with a crowd of men armed with swords and clubs. They had been sent by the leading priests and elders of the people.* **48***The traitor, Judas, had given them a prearranged signal: "You will know which one to arrest when I greet him with a kiss."* **49***So Judas came straight to Jesus. "Greetings, Rabbi!" he exclaimed and gave him the kiss.*

50*Jesus said, "My friend, go ahead and do what you have come for."*

Then the others grabbed Jesus and arrested him. **51***But one of the men with Jesus pulled out his sword and struck the high priest's slave, slashing off his ear.*

52*"Put away your sword," Jesus told him. "Those who use the sword will die by the sword.* **53***Don't you realize that I could ask my Father for thousands of angels to protect us, and he would send them instantly?* **54***But if I did, how would the Scriptures be fulfilled that describe what must happen now?"*

55*Then Jesus said to the crowd, "Am I some dangerous revolutionary, that you come with swords and clubs to arrest me? Why didn't you arrest me in the Temple? I was there teaching every day.* **56***But this is all happening to fulfill the words of the prophets as recorded in the Scriptures." At that point, all the disciples deserted him and fled.*

Jesus before the Council

57*Then the people who had arrested Jesus led him to the home of Caiaphas, the high priest, where the teachers of religious law and the elders had gathered.* **58***Meanwhile, Peter followed him at a distance and came to the high priest's courtyard. He went in and sat with the guards and waited to see how it would all end.*

59*Inside, the leading priests and the entire high council were trying to find witnesses who would lie about Jesus, so they could put him to death.* **60***But even though they found many who agreed to give false witness, they could not use anyone's testimony. Finally, two men came forward* **61***who declared, "This man said, 'I am able to destroy the Temple of God and rebuild it in three days.'"*

62*Then the high priest stood up and said to Jesus, "Well, aren't you going to answer these charges? What do you have to say for yourself?"* **63***But Jesus* remained silent. Then the high priest said to him, "I demand in the name of the living God—tell us if you are the Messiah, the Son of God."

64Jesus replied, "You have said it. And in the future you will see the Son of Man seated in the place of power at God's right hand and coming on the clouds of heaven."

65Then the high priest tore his clothing to show his horror and said, "Blasphemy! Why do we need other witnesses? You have all heard his blasphemy. 66What is your verdict?"

"Guilty!" they shouted. "He deserves to die!"

67Then they began to spit in Jesus' face and beat him with their fists. And some slapped him, 68jeering, "Prophesy to us, you Messiah! Who hit you that time?"

Peter Denies Jesus

69Meanwhile, Peter was sitting outside in the courtyard. A servant girl came over and said to him, "You were one of those with Jesus the Galilean."

70But Peter denied it in front of everyone. "I don't know what you're talking about," he said.

71Later, out by the gate, another servant girl noticed him and said to those standing around, "This man was with Jesus of Nazareth."

72Again Peter denied it, this time with an oath. "I don't even know the man," he said.

73A little later some of the other bystanders came over to Peter and said, "You must be one of them; we can tell by your Galilean accent."

74Peter swore, "A curse on me if I'm lying—I don't know the man!" And immediately the rooster crowed.

75Suddenly, Jesus' words flashed through Peter's mind: "Before the rooster crows, you will deny three times that you even know me." And he went away, weeping bitterly.

Matthew 27
Judas Hangs Himself

1Very early in the morning the leading priests and the elders of the people met again to lay plans for putting Jesus to death. 2Then they bound him, led him away, and took him to Pilate, the Roman governor.

3*When Judas, who had betrayed him, realized that Jesus had been condemned to die, he was filled with remorse. So he took the thirty pieces of silver back to the leading priests and the elders.* 4*"I have sinned," he declared, "for I have betrayed an innocent man."*

"What do we care?" they retorted. "That's your problem."

5*Then Judas threw the silver coins down in the Temple and went out and hanged himself.*

6*The leading priests picked up the coins. "It wouldn't be right to put this money in the Temple treasury," they said, "since it was payment for murder."* 7*After some discussion they finally decided to buy the potter's field, and they made it into a cemetery for foreigners.* 8*That is why the field is still called the Field of Blood.* 9*This fulfilled the prophecy of Jeremiah that says,*

"They took the thirty pieces of silver—
the price at which he was valued by the people of Israel,
10*and purchased the potter's field,*
as the lord directed."

Jesus' Trial before Pilate

11*Now Jesus was standing before Pilate, the Roman governor. "Are you the king of the Jews?" the governor asked him.*

Jesus replied, "You have said it."

12*But when the leading priests and the elders made their accusations against him, Jesus remained silent.* 13*"Don't you hear all these charges they are bringing against you?" Pilate demanded.* 14*But Jesus made no response to any of the charges, much to the governor's surprise.*

15*Now it was the governor's custom each year during the Passover celebration to release one prisoner to the crowd—anyone they wanted.* 16*This year there was a notorious prisoner, a man named Barabbas.* 17*As the crowds gathered before Pilate's house that morning, he asked them, "Which one do you want me to release to you—Barabbas, or Jesus who is called the Messiah?"* 18*(He knew very well that the religious leaders had arrested Jesus out of envy.)*

19*Just then, as Pilate was sitting on the judgment seat, his wife sent him this message: "Leave that innocent man alone. I suffered through a terrible nightmare about him last night."*

20*Meanwhile, the leading priests and the elders persuaded the crowd* to ask for Barabbas to be released and for Jesus to be put to death. **21** So the governor asked again, "Which of these two do you want me to release to you?"

The crowd shouted back, "Barabbas!"

22 Pilate responded, "Then what should I do with Jesus who is called the Messiah?"

They shouted back, "Crucify him!"

23 "Why?" Pilate demanded. "What crime has he committed?"

But the mob roared even louder, "Crucify him!"

24 Pilate saw that he wasn't getting anywhere and that a riot was developing. So he sent for a bowl of water and washed his hands before the crowd, saying, "I am innocent of this man's blood. The responsibility is yours!"

25 And all the people yelled back, "We will take responsibility for his death—we and our children!"

26 So Pilate released Barabbas to them. He ordered Jesus flogged with a lead-tipped whip, then turned him over to the Roman soldiers to be crucified.

The Soldiers Mock Jesus

27 Some of the governor's soldiers took Jesus into their headquarters and called out the entire regiment. **28** They stripped him and put a scarlet robe on him. **29** They wove thorn branches into a crown and put it on his head, and they placed a reed stick in his right hand as a scepter. Then they knelt before him in mockery and taunted, "Hail! King of the Jews!" **30** And they spit on him and grabbed the stick and struck him on the head with it. **31** When they were finally tired of mocking him, they took off the robe and put his own clothes on him again. Then they led him away to be crucified.

The Crucifixion

32 Along the way, they came across a man named Simon, who was from Cyrene, and the soldiers forced him to carry Jesus' cross. **33** And they went out to a place called Golgotha (which means "Place of the Skull"). **34** The soldiers gave Jesus wine mixed with bitter gall, but when he had tasted it, he refused to drink it.

35 After they had nailed him to the cross, the soldiers gambled for his clothes by throwing dice. **36** Then they sat around and kept guard as he hung there. **37** A sign was fastened above Jesus' head, announcing the charge against him. It read: "This is Jesus, the King of the Jews." **38** Two revolutionaries were crucified with him, one on his right and one on his left.

39*The people passing by shouted abuse, shaking their heads in mockery.* **40***"Look at you now!" they yelled at him. "You said you were going to destroy the Temple and rebuild it in three days. Well then, if you are the Son of God, save yourself and come down from the cross!"*

41*The leading priests, the teachers of religious law, and the elders also mocked Jesus.* **42***"He saved others," they scoffed, "but he can't save himself! So he is the King of Israel, is he? Let him come down from the cross right now, and we will believe in him!* **43***He trusted God, so let God rescue him now if he wants him! For he said, 'I am the Son of God.'"* **44***Even the revolutionaries who were crucified with him ridiculed him in the same way.*

The Death of Jesus

45*At noon, darkness fell across the whole land until three o'clock.* **46***At about three o'clock, Jesus called out with a loud voice, "Eli, Eli, lema sabachthani?" which means "My God, my God, why have you abandoned me?"*

47*Some of the bystanders misunderstood and thought he was calling for the prophet Elijah.* **48***One of them ran and filled a sponge with sour wine, holding it up to him on a reed stick so he could drink.* **49***But the rest said, "Wait! Let's see whether Elijah comes to save him."*

50*Then Jesus shouted out again, and he released his spirit.* **51***At that moment the curtain in the sanctuary of the Temple was torn in two, from top to bottom. The earth shook, rocks split apart,* **52***and tombs opened. The bodies of many godly men and women who had died were raised from the dead.* **53***They left the cemetery after Jesus' resurrection, went into the holy city of Jerusalem, and appeared to many people.*

54*The Roman officer and the other soldiers at the crucifixion were terrified by the earthquake and all that had happened. They said, "This man truly was the Son of God!"*

55*And many women who had come from Galilee with Jesus to care for him were watching from a distance.* **56***Among them were Mary Magdalene, Mary (the mother of James and Joseph), and the mother of James and John, the sons of Zebedee.*

The Burial of Jesus

57*As evening approached, Joseph, a rich man from Arimathea who had become a follower of Jesus,* **58***went to Pilate and asked for Jesus' body. And*

Pilate issued an order to release it to him. **59**Joseph took the body and wrapped it in a long sheet of clean linen cloth. **60**He placed it in his own new tomb, which had been carved out of the rock. Then he rolled a great stone across the entrance and left. **61**Both Mary Magdalene and the other Mary were sitting across from the tomb and watching.

The Guard at the Tomb

62The next day, on the Sabbath, the leading priests and Pharisees went to see Pilate. **63**They told him, "Sir, we remember what that deceiver once said while he was still alive: 'After three days I will rise from the dead.' **64**So we request that you seal the tomb until the third day. This will prevent his disciples from coming and stealing his body and then telling everyone he was raised from the dead! If that happens, we'll be worse off than we were at first."

65Pilate replied, "Take guards and secure it the best you can." **66**So they sealed the tomb and posted guards to protect it.

Matthew 28
The Resurrection

1Early on Sunday morning, as the new day was dawning, Mary Magdalene and the other Mary went out to visit the tomb.

2Suddenly there was a great earthquake! For an angel of the Lord came down from heaven, rolled aside the stone, and sat on it. **3**His face shone like lightning, and his clothing was as white as snow. **4**The guards shook with fear when they saw him, and they fell into a dead faint.

5Then the angel spoke to the women. "Don't be afraid!" he said. "I know you are looking for Jesus, who was crucified. **6**He isn't here! He is risen from the dead, just as he said would happen. Come, see where his body was lying. **7**And now, go quickly and tell his disciples that he has risen from the dead, and he is going ahead of you to Galilee. You will see him there. Remember what I have told you."

8The women ran quickly from the tomb. They were very frightened but also filled with great joy, and they rushed to give the disciples the angel's message. **9**And as they went, Jesus met them and greeted them. And they ran to him, grasped his feet, and worshiped him. **10**Then Jesus said to them, "Don't be afraid! Go tell my brothers to leave for Galilee, and they will see me there."

The Report of the Guard

11*As the women were on their way, some of the guards went into the city and told the leading priests what had happened.* **12***A meeting with the elders was called, and they decided to give the soldiers a large bribe.* **13***They told the soldiers, "You must say, 'Jesus' disciples came during the night while we were sleeping, and they stole his body.'* **14***If the governor hears about it, we'll stand up for you so you won't get in trouble."* **15***So the guards accepted the bribe and said what they were told to say. Their story spread widely among the Jews, and they still tell it today.*

The Great Commission

16*Then the eleven disciples left for Galilee, going to the mountain where Jesus had told them to go.* **17***When they saw him, they worshiped him—but some of them doubted!*

18*Jesus came and told his disciples, "I have been given all authority in heaven and on earth.* **19***Therefore, go and make disciples of all the nations, baptizing them in the name of the Father and the Son and the Holy Spirit.* **20***Teach these new disciples to obey all the commands I have given you. And be sure of this: I am with you always, even to the end of the age.*

What a story this is! Compile all your questions and talk to someone. Get your questions answered. When you feel that it's time to begin your new journey by accepting Jesus Christ into your heart, pray to God. Open your mind and your heart and pray the following.

"God, my life is messed up. It's a train wreck. I'm all jacked up. I have no hope except through you. I have run out of options and am ready to let you have my life. It's yours. I believe you sent your Son to live with me, feel my pain, and get to know me. I believe Jesus died for my sins so I could live eternally with joy and in peace. I believe He rose from the dead to open up heaven for me. I believe you have prepared a place for me. Thank you, God, for loving me this much and offering your grace. "Jesus I need you in my heart. Please come in at once and never leave me. Grab hold of me and shape me into what you want me to be. I can't do this on my own any longer. Amen!

Praise God—you did it! I can't wait to hear your story. I love you, brothers and sisters in Christ. What can I do for you? How can I help you? I will start by praying this for you. Dear God, I pray that this new believer fights the good fight and receive truth, faith, grace, and joy. "Hold tightly to the eternal life to which God has called you, which you have declared so well before many witnesses." (1 Timothy 6:12) AMEN!

2. Get Connected!

The devil will try to steal you back; you'll feel that tug of war once the excitement wears down a bit. Find a church quickly. Ask around if needed. Hang out with other believers. You will find they're pretty easy to hang out with. Don't delay getting connected. Hold yourself accountable to this. Get into small groups or Christian help groups or find a counselor. Connect with a pastor you trust or comes highly recommended. Do your homework; make sure the church you're attending has the correct beliefs. It must match the book of Matthew you just read.

You are in your most vulnerable state right now. Satan is a heathen who preys on the vulnerable, so beware of him. He is as real as God. Connectedness means so much more than connecting at the earthly level. There is much more in the spiritual level you must learn to connect with.

3. Avoid Temptation

Remember that in Matthew 4, Jesus was tempted. To prove just how sick Satan is, he will tempt you too. You will feel at times that you're being torn in two. God's got this. Stay strong. Stay connected. Stay around good, Christian people who will love and support you. Look to the Bible and God as soon as you feel temptation. This is Satan trying to take you back to the dark world you came from. You can fight this. You have a choice. Look to Jesus. Pray, pray, pray!

4. Pray Well and Listen to God

Take time to listen to God. He will instruct, protect, guide, and keep you. He will shine His face on you and bring you peace. Hear Him. If you were like me and had a rough life, you're gifted with heightened senses, experience, and wisdom. You have a jump-start on your relationship with God. He communicates with us in many ways. Open your ears to hear and your eyes to see. Your touch, your gut, your mind—all your senses can detect when God is communicating with you. It will borderline freak you out when it happens unless you're already a bit freaky Ha ha! You'll learn that if you pray well, God will speak to you in many different ways.

5. Follow Jesus

Jesus will do a number of things to guide you, but you must stay in His Word, the Bible. "His word is a lamp to guide my feet and a light for my path." (Psalms 19:105) He will clear the danger ahead of you and look back to keep you in His sight. He'll beckon you forward as He did His apostles. He will make you a fisher of men. Stay on track. Don't steer the train or you'll wreck it. He's got this. Let go and follow by listening and acting. Do as He commands. Remember that He commands you not to worry many times in the Bible.

6. Love Well

Learn just how much God loves you. You'll learn how to define true love and even how to love well.

7. Serve Well

Time to act. God has made you anew and has invested His all into transforming you. Jesus has helped you build a foundation. You are now strong and worthy of fighting alongside Him. It is now time to step aside from yourself and let God use you for His glory. There is no greater reward than serving. It takes everything you were and everything you are now and pulls your story all together in a perfectly woven web. This is where you will experience how God can use your soul to find many other lost souls. Where once you were beaten, mocked, sexually abused, made fun of, laughed at, ridiculed, and called a failure, now you are blessing others as a servant. There is only one thing better than all this—to bless, serve, love, and forgive those who have hurt you. Serving is powerful, holds us accountable, and gives us purpose.

8. Share Your Story

Just as I'm doing with this book, you should one day share your story. That might be hard for you, but sharing your story means that you love God so much that you would allow Him to sacrifice you to help others. This will probably put you outside your comfort zone and end up mocked, made fun of, laughed at, etc., but it will be different. You will love those who are trying to hurt you. You will be armed with a shield and sword.

I'm nervous about what others will think of my crazy life, but I'm more excited to see how God will use it for His purpose. I have learned from experience that we human beings are very tough. Our spirits, minds, and souls can heal just as our skin does. There might be scars as reminders of our injuries, but we will heal. It isn't the painful experiences themselves that can drag us into depression but the psychological weight we carry from them if we don't learn how to let them go.

I'm a victim of many bad things; I have the scars to prove it. I have a heart that has been broken many times. I had a spirit that was lost for years, but in the end, through God's perfectness, I was made perfect. At the point that my story became God's glory, I no longer suffered. That's the secret to life.

9. Take NAPs on the Sabbath

Take time to enjoy the peace, joy, and serenity that comes with being a Christian. I didn't say happiness; you aren't always going to be happy. You will, however, learn to identify and hold onto joy. It's a special moment when you first identify joy versus happiness. You no longer need quick fixes to feel better. Takes some time out for yourself and spend quiet time with God. Keep the balance. It's very important. Take NAPs—Notice, Appreciate, and Praise

10. Create Your Legacy

Your journey and relationship with Christ is different from anyone else's. I was as slow to let Christ into my life as I was with any relationship; I had been hurt too many times by people. Now that I have a deep, fulfilling relationship with Christ, I am learning that who I am becoming is worth leaving behind who I used to be. I can't keep my money, or my house, or any other of my possessions when I die, but I can leave behind a good legacy. What will people say when I'm gone? Will the things I taught my family, friends, and acquaintances be fruitful for God's purpose? Will my acts of kindness and examples leave a lasting, positive impression? I don't care about gloating over the kind things I have done, but I hope my legacy will glorify God. When you move on, will your family and friends take what wisdom you have taught them and continue to live in Christ?

Conclusion

It has been a privilege and an honor to have shared my life and passion of Christ with you. God is so good. Thank you for reading this book. I hope that you have related to it and that it helped you sort some things out and discover your real purpose.

No amount of regret or guilt will change the past. No amount of depression or anxiety will change the future. God is love, life, and joy. Let Him become your present so your present will reflect your future.

Remember my HSFT—Life Guide by Alter Pain. The ten steps will be expounded on, and you'll challenge yourself and interact with your authentic side.

"I pray for each of you that the Lord bless you and protect you. May the Lord smile on you and be gracious to you. May the Lord show you His favor and give you His peace." (Numbers 6:24–26), amen.

I'd love to get to know each of you and stay in touch. I will do my best time permitting. I'd like to hear from you about your journey and your story.

You can reach me by the following:
Website: www.HeartestStory.com

God bless you and love in Christ,
Alter Pain, your brother in Christ